The International Student Handbook

WITHDRAWN

Palgrave Study Skills

Authoring a PhD
Business Degree Success
Career Skills
Critical Thinking Skills
e-Learning Skills (2nd edn)
Effective Communication for
  Arts and Humanities Students
Effective Communication for
  Science and Technology
The Exam Skills Handbook
The Foundations of Research
The Good Supervisor
How to Manage your Arts, Humanities and
  Social Science Degree
How to Manage your Distance and
  Open Learning Course
How to Manage your Postgraduate Course
How to Manage your Science and
  Technology Degree
How to Study Foreign Languages
How to Write Better Essays (2nd edn)
IT Skills for Successful Study
The International Student Handbook
Making Sense of Statistics
The Mature Student's Guide to Writing (2nd edn)
The Personal Tutor's Handbook
The Postgraduate Research Handbook (2nd edn)
Presentation Skills for Students

The Principles of Writing in Psychology
Professional Writing (2nd edn)
Researching Online
Research Using IT
Skills for Success
The Study Abroad Handbook
The Student's Guide to Writing (2nd edn)
The Student Life Handbook
The Study Skills Handbook (3rd edn)
Study Skills for Speakers of English as
  a Second Language
Studying the Built Environment
Studying Business at MBA and Masters Level
Studying Economics
Studying History (3rd edn)
Studying Law (2nd edn)
Studying Mathematics and its Applications
Studying Modern Drama (2nd edn)
Studying Physics
Studying Programming
Studying Psychology (2nd edn)
Teaching Study Skills and Supporting Learning
Work Placements – A Survival Guide for Students
Writing for Nursing and Midwifery Students
Write it Right
Writing for Engineers (3rd edn)

Palgrave Study Skills: Literature

General Editors: John Peck and Martin Coyle

How to Begin Studying English Literature
  (3rd edn)
How to Study a Jane Austen Novel (2nd edn)
How to Study a Charles Dickens Novel
How to Study Chaucer (2nd edn)
How to Study an E. M. Forster Novel
How to Study James Joyce
How to Study Linguistics (2nd edn)

How to Study Modern Poetry
How to Study a Novel (2nd edn)
How to Study a Poet
How to Study a Renaissance Play
How to Study Romantic Poetry (2nd edn)
How to Study a Shakespeare Play (2nd edn)
How to Study Television
Practical Criticism

The International Student Handbook

HAYO REINDERS, NICK MOORE and
MARILYN LEWIS

© Hayo Reinders, Nick Moore and Marilyn Lewis 2008

First published 2008 by
PALGRAVE MACMILLAN

Palgrave Macmillan in the UK is an imprint of Macmillan Publishers Limited,
registered in England, company number 785998, of Houndmills, Basingstoke,
Hampshire RG21 6XS.

Palgrave Macmillan in the US is a division of St Martin's Press LLC,
175 Fifth Avenue, New York, NY 10010.

Palgrave Macmillan is the global academic imprint of the above companies
and has companies and representatives throughout the world.

Palgrave® and Macmillan® are registered trademarks in the United States,
the United Kingdom, Europe and other countries.

ISBN-13: 978–0–230–54519–9
ISBN-10: 0–230–54519–X

This book is printed on paper suitable for recycling and made from fully
managed and sustained forest sources. Logging, pulping and manufacturing
processes are expected to conform to the environmental regulations of the
country of origin.

A catalogue record for this book is available from the British Library.

10 9 8 7 6 5 4 3 2 1
17 16 15 14 13 12 11 10 09 08

Printed and bound in China

Short contents

Contents

Preface

Dear Reader,

Studying overseas is an exciting experience. For many students their time in another country is one of the most rewarding times of their lives. As a second-language speaker of English it can also be challenging. Understanding a new accent, reading lots of course materials and having group discussions can be both difficult and time-consuming. That's where this book will be of help. The chapters that follow will offer you both advice and a chance to practise the skills you will need to make the most of your studies overseas. The examples will give you an idea of what to expect and the tasks are a fun way to check your understanding.

The authors of this book have first-hand experience in travelling, studying and working in other countries. Your first author, Hayo, writes:

Studying languages has been the most valuable experience of my life. It has allowed me to really get to know the people in the countries I have visited and, eventually, to settle in another country. I wish I had had the advice in this book when I studied overseas, though. It would have certainly made things easier!

Nick writes:

Studying part of my first degree in Italy was a fantastic adventure and one of the things that made me eventually become a language teacher. It was so much fun and such a rich learning experience – everything was different from universities in the UK and the biggest difference, of course, was the language!

Marilyn writes:

I crossed to the other side of the world to study in a language that was familiar from years of study. Did all that study help? Yes, it meant I understood the written word and could write reasonably well. What was not so familiar was the spoken language. It took a while to become accustomed to the speed of people's speech.

We would have liked to have learned from the experiences of other students. We would also have been interested to hear what our teachers expected from us. That is why we have included our own experiences as students and teachers at universities in different countries. Between us we have studied and taught at universities in twelve different countries. However, we have not limited the examples in this book to our own experiences. You will read advice from many, many other students and teachers.

So where to start? Of course, you can read the book from start to finish. But perhaps there are some topics that are more important to you than others, or more urgent. Use the Contents page to find what you need. There is also a glossary at the end that explains the key terms in this book and which you can use to look up information on specific topics. If you are not sure where to start, read the first chapter of the book. It contains a number of case studies where students from around the world talk about their experiences. We use their stories to identify some common problems and then recommend particular chapters throughout the book. You can also read the introduction to each chapter, where we highlight the main topics that will be covered.

We hope this book will help to make your time overseas more successful and more enjoyable. Read, enjoy your study and be ready to add to a book, one day, with your own experiences.

Hayo Reinders, Nick Moore and Marilyn Lewis

Chapter 1

Case studies: these people need help!

CHAPTER OVERVIEW

In this chapter you will meet a number of students we have worked with over the years. Each one speaks English as a second language, and each one is concerned about some aspect of studying at university. At the end of the profile you will read some questions to help you identify the problems they faced.

When you have thought about your own ideas, look at the suggestions at the end of the book (pp. 201–3). If it turns out that you are concerned about the same thing, then follow the directions to the chapter or chapters that will help you.

Case study 1 **Chamroeun**

Chamroeun is studying for an undergraduate degree. Although most of his lectures are large, and a bit impersonal, he is pleased to be in one class that is small enough for the lecturer to know the students by name. This lecturer encourages everyone to ask questions in class and even to go to her office if they have additional problems with their assignments.

Chamroeun takes up the offer every time and is a constant visitor to the lecturer's office. At first his questions are all about his assignments but gradually, as he realises how kind she is, he starts talking to her about problems with his girlfriend. Lately he senses that she is not so keen to talk about his personal problems, although she continues to be helpful with questions about his assignments. She has even suggested that he might like to see a counsellor.

He is puzzled. In his country staff members are very interested in every aspect of a student's life. Why is this person suggesting he should see a counsellor. 'I'm not going mad,' he says to himself. 'Why on earth would she suggest such a thing?'

QUESTIONS

1   How many problems does this student seem to have?
2   Can you explain the lecturer's attitude?

Case study 2 **Hanna**

Hanna is always surprised when her assignments are returned. Sometimes the mark is much higher than she had expected but the reverse also happens. For instance, last week she got back an assignment that she had worked on solidly for a week. Yet, she only got a B. The big surprise, though, was the lecturer's comments. The lecturer praised several aspects of the assignment. How could he possibly praise her for such a low mark? It doesn't make sense.

Hanna doesn't know how to tell her parents about this terrible grade. When she did her first degree in her own country she always had top grades, which is why she was given a scholarship to study overseas. Now, in her postgraduate studies, here comes this disgrace. She feels lonely and ashamed.

QUESTIONS

1   How many problems is Hanna facing?
2   Who could help her with them?

Case study 3 **Tanako**

Tanako is a popular student who has had no trouble making friends in her new country. People are always complimenting her on her English and saying things like 'We can understand everything you say.' What's more, she never has to ask people to repeat themselves. She gets their meaning the first time.

When it comes to her assignments, however, the lecturers are often making suggestions about her getting some help with her writing. How can they say this when all her friends understand her so well? It doesn't make sense.

QUESTIONS

1   Can you explain why her friends and the markers of her assignments are giving her different messages?
2   What advice would you give to Tanako?

Case study 4 **Laura**

Laura is extremely shy. She was horrified to discover that tutorials meant discussion time. What is worse, the tutor sometimes calls on students to answer by name. She finishes each tutorial feeling embarrassed and stupid. The other students probably think she understands nothing, but that's not true. She understands most of what the other students and the tutor are saying but she is scared to speak.

She is thinking that it might be best to avoid tutorials altogether except when an assignment is being given out. That would save her being constantly embarrassed.

QUESTIONS

1   How many reasons can you suggest for Laura's attitude?
2   What advice would you give her?

Case study 5 **Phond**

Phond has come to a Western university for just one year to do a postgraduate diploma. She doesn't really need this for her chosen career but her parents believe having a foreign qualification will help her to find a really good job in her own country.

After the first class test this student is shocked to find that her grade is B–. Immediately she goes to see the lecturer, feeling sure that this kind person will understand. She starts explaining:

> 'This qualification doesn't mean much to me but it does to my parents and they have spent a huge amount of money sending me here. Would you be able to adjust the mark please?'

To her shock the lecturer looks quite severe and says "No, definitely not." The lecturer also says he considers B- a good mark for the first test in a new country and a new course.

QUESTIONS

1   Who is being unreasonable here: the lecturer or the student, and why?
2   What would you suggest the student does next?

Case study 6 **Ken**

Ken is concerned because he cannot take down everything that is said during lectures. However fast he writes he cannot keep up. What is worse, when he goes to read his notes later they don't make sense. He is afraid that without understanding the lectures he will fail the course.

QUESTIONS

1   Is Ken right that without lecture notes he will fail the course?
2.   What suggestions would you make for overcoming his problems?

Case study 7 **Fukang**

Fukang is having a hard time getting used to living in the new country. In his home country he usually studies with others in groups or at least spends time with them after class. Every student joins a club of some sort, either sports or a hobby. Here students immediately rush off after class without paying much attention to each other. Although there are some university clubs, often people seem to arrive together in pairs or small groups and it is difficult to talk to them. Fukang is starting to feel lonely and is also finding it hard to motivate himself to study alone.

QUESTION

1   How can Fukang connect with people and avoid becoming isolated?

Case study 8 **Tanya**

Tanya is enjoying her university studies in her new country except for one thing: oral presentations. Whenever the tutor announces that next week students will start presenting their assignments to the rest of the class, she starts to feel unwell. She gets headaches, her throat goes dry and she feels physically ill. The main reason for this is that her spoken English is not as good as her understanding of other people's speaking. On top of this, even in her own language she never enjoyed public speaking. She thinks it might be a good idea to ask the tutor what she needs to do to be excused from oral presentations.

QUESTIONS

1   What do you think of Tanya's solution to the problem?
2   If you were her friend, what would you advise her to do?

Case study 9 **Marco**

Marco's problem is the amount of reading that is expected for the course. He reads English quite well, but not fast. Staying up later and later doesn't seem to be helping. In fact, he is now having trouble waking up early enough to get to his first lecture of the morning.

One day he asks a friend, 'Why can't the lecturers hand out summaries of all our text books? That's what they used to do in my country.'

QUESTIONS

1   Why do you think lecturers don't hand out summaries?
2   If you were the friend, what would you suggest to this sleepless student?

Case study 10 **Umut**

Umut found a wonderful article on the very topic of her assignment. She used large pieces of this article in her essay and now has received what looks like a very urgent email from the person marking the assignment. The email is full of words like 'serious', 'plagiarism' and 'explanation'. Even though she doesn't know the meaning of the word 'plagiarism', she can understand that there is a major problem (see Chapter 12 for more on Umut's case).

QUESTIONS

1   Do you think this student has been dishonest?
2   How would you explain the word 'plagiarism' to her?

Chapter 2

Planning your studies

Introduction

You have decided you want to study overseas. Good for you! This will be one of the most exciting and rewarding times of your life. To make the most out of that time it is important that you carefully consider what to study, and where.

Where to go

Here are some common reasons for deciding to study overseas. How important are these reasons for you?

Knowing your reasons for going overseas will help you decide where to go. Look at the most important of the ideas for you from the table on the right, and then ask yourself further questions to narrow down the choices. There are some examples for you in the chart in Figure 1.1.

This chart will help you come up with an ideal list of places to study. But, of course, there are also many practical questions to consider. Let's use the table below to find out how these affect

Reason	How important		
	not at all	a little bit	very
To improve my English			
To study at a famous university			
Because the study I want to do is not available in my country or the quality is not good enough			
To experience another culture			
To take a break and study at the same time			
Because the study I want to do is easier to enter/complete in another country			
Because I will be able to get a better job in my home country if I have studied overseas			

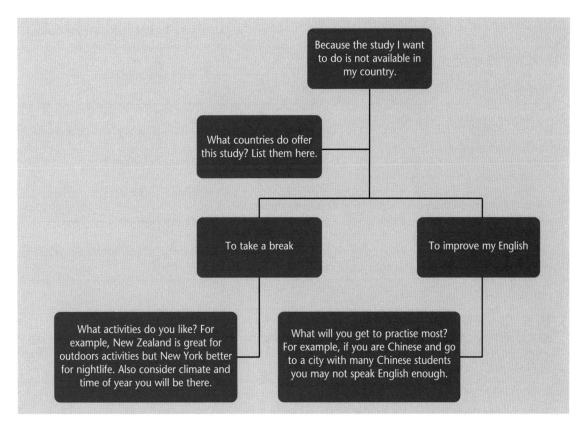

Figure 2.1   Reasons for studying overseas

your choice. First list your top three ideal choices:

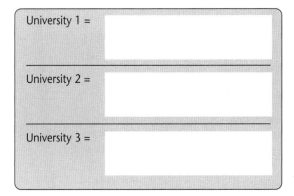

University 1 =

University 2 =

University 3 =

Next, consider each of the following practical points. For example, if one of your preferred universities has very high tuition fees and this is a problem for you, that university gets 0 points. If its tuition fees are reasonable, it gets 1 point. If its fees are low, then it gets 2 points. If a question is not important for you (for example, whether you can meet people of your own culture), then simply don't answer that question.

When you are finished, add up the score for each university. Do you have a clear winner? Then you know which option is the best one for you.

	University 1	University 2	University 3
What are the tuition fees like?			
How much does it cost to live in that country?*			
Is it possible to get a scholarship to go there?			
How easy is it to get a visa?			
Are there people who speak your language?			
Do you know anyone there (friends or family) who can support you?			
Is it dangerous to live there?			
Is the climate right for you?			
How difficult is it to be accepted at the university?			
Are the start and finish dates suitable for you – for example, if you want to continue to study in your own country when you finish?			
Total score			

*See the end of this chapter (p. 13) for ways of finding out the cost of living in a country.

Applying for a scholarship

For many students, a scholarship is a necessity if they want to be able to study overseas. Luckily there are many opportunities available to eager students (see below). Your chances of getting a scholarship depend on many things, not the least the quality of the documentation you submit. If the information you prepare is well written, looks as if it has been prepared carefully and gives a good impression of yourself, your chances are that much better. Your cover letter (or 'personal statement') is particularly important to show why you are the right candidate for the scholarship. Have a look at this sample letter from one student. What do you think of it?

What do you feel is missing from this letter?

Hello!

My name is . . . and I am a student at . . . in . . .

I am very interested in the . . . scholarship. I love to study and to travel abroad. My dream is to be a . . . one day.
I have studied . . . for three years and next year I hope to graduate.

The . . . scholarship is right for me as my family is poor and I don't have a chance to study overseas. I hope you will give me the money. I will be a good student and work very hard.

Thank you very much
Stu Dent

Here are some key things to include:

- the reason why you want the scholarship (your motivation)
- why you are the best candidate to get it
- why this scholarship is the best one for you (compared with others)
- what you will do after you complete the scholarship
- show that you meet all the requirements

In addition to this, your letter needs to be clear and well written. You want to check very carefully for language mistakes. Always ask someone (preferably a native speaker) to proofread your letter. Also, make sure you include all the relevant documents, such as recommendation letters, copies of your qualifications etc.

A model letter

In the model letter on the right you will find all the elements listed above. But there are some gaps. Fill them in with information about yourself and your studies. Also make any other changes to the text as you find necessary. There is no answer key for this task as your 'answers' will depend on the specific scholarship you are applying for.

What do you think? Is this an improvement over the other example?

Which language test is right for me?

There are many language tests in use around the world. Table 2.1 gives some information about the most common ones that are used internationally.

Dear Madam/Sir

In a recent newsletter from the University of _____ I read about the scholarship. Having nearly completed my undergraduate degree in the area of _____ I am now very keen to get the practical experience the scholarship will give me. It is my goal to one day work as _____ and be really able to make a difference in _____ I think this scholarship will give me a wonderful chance to develop myself further and to learn __

I am a hard-working student. I have received _____ grades and taken several extra courses, including _____ In addition, I have been class rep three times, been a member of the student board and have assisted with producing our department's magazine. During the last summer I worked as an intern at _____ Although I did not get paid for this job I was eager to learn the practical skills in this field. During my internship I have learned _____ and further developed my _____ skills.

The information about the _____ scholarship says it aims to '_____' and I feel that I fit this description. It also specifically mentions candidates who have experience in _____ and from my attached CV you will see that I have taken courses in all these subjects. I strongly agree with the scholarship's goals to _____ as these are also some of my personal goals.

After I finish the scholarship I plan to _____ and to put into practice the skills I will have learned from this scholarship by _____

Please find attached a copy of all the required documentation. I have checked and am eligible to apply as I am under _____ years of age and have already completed my _____ degree. I hope through this letter I have shown you some of my enthusiasm and motivation for applying for this scholarship.

Yours sincerely

© Hayo Reinders, Nick Moore and Marilyn Lewis (2008),
The Internatiuonal Student Handbook, Palgrave Macmillan Ltd

Your own government may sponsor people to study overseas by paying travel expenses as well as tuition fees. A good place to look is at the website of the Ministry of Foreign Affairs or the Ministry of Education.

There are also scholarships given by international organisations such as the United Nations. These are usually awarded to students from certain countries or for students who cannot afford the tuition fees. A good place to start looking is one of these sites:

www.iefa.org
Here, international students can search for scholarships by area of study, by their country of origin, by the region where they want to study, or by the name of the university.

www.globalgrant.com
Although this site charges a fee to help you find a scholarship, this kind of service may be useful when you don't have access to a university or if your university does not have someone to help you with your scholarship.

Table 2.1 Language tests

	Where is it used?	Which version?	Other information
TOEFL	Around the world. Especially in the United States.	There are three versions. More and more testing locations will move to use the internet-based test, while others still use the computer-based or the paper-based test.	It is a test of your global English proficiency. The new internet-based test includes a speaking part for the first time (you talk into a computer) and a compulsory writing section. **See toefl.org**
TOEIC	Worldwide.	Most countries use only one version of the TOEIC. Japan and Korea are now using an online version which will gradually become available in other countries too.	This is the Test of English for International Communication. It is also a test of your global English proficiency but covers more business, rather than academic, topics. It includes both spoken and written components. **See ets.org**
IELTS	Great Britain, Canada, Australia, New Zealand and many other countries that also accept TOEFL.	There are two versions: one general and one academic. You will need the academic one for entry into most universities.	This is the International English Language Testing System. It tests either your general or your academic English proficiency. There are four parts: reading, writing, listening and speaking. **See ielts.org**
Cambridge	Worldwide and especially in Europe.	KET: elementary level PET: intermediate FCE: upper-intermediate CAE: advanced CPE: very advanced Others include tests for legal or business English.	These are general English (not academic English) exams. There are five parts: reading, writing, listening, speaking and use of English (which includes grammar and vocabulary). **See cambridgeesol.org/exams/ index.htm**

Table 2.2 A comparison of the TOEFL and the IELTS tests

	Possible scores	Common scores required for university entry
TOEFL (paper-based version)	310–677	550
TWE	1–6	4.5
TOEFL (computer-based version)	0–300	215
TOEFL (computer-based version) writing section	1–6	4.0
TOEFL (internet-based version)	0–120	Some require a certain total score (which can vary considerably, from as low as 54 to as high as 90), or a minimum score for each of the four skills, or a combination of the two. Check with your university.
IELTS (no band below 5.5)	1–9	6.0

Which one is right for you depends on what you need to take the test for. To simply get an idea of your level you may just want to borrow a practice book from your school or library to avoid having to pay for an expensive test. If you need a test score for university entrance or for immigration purposes, they will be able to tell you which tests they accept.

How do scores on TOEFL and IELTS compare?

Table 2.2 compares the possible scores for the two most commonly accepted tests by universities, the TOEFL and the IELTS tests. It also shows you common minimum scores for university entry.

Table 2.3 shows you what the various scores mean and how they compare between IELTS and TOEFL.

Table 2.3 How do the tests compare?

Description	IELTS (academic + general)	TOEFL (paper)	TOEFL (computer)	TOEFL (internet)
9.0 **expert user** Has fully operational command of the language: appropriate, accurate and fluent with complete understanding	9.0	(700)	300	120
8.0 **very good user** Has fully operational command of the language with only occasional unsystematic inaccuracies and inappropriacies. Misunderstandings may occur in unfamiliar situations. Handles complex detailed argumentation well.	8.0	650 647 643 640 637 633 630	280 277 273 270 267	106

Table 2.3 *continued*

Description	IELTS (academic + general)	TOEFL (paper)	TOEFL (computer)	TOEFL (internet)
7.0 good user Has operational command of the language, though with occasional inaccuracies, inappropriacies and misunderstandings in some situations. Generally handles complex language well and understands detailed reasoning.	7.0	627	263	93
		623	260	
		620		
		617		
		613	257	
		610	253	
		607		
	6.5	603	250	87
		600	247	
		597		
		593	243	
		590		
		587	240	
		583	237	
		580		
		577	233	
		573	230	
		570		
		567	227	
		563	223	
		560	220	
		557		
		553	217	
6.0 competent user Has generally effective command of the language despite some inaccuracies, inappropriacies and misunderstandings. Can use and understand fairly complex language, particularly in familiar situations.	6.0	550	213	80
		547	210	
		543	206	
		540		
		537	203	
		533	200	
		530	197	
		527		
		523	193	
		520	190	
		517	187	
		513	183	
		510	180	
		507		
		503	177	
	5.5	500	173	
5.0 modest use Has partial command of the language, coping with overall meaning in most situations, though is likely to make many mistakes. Should be able to handle basic communication in own field.	5.0	450	133	66

Source: Adapted from 'What is IELTS' – htttp://www.ielts.org/format.htm and LSE Language)

Foundation courses

When you apply for some university courses you may be told you need to do a foundation course. This section answers some common questions about foundation courses.

What is a foundation course?

It's a course run either by a university or by a college linked to a university that some students need to take before they start at university. Sometimes you can do a foundation course in your own country before going to study in an overseas university.

Why do students have to do foundation courses?

You may need to do one if you haven't got the academic qualifications to do the course you want to study at university, and/or your English is not good enough. For example, you may come from a country where most students study for 12 years at school and you want to study in a country where it is normal to study for 13 years before starting university. You may not have completed high school, or your high school grades may not be good enough for university entry. For international students, you often learn English at the same time.

What do you learn on a foundation course?

Depending on your needs, you can learn a combination of . . .

Course content: relevant to the university course you want to study – e.g. calculus or trigonometry, chemistry, basic statistics. This is usually at the same level as in year 13 at school in the country where you wish to study.

Academic English: how to write an essay, listen to a lecture, participate in tutorials. This part of the course often also helps you prepare for the IELTS or TOEFL exam.

Study skills: e.g. critical thinking, how to use a library, how to manage deadlines.

Information Technology: e.g. using word processing software or spreadsheets.

How long do foundation courses last?

Usually a year, but sometimes longer or shorter. It depends on your academic skills and language skills when you start. Often foundation courses for international students have different start dates, depending on your English language level when you enrol and your academic record. For example, you may need to study for 12 months if your IELTS level is 4.5 but only 6 months if your IELTS score is 5.5.

What happens at the end of the course?

You are assessed on the academic part of the foundation course and sometimes on your English level. Sometimes you may need to take an IELTS or TOEFL test as well. If you are successful you may go directly to university. If you are not successful, you may need to keep studying and retake some units.

How do I find out more?

Make contact with the international student office at the university where you want to study. Tell them about your academic record and your language level. They will tell you if you need to do foundation studies and possibly recommend one or more places.

Case studies

One way of thinking about your university studies is to learn from the experiences of others. Here are some examples of students at different stages of their studies. After each one we have put some questions to help you consider your situation. There is no answer key at the end of the book for this section because choices about study do not have just one right answer.

Before studying

Vijay is at the stage of enrolling for university. His family really wants him to be a doctor but he knows that medicine is not an easy course to be accepted into. Also his uncle is a doctor who works very hard for long hours and he's not sure if that's the life for him. The university offers a number of other courses, such as a year's study in bio-medical subjects, which could lead to medicine or to other fields of study.

QUESTIONS

1 Is there anything about Vijay's story that sounds like your situation?
2 How many options does Vijay have?
3 If you were Vijay, what option would you take and why?

Malwina has always been good at languages and had imagined she would study them at university but now her friends have raised some doubts. 'What could you do with languages for a job later?' they say.

QUESTIONS

Which of these steps would you recommend for Malwina?

- Go to discuss the future with a careers counsellor.
- Look on the website of languages departments to see what careers they mention.
- Study just one language but choose other subjects that seem to have a more professional focus.
- Talk to someone who has studied languages and ask them about their career.
- Ignore the friends and study the subjects you are good at.

Miyako has already completed her undergraduate degree in Commercial Law. She is now considering doing a Master's but her friends don't agree. They think she should get some work experience first.

QUESTIONS

If you were this student's friend, or if you are in a similar position, here are some questions you could ask her:

1 Are you eligible for a Master's programme? Were your grades good enough?
2 What do you hope to get out it? Do you enjoy studying or is your goal to get a higher salary or a better job?
3 Have you spoken with someone who works in your field? What do they think doing a Master's will do for your career opportunities?

While studying

Robert has just completed the first year of his degree. He passed in all but one subject. He is being given different advice by different people.

His lecturer says, 'Plenty of people miss one subject in their first year. It doesn't mean anything. Just keep on with your second year subjects and repeat the one you missed.'

His friend says, 'This course obviously doesn't suit you. How about changing to something easier?'

His older sister says, 'You only took that failed subject because someone else thought it would be good for you. Drop that and continue with the others.'

QUESTIONS

Talk about this advice with a friend. What do you think of each comment? If you were Robert, which would you follow? Why?

Ly had planned to major in certain subjects. She had had this idea ever since her schooldays. When her first year results came out the head of department called her in and said that she had done extremely well in one particular subject and that she would be eligible for a scholarship for her fees if she advanced it. Actually this was the subject she had been least interested in all year, mainly because she found the lecturer boring.

QUESTIONS

Which of these options would you recommend? Why?

1 Take the scholarship and hope to get a different lecturer.
2 Check out who would be teaching the course before agreeing to the scholarship.
3 Ignore the offer and drop the subject.

Many universities will tell you on their website how much you can expect to pay for living expenses – rent, transport, food, entertainment etc. as well as student fees.

If you are not sure where you want to study, you can get an idea of typical living expenses by trying some of these websites. Many of them have useful cost-of-living calculators.

University of Adelaide – www.international.adelaide.edu.au/

Melbourne, Australia – www.studymelbourne.vic.gov.au/living/calculator/default.aspx

studying in the UK – UKstudentlife.com/Prepare/Cost.htm

Victoria University, Wellington, New Zealand – www.victoria.ac.nz/international/Tools/costs.aspx

University of Toronto, Canada – www.isc.utoronto.ca/preparingforuoft/costofliving.htm

Graduate School, Massachusetts Institute of Technology, USA – web.mit.edu/gsc/www/programs/costofliving/index.shtml

When using these cost of living calculators, check what is included and what is not. Also, remember that while all international students at a university taking one course will pay the same, basic course fees, there may be a big difference between two students' weekly expenses!

Another useful online tool is a currency calculator (such as www.xe.com/ucc/ which can help you work out exchange rates.

Ahmed has started a postgraduate diploma and now has a choice between doing coursework only or doing some coursework and writing a thesis. He is not sure what to do.

QUESTIONS

What would you want to know about this student before recommending either of the options?

- Whether he is disciplined to work on his own.
- Whether he likes doing research.
- What his writing skills are like.
- What he will do after completing his studies.

After studying

Ricardo has completed his degree. Now his parents have said they would like him to continue and do a PhD. In his opinion he is only an average student and anyway he wants to start earning money.

QUESTION

With a friend, work out all the options for Ricardo. If that were you, which would you do?

Enrolling in a university

It is not always easy to enter the university of your choice. There may be only limited places available and you will almost certainly have to meet a large number of requirements. Here is a checklist that will help you to make sure that you include all the relevant information when you submit your application. Check for specific information with the department.

Information to submit	Type of proof/documentation	OK?
English language level	An official copy of your IELTS, TOEFL, or other **accepted** test result.	
Previous qualifications	Diplomas and certificates. These often need to be (1) translated, and (2) verified (in the case of copies) by a Justice of the Peace or similar.	
Transcripts	In addition to (a copy of) your qualifications you will generally need to provide official transcripts that show the courses you took and your results.	
Previous work experience	Some studies, especially at postgraduate level, require evidence of work experience in a relevant field. You will need to provide some sort of evidence, for example in the form of a statement from the employer.	
References	Some universities require one or more references. These can be academic, personal, or professional. An academic reference gives comments on your abilities as a student, whether you are conscientious, prepare your work on time, work well with other students, etc. A personal reference gives information about you as a person, your social and communication skills, etc. A professional reference gives information about your work experience.	
Personal statement	Many programmes require you to give information about yourself, your reasons for choosing this study and university and your personal and professional goals. You can use the tips earlier in this chapter (p. 7) on how to write an application for a scholarship for this part.	
Copy of passport	Almost always needs to be a verified copy. This means that a Justice of the Peace or a solicitor needs to view the original and the copy and needs to sign it.	
Evidence of your ability to obtain a visa	It often happens that students cannot travel to their chosen country because they cannot get a visa. Some universities require you to show that you are eligible to enter the country.	
Financial situation	You may be asked to give evidence of your ability to support yourself financially during your studies.	

© Hayo Reinders, Nick Moore and Marilyn Lewis (2008),
The International Student Handbook, Palgrave Macmillan Ltd

Chapter 3

Improving your English

CHAPTER OVERVIEW

This chapter will help you to:

- find out what language skills are the most important ones for you
- find out your current English level
- set your English language learning goals
- find out what kind of learner you are
- find the best language school
- get to know about your university's language support
- build a language portfolio
- keep a language journal
- find excellent ways to learn English . . . while having fun!

Introduction

One of the most important steps in becoming successful in your overseas studies is to make sure your English is good. Research confirms what many students have told us: having a low level of English means getting lower marks and failing courses. So it is a good idea to invest your time before and during your studies to improve your English as much as you can. In this chapter we will look at some ways to do that.

What language skills do you need to improve?

Improving your English starts with knowing what your weak areas are. The better you know what to focus on, the less time you will waste and the better you will know where to look for help.

How will you know what areas to work on first? Here are some ways to find out:

Rate your own English

You can use the self-assessment grid in Table 3.1 to rate yourself in different areas of English. You can then use this to decide what to work on first.

Ask your teacher, or a previous teacher if you are not currently taking classes. Write down his/her comments here:

Look at your (university) grades and especially any grades from English classes you may have taken. Write down your grades here:

If you are already taking courses at university, look at the feedback from your lecturers on your writing. Are there any comments specifically about the language? Also look out for words like 'unclear', 'messy', 'difficult to follow', 'unstructured', 'chaotic', 'imprecise'. Copy the comments here:

Take a test such as IELTS or TOEFL (see Chapter 2). Many libraries have books with practice exams so you don't have to pay to do the test. Often these give you an overall score as well as a component score for different English skills. Write down the overall and the individual scores here:

Overall score: Writing:

Listening: Vocabulary:

Speaking: Others:

Reading:

Rate yourself (see below) or ask others to rate you.

Do a needs analysis (see below).

Table 3.1 Self-assessment grid I

	Reception		Interaction		Production	
	Listening	Reading	Spoken Interaction	Written Interaction	Spoken Production	Written Production
C2	I have no difficulty in understanding any kind of spoken language, whether live or broadcast, even when delivered at fast native speed, provided I have some time to get familiar with the accent.	I can read with ease virtually all forms of the written language, including abstract, structurally or linguistically complex texts such as manuals, specialised articles and literary works.	I can take part effortlessly in any conversation or discussion and have a good familiarity with idiomatic expression and colloquialisms. I can express myself fluently and convey finer shades of meaning precisely. If I do have a problem I can backtrack and restructure around the difficulty so smoothly that other people are hardly aware of it.	I can express myself with clarity and precision, relating to the addressee flexibly and effectively in an assured, personal style.	I can present a clear, smoothly flowing description or argument in a style appropriate and with a logical structure which helps the recipient to notice and remember significant points.	I can write clear, smoothly flowing text in an appropriate style. I can write complex letters, reports and articles, which present a case with an effective logical structure, which helps the recipient to notice and remember significant points. I can write summaries and reviews of professional or literary works.
C1	I can understand extended speech even when it is not clearly structured and when relationships are only implied and not signalled explicitly. I can understand television programmes and films without much effort.	I can understand long and complex factual and literary texts, appreciating distinctions of style. I can understand specialised articles and longer technical instructions, even when they do not relate to my field.	I can express myself fluently and spontaneously without much searching for expressions. I can use language flexibly and effectively for social and professional purposes. I can formulate ideas and opinions with precision and relate my contribution skilfully to those of other speakers.		I can present clear, detailed descriptions of complex subjects integrating sub-themes, developing particular points and rounding off with an appropriate conclusion.	I can express myself in clear, well-structured text, expressing points of view at some length. I can write detailed expositions of complex subjects in an essay or a report, underlining that I can write different kinds of texts in a style appropriate to the reader in mind.
B2	I can understand extended speech and lectures and follow even complex lines of argument provided the topic is reasonably familiar. I can understand most TV news and current affairs programmes. I can understand the majority of films in standard dialect.	I can read articles and reports with contemporary problems in which the writers adopt particular stances or viewpoints. I can understand contemporary literary prose.	I can interact with a degree of fluency and spontaneity that makes regular interaction with native speakers quite possible. I can take an active part in discussion in familiar contexts, accounting for and sustaining my views.	I can write letters highlighting the personal significance of events and experiences.	I can present clear, detailed descriptions on a wide range of subjects related to my field of interest. I can explain a viewpoint on a topical issue giving the advantages and disadvantages of various options.	I can write clear, detailed text on a wide range of subjects related to my interests. I can write an essay or report, passing on information or giving reasons in support of or against a particular point of view.

Table 3.1 continued

	Reception		Interaction		Production	
	Listening	Reading	Spoken Interaction	Written Interaction	Spoken Production	Written Production
B1	I can understand the main points of clear standard speech on familiar matters regularly encountered in work, school, leisure, etc. I can understand the main point of many radio or TV programmes on current affairs or topics of personal or professional interest when the delivery is relatively slow and clear.	I can understand texts that consist mainly of high frequency everyday or job-related language. I can understand the description of events, feelings and wishes in personal letters.	I can deal with most situations likely to arise whilst travelling in an area where the language is spoken. I can enter unprepared into conversation on topics that are familiar, of personal interest or pertinent to everyday life (e.g. family, hobbies, work, travel and current events).	I can write personal letters describing experiences and impressions.	I can connect phrases in a simple way in order to describe experiences and events, my dreams, hopes & ambitions. I can briefly give reasons and explanations for opinions and plans. I can narrate a story or relate the plot of a book or film and describe my reactions.	I can write straightforward connected text on topics, which are familiar, or of personal interest.
A2	I can understand phrases and the highest frequency vocabulary related to areas of most immediate personal and family information, shopping, local geography, employment. I can catch the main point in short, clear, simple messages and announcements.	I can read very short, simple texts. I can find specific, predictable information in simple everyday material such as advertisements, prospectuses, menus and timetables and I can understand short simple personal letters.	I can communicate in simple and routine tasks requiring a simple and direct exchange of information on familiar topics and activities. I can handle very short social exchanges, even though I can't usually understand enough to keep the conversation going myself.	I can write short, simple notes and messages relating to matters in areas of immediate need. I can write a very simple letter, for example thanking someone for something.	I can use a series of phrases and sentences to describe in simple terms my family and other people, living conditions, my educational background and my present or most recent job.	I can write a series of simple phrases and sentences linked with simple connectors like 'and', 'but' and 'because'.
A1	I can recognise familiar words and very basic phrases concerning myself, my family and immediate concrete surroundings when people speak slowly and clearly.	I can understand familiar names, words and very simple sentences, for example on notices and posters or in catalogues.	I can interact in a simple way provided the other person is prepared to repeat or rephrase things at a slower rate of speech and help me formulate what I'm trying to say. I can ask and answer simple questions in areas of immediate need or on very familiar topics.	I can write short, simple postcards, for example sending holiday greetings. I can fill in forms with personal details, for example entering my name, nationality and address on a hotel registration form.	I can use simple phrases and sentences to describe where I live and people I know.	I can write simple isolated phrases and sentences.

Source: Adapted from Council of Europe, Common European Framework of Reference for Languages (CEF).

Table 3.2   Self-assessment record

Comprehension	Conversation	Transaction	Discussion	Description
Level:	Level:	Level:	Level:	Level:

If you think you need to especially improve your speaking and listening skills, then use Table 3.2 to help you decide what aspects of your speaking you should work on first. Record yourself and see where you fit in this table for each of the aspects related to speaking. You can use Table 3.3 to record your level.

> **TIP**   *Taking a computer-based test*
>
> If by looking at Table 3.3 you can't tell at what level your English is, then try taking an online diagnostic assessment. This is a test designed to tell you your level for grammar, vocabulary and listening skills. To find out your level for speaking skills see the section further down in this chapter (p. 20). You can find the test here: www.britishcouncil.org/learnenglish-central-test-test-your-level.htm

Planning your learning: setting goals

Now that you have an idea of your level it is time to set some specific goals. This will help you to keep track of your progress so that you know exactly how much more work you have to do. There are a few steps to find this out:

1 Write down all the skills you want to improve (both general English such as 'pronunciation' and 'listening skills', as well as academic English skills such as 'speaking in tutorials', 'writing an argument essay').

2 Write down both the level you have now and your goal level. Your goal level is how good you think you will have to be at that skill. You do not need to have an excellent level for all skills, certainly not in your first year! It is easiest to use scores from 1 (bad) to 10 (excellent).

General English skills	Level now	Goal level
1		
2		
3		
4		
Academic English skills		
1		
2		
3		
4		

The next step is to work out which skills to concentrate on first. For this you choose how urgent each skill is. For example, even though your speaking skills may be poor, if you mainly expect to study online this would not be a very urgent skill for you to improve. However, if you know you will need to do a lot of reading from the first week, then reading might be a more urgent skill for you. Go on to step 3 (see p. 21).

Table 3.3 Self-assessment II

	Beginner	Pre-intermediate	Intermediate	Upper-intermediate	Advanced
Comprehension	I can understand what is said clearly, slowly, and directly to me in simple everyday conversation. I can be made to understand, if the speaker takes the trouble to explain to me.	I can generally identify the topic of discussion around me if it is conducted slowly and clearly. I can generally understand clear, standard speech on familiar matters directed at me, provided I can ask for repetition or reformulation from time to time.	I can generally follow the main points of extended discussion around me, provided speech is clearly articulated in standard dialect. I can follow clearly articulated speech directed at me in everyday conversation, although I sometimes have to ask for repetition of particular words and phrases.	I can, with some effort, catch much of what is said around me, but may find it difficult to participate effectively in discussion with several native speakers who do not modify their language in any way. I can understand what is said directly to me, provided the speaker avoids very idiomatic usage and articulates clearly.	I can follow discussions with several interlocutors on most general themes and on matters related to my field, identifying accurately the key points expressing a point of view. I can understand in detail what is said to me in the standard spoken language even in a noisy environment.
Conversation	I can handle very short social exchanges. However, I am rarely able to understand enough to keep conversation going freely in the way I want to.	I can participate in short conversations in routine contexts on topics of interest.	I can enter unprepared into conversation on familiar topics. I can maintain a conversation or discussion but may sometimes be difficult to follow when trying to say exactly what I would like to.	I can interact competently on informal social occasions. I can maintain conversation with unfamiliar people (e.g. visitors) on subjects of immediate relevance or areas related to my interests or field.	I can engage in extended conversation on most general topics in a clearly participatory fashion, even in a noisy environment with native speakers, without requiring them to behave other than the way they would behave with a native speaker.
Transaction	I can communicate in simple and routine tasks requiring a simple and direct exchange of limited information on familiar and routine matters to do with work and leisure time. I can make simple transactions (e.g. buying something) in shops, post offices, banks, and so on.	I can make myself understood and exchange information on familiar topics connected with common aspects of everyday living such as travel, accommodation, eating and shopping.	I can deal with most transactions likely to arise while travelling, arranging travel or accommodation, or dealing with authorities (e.g. extending a visa) during a foreign visit. I can find out and pass on straightforward factual information and obtain more detailed information when necessary.	I can understand, exchange, check and confirm and summarise straightforward factual information and deal with difficult, less routine situations, although I may occasionally have to ask for repetition if the other person's response is rapid or extended.	I can understand and exchange detailed information reliably, explain a problem, and make it clear in a disagreement that a concession is necessary.
Discussion	I can discuss everyday practical issues in a simple way when addressed clearly, slowly, and directly.	I can say what I think about things when addressed directly, provided I can ask for repetition of key points if necessary.	I can discuss topics of interest. I can express belief, opinion, and disagreement politely	I can explain why something is a problem, and can compare and contrast different alternative suggestions or solutions, commenting on the views of others.	I can take an active part in formal and informal discussion and put a point of view clearly. I can account for and sustain my opinions by providing relevant explanations, arguments and comments.
Description	I can describe my family, living conditions, education, or most recent job.	I can describe everyday aspects of my surroundings and background (e.g., people, places, a job, or study experience). I can describe plans and arrangements, habits and routines, likes and dislikes, activities, and personal experiences.	I can give detailed accounts of experiences and real or imaginary events, and can narrate stories and film/book storylines, describing feelings and reactions. I can also describe dreams, hopes and ambitions.	I can give straightforward descriptions on a variety of familiar subjects within my field of interest. I can describe in detail unpredictable occurrences (e.g. an accident).	I can give clear detailed descriptions on a wide range of subjects related to another person's field of interest.

Source: Adapted from B. North, 'Defining a Flexible Common Measurement Scale: Descriptors for Self and Teacher Assessment', in G. Ekbatani and H. Pierson (eds), *Learner-Directed Assessment in ESL* (Mahwah, NJ: Lawrence Erlbaum, 2000).

The International Student Handbook

3 Choose for each skill how urgent it is, writing 1 (not urgent), 2 (a little bit urgent) or 3 (very urgent) in the column for 'urgency' in the chart on the right.

4 Next, look at the table above and take your 'goal level'. Take away this number from your 'level now' and write down the result below, under 'level'. For example, if for the first skill your goal level is 8 and your level now is 5, then you would write 3.

5 Now multiply 'urgency' by 'level' and write down the result in the column for 'total'.

6 Now rank your answers. The skill with the highest number in the 'total' column will have a rank of 1, the next highest score will be ranked 2, etc.

The numbers in step 6 show you which skill you need to work on first, which one next, etc. The final step is to set some specific goals and to list the ways you intend to improve your top priority skills. Let's focus on the top four skills. Write them down in order of rank. Next, write down what it is you find difficult about each skill.

With this information you can start studying in an effective way. Read the rest of the chapter for tips on how to start.

Urgency	Level	Total	Rank

Skill	What I find difficult about this skill	What I can do to improve

What kind of learner are you?

Everyone learns in a different way. Some of us study lying on a couch with the TV on in the background while others can only study sitting down at a desk in absolute silence. The same is true for language learning. There is no one right or wrong way but it is good to know what your own preferences are. Answer the questions below and then add up your score. You can look up your results on page 203.

	(0) I don't know	(1) No, it's not true	(2) It is partly true	(3) Yes, it is true
(A) The most important part of learning English is to study grammar rules.				
(B) Learning new words by using vocabulary lists is helpful.				
(C) I need to learn new words and grammar rules by heart.				
(D) Having a good teacher is very important.				
(E) When I read I look up all the words I don't know in a dictionary.				
(F) When I make a mistake, I want to have it corrected immediately.				
(G) I often feel I don't have enough time to think before I speak.				
(H) It is important to keep a well-structured notebook when learning English.				
(I) It is important to take every opportunity to speak English.				
(J) Languages follow grammar rules but because native speakers often don't know these rules, I don't need to learn all of them.				
(K) Listening to the radio and watching TV are good ways to learn English.				
(L) The best way to learn English is to pretend to be an English speaker and then act out a dialogue with a partner.				
(M) When I read I usually just guess the words I don't know.				
(N) It doesn't matter if you make mistakes. The important thing is to speak as much as possible.				
(O) Whenever I meet a native speaker I try to practise my speaking.				
(P) The teacher can help but I am the one responsible for my learning.				

Do you prefer to learn through images, through sounds, by reading and writing or by touch? Find out by doing the VARK questionnaire. Then read some study tips that will be relevant to your learning style. You can find the questionnaire here:

www.vark-learn.com/english/page.asp?p= questionnaire

Here is another questionnaire that will help you find out what kind of learner you are. This one is not specific to language learning so it may also be helpful to you in learning more about your general study preferences:

www.engr.ncsu.edu/learningstyles/ilsweb.html

Are you a strategic learner?

If you can understand the English in this book you have already come a long way as a language learner. Do you know how you did it? Probably you attended courses, read a lot, memorised words, maybe listened to music and watched English movies. But you did much more than that. You also used *language learning strategies*. Strategies are techniques or ways that help you to learn faster or learn more. An example is when you learn new vocabulary by writing it down or by forming new sentences with it. Often we are not even aware of the strategies

that we use. We know, however, that strategic learners are far more successful than non-strategic learners. Let's look at some types of learning strategies. You will find more examples throughout this book, for example in the chapter on vocabulary.

Memory strategies

When you meet someone new, how do you try to remember their name?

> I write it down.
> I repeat it in my mind.
> I find a word it rhymes with.

These are examples of memory strategies and we use them every day. We also use them for language learning. In order to understand how best to memorise new language, let's take a look at how your brain works (see Figure 3.1).

As you can see, your brain has three memory stores. The first one is called your 'sensory memory'. 'Sensory' means anything to do with your senses, i.e. anything you touch, smell, taste, hear, or see. This memory store can only hold information for a very short time, often even less than one second. If you do not pay attention to the information you hear or read – say, for example, a new word – your sensory memory loses it very quickly. If you do pay attention to it, the new word has a chance to move on to your 'working memory'. It is called this because your working memory works for you. This is where your brain does something with the language. Maybe you repeat the word

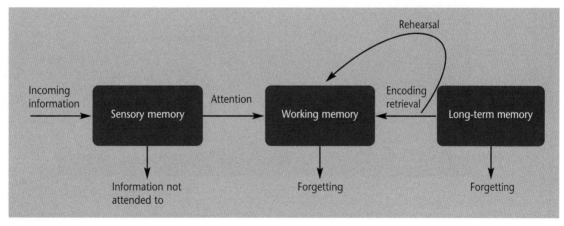

Figure 3.1   How the brain works

silently to yourself, maybe you quickly write it down, maybe you spell it out – whatever you do, by working with it you are transferring it to your third memory store, your 'long-term memory'. Items in your long-term memory can be remembered for a very long time.

Many learners make two mistakes:

1 They do not pay enough attention to the language. They think that watching a movie while drinking a beer or half-falling asleep will help them learn English. Maybe you will learn a little bit but unless you try to actively pay attention to the language you hear (or read in the subtitles) during the movie, your sensory memory will not keep that information. In other words: it has no chance to move on to your working memory.

2 Many learners also do not use their working memory. They listen to a teacher explaining a new grammar point and maybe even pay close attention. But then, as the teacher moves on to a new point or as the class finishes, they forget about that point. The brain then does not have time to work with the new information and cannot transfer it to their long-term memory. You will probably forget a lot of what you have heard.

So, if you want to learn something you have to be active, concentrate and pay attention to the language.

Another point is that without reviewing, whatever you learn will be lost quickly. Have a look at the graph in Figure 3.2. It shows you how quickly you forget things. The other thing it shows you is that one review is not enough. You need several reviews and they need to be spaced so that they are further and further apart. Do you do this in your language learning?

Communication strategies

Ken has recently arrived in London and will start studying soon. He has studied English for many years but this is his first time in an English-speaking country on his own and he finds it hard to communicate with people. Read this brief conversation between him and Susan, who will soon be his classmate. What strategies do you think Ken is using? List them below. The answers are in the text that follows, so you may want to cover that while you read the conversation.

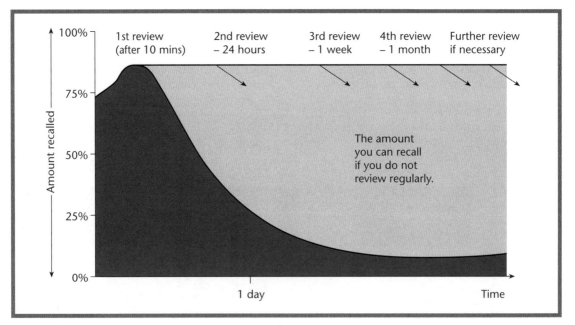

Figure 3.2 How quickly we forget

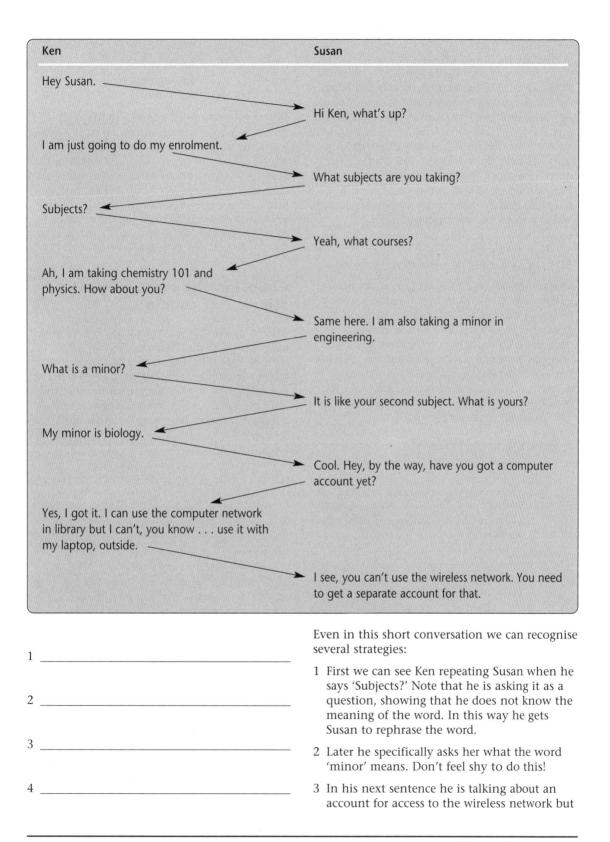

Ken	Susan
Hey Susan.	
	Hi Ken, what's up?
I am just going to do my enrolment.	
	What subjects are you taking?
Subjects?	
	Yeah, what courses?
Ah, I am taking chemistry 101 and physics. How about you?	
	Same here. I am also taking a minor in engineering.
What is a minor?	
	It is like your second subject. What is yours?
My minor is biology.	
	Cool. Hey, by the way, have you got a computer account yet?
Yes, I got it. I can use the computer network in library but I can't, you know . . . use it with my laptop, outside.	
	I see, you can't use the wireless network. You need to get a separate account for that.

Even in this short conversation we can recognise several strategies:

1 First we can see Ken repeating Susan when he says 'Subjects?' Note that he is asking it as a question, showing that he does not know the meaning of the word. In this way he gets Susan to rephrase the word.

2 Later he specifically asks her what the word 'minor' means. Don't feel shy to do this!

3 In his next sentence he is talking about an account for access to the wireless network but

1 _____

2 _____

3 _____

4 _____

© Hayo Reinders, Nick Moore and Marilyn Lewis (2008),
The International Student Handbook, Palgrave Macmillan Ltd

he doesn't know that word. So he describes what he means and Susan can guess.

These are all excellent communication strategies. One of the most successful ones is simply to get out there and speak without worrying about mistakes! We have often found that our students do not leave the house, or only mix with students from their own countries and do not speak very much English outside their classes. This will not help you in the long run. It is good to realise that by using some simple strategies, you can improve your understanding.

Strategies for managing your learning

One important type of strategy is about how you *manage* and organise your learning. Good language learners are people who are good at managing themselves and their learning. This becomes even more important once you move overseas. When you start studying you may not have time to take language classes and you will do most of your learning by yourself. Take the brief questionnaire below, to see how strategic you are about managing your learning.

Which of the strategies below do you use?

Choose 1   for 'never'
         2   for 'sometimes'
         3   for 'often'

When you have finished, add up the total number. If your score is under 24, have a look to see if any of these strategies sound like you might want to try them out. Although being a strategic learner is not just about the number of strategies you use, it certainly doesn't hurt to know a few more. You can use the tips in this and other chapters to help you use some of the other strategies.

Choosing the right language school and course

Choosing the right place to study is a very important decision. You are likely to spend considerable time and money so take the time to get the choice right. But choosing a school is not enough. You also need to know what the right type of course is for you. For example, do you need to work on general English skills first

	I plan my language learning.
	I know how to check if I have improved, and regularly do so.
	I work on language-learning tasks with other people (e.g. friends, people on my course) as well as on my own.
	I try to find opportunities to practise speaking (even to myself) to improve my fluency.
	I set specific weekly or monthly language-learning goals.
	I try to adopt an active approach towards my language learning; I don't just study when I have to.
	I think about what I need to learn to meet my goals.
	I think about how I learn, so I can improve my learning methods.
	I am willing to take risks and be adventurous with language to try out my skills.
	I try to learn from the mistakes I make.
	I motivate myself to learn and to keep learning even when it is not going well.

Source: Adapted from www.lang.soton.ac.uk/resources/key.htm

or go straight into academic English? Do you need an intermediate or an advanced course? Use the other sections in this chapter that help you find out your English level. Schools will also test your English to find out which class you should go into. Then use the following checklist to help you decide the best school. Only fill in the first part once and then the rest for each school you are considering.

Content

My current overall level is:

The most important skills for me are:

1

2

3

4

I will use English in the following situations, for the following purposes:

I need practice for the following language test:

I need to reach the following level:

I have ____ weeks/months to reach this level.

Quality

Average teaching experience of the teachers:

Maximum and average class sizes:

Nationality mix of students:

Teacher qualifications:

Reviews (from other students or the internet).

Facilities and services

Does the school have:
- a resource room Yes ☐ No ☐
- resources you can borrow Yes ☐ No ☐
- good computer facilities Yes ☐ No ☐
- a self-access centre Yes ☐ No ☐
- a common room/lounge Yes ☐ No ☐

Is there a language/course advisor to help you plan your learning? Yes ☐ No ☐

You may also want to ask about activities and other services. Does the school:
- help with finding homestays and accommodation? Yes ☐ No ☐
- offer trips? Yes ☐ No ☐
- offer after-class activities? Yes ☐ No ☐

Practical and financial questions

The maximum amount I can pay per week is:

Price for this school:

Extras:

Can I get a refund if I stop early? Yes ☐ No ☐

If yes, then what percentage?

Can I attend some classes to see if I like the school? Yes ☐ No ☐

Do students at this school have privileged entry into a specific university or college? Yes ☐ No ☐

Are the course times suitable for me? Yes ☐ No ☐

Other comments/observations:

What kind of English course do you need?

Whether you need to do an English course before your university course will depend on the level of your English to a certain extent. However, even if you have a high enough TOEFL or IELTS score to get onto your course, it may still be a really good idea to spend some time taking English classes before you go to university, to build up your confidence, get used to using English all the time, and particularly to improve your academic English skills. Remember that once you start your university study, you may have little time to concentrate fully on improving your English. Here are some different types of courses:

1 A General English course aimed at improving your English communication. This will help you with skills (reading, writing, listening and speaking) and language (grammar, vocabulary and pronunciation).

2 An EAP (English for Academic Purposes course), which is similar to a General English course except that the topics studied will be more academic and the skills and language you will learn will be more like the skills you will need at university and those covered in this book. These courses are taught by language teachers (not academics) and the other students may all plan to do different courses at university. Often you will need to be at intermediate level or above to enter one of these courses.

3 An exam preparation course (IELTS or TOEFL). This will teach you about the exam you are going to take and give you practice in answering exam-type questions.

4 A foundation studies programme including an English language programme. This is a much more general academic programme, so it will include other content as well as English language classes.

Read the following case studies. Decide which type of language course would be most suitable for each student. Then read the advice given by an academic counsellor on page 204. Do you agree?

Waleed (Saudi Arabia): 'My English is low intermediate level and I need 6.0 points at IELTS as soon as possible to go to university. I don't have much confidence in my English – my speaking and listening are OK, but my writing and my spelling is bad. I think I will go to another country to study English so I can go to university. My parents expect me to start my university course next semester. What English course should I take?'

Li Ping (China): 'I need 6.5 points at IELTS to get into university. I've done an IELTS preparation course and studied hard for IELTS but my scores are not improving and I'm bored with preparing for IELTS. What sort of course should I do?'

Sun Woo (Korea): 'My English is roughly upper intermediate level but I haven't studied at university before – I graduated from high school last summer. Of course I need to do IELTS but I am also worried. My friends say that studying at university in an English-speaking country is very different from studying in high school in Korea. I would like to know what other students know before I start university.'

Ekaterina (Russia): 'I think my English is good enough to get the TOEFL points to get into university but I'm not sure if I have the skills to write long essays, read articles and give presentations. I previously studied at university in Russia so I know what it's like! I have three months before my course starts. Should I take a TOEFL preparation course?'

Ernesto (Chile): 'My English is pretty good. I did an advanced course a couple of years ago but I've forgotten a lot and need a refresher. I want to be able to get on with my colleagues on the course. I start my Master's in a few months. I also need TOEFL to get into university. I don't want to do lots of essay writing – I've already done a degree and will have to do all that when I start my Master's.'

Getting to know your language centre

Many, if not most, universities these days have one or more places where students can get help with their English. In some universities these are called a

● self-access centre (SAC), or
● independent learning centre, or

Cont. on p. 33

Using the SAC

What times is the SAC open? _____

When are there staff members to help you? _____

Finding materials

How can you find the right materials? See if:

1 There is a computer catalogue to search for materials by topic, level, or skill.
2 You can browse through the materials on the shelves. Find out how they are organised (e.g., by skill or topic).
3 The centre offers language-learning activities.

Find out what resources there are that will help you with the following skills:
Pronunciation skills at the intermediate level:

1 _____

2 _____

Using relative pronouns at the advanced level:

1 _____

2 _____

Conversation skills at the upper-intermediate level:

1 _____

2 _____

Imagine you want to write an academic essay. What resources does the centre have that can help you?

Getting help

Is there someone in the centre who can help you with the following?

1 To advise you on borrowing books.
2 To look at the work you complete in the centre.
3 To help you plan your independent learning?

Manage your learning

Successful learners plan and reflect on their learning. Many self-access centres offer students help with this. Does the centre have:

• Books on 'learning to learn' or 'study skills'
• Worksheets that help you develop your language learning strategies?
• Staff who you can ask questions?
• A language 'consultant' or 'advisor' who will help you to develop a language-learning plan?
• Computer resources such as a 'needs analysis' that will help you identify the areas you need to work on and help you develop a learning plan?

© Hayo Reinders, Nick Moore and Marilyn Lewis (2008),
The International Student Handbook, Palgrave Macmillan Ltd

Language portfolio

Name:

Language: English

Years I have studied English

0–1 years ☐

1–2 years ☐

2–5 years ☐

More than 5 years ☐

Total time I have spent in English-speaking countries

0–1 month ☐

1–6 months ☐

6–12 months ☐

More than 12 months ☐

For each overseas stay describe:

● Country/place visited
● Length of visit
● Main purpose of trip (if English course, describe course level and aims)

I use English . . .

. . . minutes/hours per week (you can include time spent reading newspapers or watching movies in English)

My main purpose for using English is to . . .

Experience in using English

Describe any other experiences you have with using English. For example, you could mention writing with an English-speaking pen-pal, or doing a project in school where you had to produce materials in English.

▼

Courses I have taken

Certificates and diplomas (English)

Self-study courses I have completed

Name of course:

Date:

Test scores (e.g. TOEFL, IELTS)

Test:	Test:
Score:	Score:
Date:	Date:

Other scores

My reading speed for academic texts is . . . words per minute (see Chapter 7).

My vocabulary is at the . . . word level (see Chapter 4).

My skills

My strong points in English are:	The points I want to improve are:
1	1
2	2
3	3

My goals

My goals in studying English include (include a target date/year):

1

2

3

4

- writing centre, or simply
- language centre.

These are excellent places to improve your English, ask questions and get feedback on your progress. Take a bit of time to get to know your centre. It will be well worth your time.

Take the sheet on p. 30 and find out the answers to the questions. This way you will get to know about the resources available in your centre. Perhaps you can give your answers to a staff member there.

Building a language portfolio

A portfolio is a tool to help you record your language-learning achievements. It is a way for you to record your progress and to show this to others, such as your language teachers (if you have them) and future employers. Here are some reasons to keep a portfolio:

- to get feedback from a teacher;
- to show it to your new language school or teacher;
- to include it when sending your CV for a job interview.

A sample portfolio

Here is a sample language portfolio (on pages 31 and 32) that you can photocopy and fill in, or use to make up your own. In this example we use English as the language but of course you can use it for other languages too.

Keeping a language journal

Keeping a language journal can be a great way to record what you learn and to see your progress. A journal can help you in the following ways:

- to plan your learning
- to record your progress
- to think about what went well and what did not
- to find out which areas you need help with

- to make sure you are working on the right language skills
- to make sure you meet your goals
- to practise your writing skills

A sample journal

Here is a sample language journal (on pages 34 and 35) that you can photocopy and fill in, or use to make up your own.

Learning English the relaxed way

Learning English does not have to be all hard work. Many successful learners say they have picked up a lot of new words from reading magazines, improved their speaking skills over a coffee with friends or become better at understanding different accents by watching movies. Here are some useful tips on improving your English in a relaxed way.

Have MP3? Will listen!

If you have an MP3 player then why not download one of the hundreds of podcasts that are available for free? There are also many podcasts specifically aimed at language learners, such as http://iteslj.org/links/ESL/Listening/Podcasts/

In addition to these podcasts, you can also learn a lot through music, especially if your MP3 player can display the lyrics. This way you can read along while listening.

Some songs are more suitable than others. If you are trying to get used to a specific accent (say, Australian English) you can choose bands from that country. Some computer software lets you change the speed of the song when you play it back without changing the pitch (the tone). Often this is used by musicians who want to practise, but of course it can be a fantastic help to language learners too. Here is one free programme that you can download: http://renegademinds.com/Default.aspx?tabid=65

Another excellent site is by the BBC. They have a section on learning English with music, interviews with artists, video clips and more: www.bbc.co.uk/worldservice/learningenglish/help/

Language journal

Name:

Language: English

Today/this week I studied the following skills:

I used the following materials:

Time planning

Times I planned to study

Mon ☐ Tues ☐ Wed ☐ Thurs ☐ Fri ☐ Sat ☐ Sun ☐

Times I actually studied

Mon ☐ Tues ☐ Wed ☐ Thurs ☐ Fri ☐ Sat ☐ Sun ☐

I did/did not have a chance to practise my spoken English.

If you did, describe the situation where you used the language.

The things that went well were:

The things I want to improve more are:

⬇

© Hayo Reinders, Nick Moore and Marilyn Lewis (2008),
The International Student Handbook, Palgrave Macmillan Ltd

Some ideas I can try out:

I would like someone to help me with:

Now re-read your previous journal notes. Did you work on the points you wanted to improve last time/last week?

Did you try out some of your ideas?

Did you get help from a teacher?

My goals for next time/week are:

The amount of time I intend to spend is:

Mon ☐   Tues ☐   Wed ☐   Thurs ☐   Fri ☐   Sat ☐   Sun ☐

If you would like to practise your listening skills but can't find any good podcasts, or instead want to listen to your own texts, then either download an audiobook or use a text-to-speech programme to have any text on your computer read out to you by a computer voice. The better voices sound very natural. So, for example, you could copy the text from any website (say a newspaper or online magazine) and then have the computer read it, save that as an audio file and play it while you are waiting for the bus! A good programme is: www.nextup.com

Speak online!

Why not join a Skypecast and have a discussion with others (http://skypecasts.skype.com)? A Skypecast is an online meeting between two or more people. Everyone joins the discussion at a set time and uses Skype to be able to speak with others. The discussion leader decides who can talk when. This is a great way to practise speaking before you leave your home country. And as it is anonymous you don't have to be embarrassed about your English.

Watching movies and TV

Movies are a great way to improve your listening skills. By using the tips below, you can get even more out of your movie-watching experience.

Strategies for watching movies

Watching a movie in English can be quite difficult, especially when people speak with an accent or speak fast. Just watching movies and trying to understand them will definitely help you, but by using some strategies you can make it easier for yourself to understand what is being said. It may take a bit more time this way, but you'll learn a lot more!

Before you start watching

Because English is not your first language, you need to prepare for watching a movie. Try to find as much information as possible about the movie that can help you to understand what it is about. For example, you can use

- The title of the film (What do you think the movie will be about?)

- The blurb (information about the movie that appears on the cover of the video/DVD)
- Any other information you can find such as screenplays (the full written text of the movie), exercises, quizzes etc. Often, a quick internet search will bring these up. (One good place to start is: www.simplyscripts.com).
  Here you will find movie and TV scripts and information about the characters, etc.
- Your background knowledge of the topic which the movie addresses. What do you know about the country where the movie takes place, the people, their culture?

While you watch

Of course you can just sit back, relax and enjoy the movie. But you'll learn better if you're a bit more active. Research has shown that the best language learners are actively involved in the learning process. They are constantly looking for new information and compare it with what they already know. Some hints:

- Ask yourself what will happen next – challenge yourself.
- If you don't understand, then stop the movie and rewind. Don't do this too often (see next point).
- Watching movies helps to improve your *extensive* listening skills. Therefore, you should try to keep listening and not focus on vocabulary too much. If an unfamiliar word keeps coming back or seems to be very important, then you can look it up. If you are watching a DVD on a computer, pause the movie and use one of the online dictionaries (see p. 197) to look it up.
- Use the subtitles if you have difficulty in understanding the movie. Try not to use them, though. If, after having used them for a while, you feel more comfortable, try to turn the subtitles off again.
- Try to focus on specific language aspects when watching a film. This could be a particular accent, or particular forms of language use (e.g. types of greetings, compliments, thanking etc).

After you finish watching

Your learning is not over when the movie finishes. By reflecting on the story and actually *doing* something with what you have seen and learned, you will remember much more.

- Talk to your friends about the movie.
- Email a friend and describe what happened in the movie and your opinion about it.
- If you had to use the subtitles (and liked the movie!) then try watching it again some time, but without the subtitles. How much can you understand now?
- Stop to think for a moment what you found most difficult about the English in the movie. Was it the accent? Words you didn't know? The speed with which the characters spoke? By thinking about this you know what to work on next.

In addition to the general guidelines above, here are some further exercises you can do to work on specific skills.

Summarising

How can you improve your English by watching a movie? Summarising is a skill that is important at university. You will often have to read a book or article and then summarise it for an assignment.

- Select a movie.
- Write down some key words or phrases while you watch the movie.
- After you have watched the movie, write a summary of it (briefly describe what happened). The key words that you have written down will help you remember.

Possible ideas to include:

- I liked/didn't like the movie because . . .
- It made me feel . . .
- I'd recommend this movie to_____ because . . .
- The main character is . . .

Language exchanges

Another great way to learn a language in a fun way is to do a language exchange. You find a partner who speaks English and who wants to learn your native language, and then you speak in each language half of the time. This has advantages for both of you as you can practise conversation (and other) skills without having to pay. Some students meet face-to-face while others prefer to meet online. This works well if

---

Describing and comparing

1 What is the name of the movie?

2 Describe the main character.

3 Would you like to meet this character? Why, or why not?

4 Write a paragraph to compare this person to someone that you know. Think about physical appearance, mannerisms, and personality

---

Building vocabulary

- As you watch the movie, write down some words that you do not know. Next, rewind the video or DVD a little and watch again. Can you understand what the word means now? Pay attention to how the word is used. Does it sound polite, impolite or neutral? Is it used between friends or in a more formal situation?
- After you finish watching the movie, spend a few minutes looking the new words up in the dictionary. Did you get the meaning right? Then try using them in a sentence.

1   New word

   Meaning

   Example sentence

2   New word

   Meaning

   Example sentence

3   New word

   Meaning

   Example sentence

4   New word

   Meaning

   Example sentence

Working with a friend

This is a really good exercise to practise your listening and also your speaking skills. You each watch half of the movie and then meet to find out what happened in the other half.

Student A

- Choose a movie that neither you nor your partner has seen.
- Sometime during the week, watch the first half of the movie only.
- Make some notes to help you remember what happened.
- Write down a list of questions to ask your partner, to find out what happened in the second half.
- Meet with your partner and ask each other your questions. You can both only answer questions with 'yes' or 'no'. You can take notes.

Movie

Meeting time and date

Notes from the first half of the movie

Student B

The same as student A, but watch only the second half of the movie.

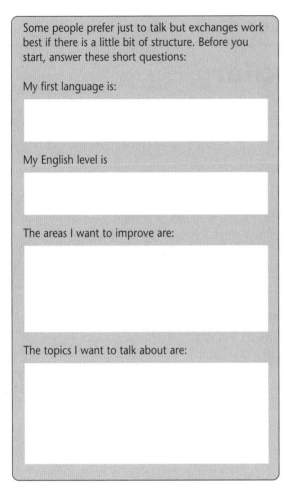

Some people prefer just to talk but exchanges work best if there is a little bit of structure. Before you start, answer these short questions:

My first language is:

My English level is

The areas I want to improve are:

The topics I want to talk about are:

you want to start practising before you go overseas. A great starting point to find a partner is www.mylanguageexchange.com

Make sure to keep track of the time so that each of you gets to practise for half of your meeting. It is best to decide beforehand what you will talk about so that you can both prepare. It may be useful to talk a bit about your preferences:

- Do you prefer to be corrected every time, or would you rather that your partner take some notes and that you go over them later?
- Do you want your partner to speak naturally, or a bit more slowly?
- Would you like your partner to explain English points or would you rather have a natural conversation?

By talking about these points beforehand you will not be disappointed.

Playing computer games

Can you learn English through computer games? You certainly can! You can buy special English 'educational games' but many students do not find these very exciting. A better alternative may be to use the games you normally use and use them as a way to practise your English.

If you normally play games in your first language, see (on the setup screen) if it lets you change the interface language, such as the language of the instructions, to English.

With games that you play online against others, change the language in your profile to English. This way you will meet others who speak English and you can interact with them, for example via chat or Skype. Some games, such as the Sims, are based on communicating with others and these may be your best bet.

Other useful games are online environments like Second Life and MySpace. If you enjoy such environments, then why not use them to improve your English? If you play them on your computer, have an online dictionary (see Chapter 4) open so you can quickly look up words that stop you from understanding what goes on. Another option is the language games such as Scrabble®. You can play these as boardgames but often also online.

A final tip is to see if you like interacting with so-called chatbots. A chatbot is a small programme made to look like a person, which you can converse with. Sometimes the interaction is surprisingly natural. There are some specifically for second-language learners. We don't recommend you use this as the main basis for improving your English but it may be useful as one way of helping you practise more. A good starting point is www.daden.co.uk/chatbots.html

There are also some computer games that require you to use language, for example, to persuade others to do something. 'Ace Attorney' is a good example. In this game you are an attorney who has come up with good arguments in order to win his cases. Great fun and great learning!

Chapter 4

Vocabulary

CHAPTER OVERVIEW

This chapter will help you to:

- find out what 'knowing a word' means
- learn about different types of vocabulary
- find out what your vocabulary level is
- find out what vocabulary you use in your writing
- find out how to learn new words
- work out the meaning of new words

- use flashcards to remember words
- make the most of a dictionary
- learn how to use a thesaurus
- choose an electronic dictionary
- learn how to use a corpus

Introduction

Words, words, words. Why are there so many in English? No one knows for sure how many words there are exactly and how many of those the average person knows, but we do know that the average person has a working knowledge of about 20,000 word families (for example, words like 'study' and 'student' are in the same family).

Luckily we don't need that many words to be able to understand and use the English language. The 1000 most common words in English cover over 70 per cent of all words in academic texts and the total estimate for the number of words we need, to understand entry-level academic texts, is about 7000. This will give you enough knowledge to be able to understand most of the other words from the context. A good point to realise is that the more words you know, the more you will learn from the context, with little or no effort. So, it pays to increase your vocabulary!

What does this word mean?

Do you know the word 'commendation'? Your answer depends on what the question means.

1 Do you know the meaning of the word and are you able to translate it into your language?
2 If so, do you know it for sure or only approximately?
3 Do you know the word well enough to *use* it in your own writing or speaking?
4 Do you know if the word is normally used in writing or speaking?
5 Can you pronounce it? Spell it? (Don't look back at the word!)
6 Do you know what words normally go together with this word (which words 'collocate' with it)? For example, do we *give* a commendation or *offer* a commendation, or can we use either?
7 Do you know whether it can take a preposition? (e.g., is it 'a commendation for', or 'a commendation with'?)
8 Does it have a positive or a negative sound? Would you use it in formal or informal situations?

Even if you don't know the word, you probably know the word '*recommendation*'. Knowing that word, you can probably partly figure out the meaning of the word 'commendation'. At least you will know that it is probably something positive. So, even if you don't 'know' the word, you know more than you do!

As you can see, there is a lot to knowing a word completely. The question is: how much of each word do you *have to* know? Do you really need to be able to *use* each word or is it okay, for some words, to only be able to *recognise* them?

TIP

By not having to learn everything about every word, you can save yourself a lot of time! Some dictionaries give you information about which words are more, or less, common. For example, the Collins Cobuild uses little symbols in the shape of diamonds to show how common words are. Other dictionaries use other systems. This is very helpful information when you have to learn a lot of words.

Different types of vocabulary

You have probably found that some words are more common in some situations. Words like 'okay' and 'great' are common in conversations, for example. Other words are only used in written English; some are mainly used in formal situations such as lectures, or in informal situations, for example when talking with friends.

Researchers have found that some words (like 'the' and 'is') are very common in all situations. In fact, even in academic texts, the same 1000 words make up over 70% of the text. So make sure you know these words before all others (to find out what they are, see below). You probably already do, if you can understand this book! The second 1000 words occur about 5% of the time, so together you have more than three-quarters of the text covered.

Academic words are, as you would expect, very common in university texts. They make up about 10% of the total but these words carry a lot of the meaning so you will certainly need to know them. Below you can complete some exercises to make sure you do. Read through the

Section on the Academic Word List (on p. 45) and ensure that you understand all the vocabulary.

University texts also include technical terms that are specific to your subject. Examples include words like 'merger' in the area of finance, and 'osmosis' in the area of biology. These words are usually explained in your textbooks and many of them will be new to native speakers too, so they are often a bit easier to learn as the lecturer is likely to cover them in class or they are explained in your course book.

Four categories of vocabulary

So, to summarise: vocabulary can be categorised into the following types:

Type	Description	Examples
Everyday vocabulary	These are the most common words in general use. They are not specific to academic vocabulary.	and, so, but, because, the, big, must
Academic vocabulary	These are words that are used frequently in academic writing but are not specific to any subject.	research, define, analyse
Technical subject-specific vocabulary	These are words that will be extremely important for your university subject but may not be very frequent. The words may be used in a technical sense.	(for anatomy students) metatarsal, mesothorax, cadaver, glottis
General low-frequency vocabulary	These words are not specific to academic texts, and not very common.	cronyism, mewling, crowbar

Types of vocabulary

Read the following text. It is from an introductory textbook called *Botany for Gardeners*. First answer this question: *According to the passage, in what ways are plants adapted for water storage?*

ADAPTATIONS FOR WATER STORAGE

To obtain water, perennial species in arid regions either develop a long tap root to reach underground sources or, as is common among many species of cactus, spread horizontal mats of fibrous roots, just below the soil surface. Although shallow roots become parched and lifeless in the heat of summer, they quickly return to growth and full metabolic activity within hours after rain has soaked the soil. Having taken full advantage of infrequent and unpredictable water supplies, many desert plants survive periods of drought by using water stored in leaves or stems. The succulent leaves and stems of such genera as Mesembryanthemum, Sedum, Crassula, and Echeveria contain enlarged water-storage cells capable of supplying the plants' basic needs for many months. Stem succulents, such as cacti and cactus-like Euphorbias, sometimes store sufficient moisture to last for years. As much as 95% of the total volume of succulent plants is devoted to water storage.   (From: B. Capon *Botany for Gardeners: An Introduction and Guide* (Portland: Timber Press, 1990), p. 107.

Now look at the words in the text. Try to find 3 examples of each of the types of vocabulary listed above:

The answers for this task are at the end of the book on p. 205.

Type	Examples	
Everyday vocabulary	1	
	2	
	3	
Non-technical academic vocabulary (see the Academic Word List)	1	
	2	
	3	
Technical subject-specific vocabulary	1	
	2	
	3	
General low-frequency vocabulary	1	
	2	
	3	

Formal and informal language

In addition to the different word types and frequencies, words also differ in how formal or informal they are. For example, you could say:

I need to exit the premises in order to purchase supplies.

Or you could say:

I'm going out shopping.

Academic language is often rather formal because the meaning needs to be as precise as possible, and we would not use academic words in everyday conversations very often. That does not mean that you need to write in the most complicated way possible, simply that you need to be able to tell which words are more likely to be used in an academic essay than others.

A   Can you tell which word in the following pairs is more likely to be used in academic texts?

Think about	Consider
Summarise	Put together
Investigate	Find out
Establish	Find that . . .
Describe	Talk about
Very small	Minute

Check your answers on p. 205.

Formal text is often less 'emotive'. In other words, it is based more on facts and less on our feelings. A good exercise to become aware of the difference is, to look at the difference between a newspaper report and a personal story. When you read the newspaper you should get the facts. Then, when you watch TV and see an interview with someone who was present at the event, compare the two and decide what, if anything, makes the second story more 'emotive'.

You will need to get a feel for which words have greater emotive value than others. For example, some words can mean the same thing but they do not have the same 'feeling'.

B   Which word is stronger, do you think?

killed   assassinated   butchered

Here are some other words. Can you put them in order, from less to more emotive? (See p. 205 for answers.)

explosion / growth / big increase

huge success / successful outcome / victory

great / fantastic / good

insulted / trashed / embarrassed

C   However, it is not just about the individual words, but the tone of the whole sentence or text. Have a look at these examples. How would you rewrite them to make them sound less emotive? (See p. 205 for answers.)

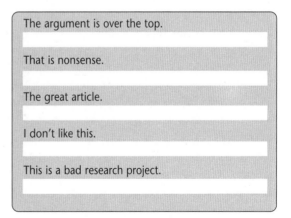

The argument is over the top.

That is nonsense.

The great article.

I don't like this.

This is a bad research project.

One thing we do is 'hedge' our language by using words like 'could' and 'might', 'maybe' and 'it appears that', to show that there may be other explanations and possibilities. You will learn more about this in Chapters 8 and 9.

What is your vocabulary level?

Without a good level of vocabulary your life at university will be much harder. But what exactly is *your* level? Here is an easy way to find out:

1 Go to: www.er.uqam.ca/nobel/r21270/levels/
2 Choose test A or B
3 Choose the word level you want to test: 1000 words means that the test only looks at the 1000 most frequent words in English.
4 Make sure to include the University Word list
5 Write down your answers below

Test (A or B)	Level	Score

The website recommends that you get at least 83% on each test. As a university student you will want to pass the tests for the 5000 and University Word lists. You may want to work on the 10,000 word list too.

What vocabulary do you use?

What is your vocabulary use like? Your word processor will tell you how many words are in your essay but it will not tell you how many different words you use, or how often you use the same word. For that we can use the VocabProfile website: www.er.uqam.ca/nobel/r21270/textools/web_vp.html

To use the website, do the following:

1 Copy the text (for example, an essay you have written for your course) from your computer screen.
2 Go to the above website and paste the text in the textbox.
3 Click 'do it' to get your results.

The results can be a little bit confusing, so let's look at an example (see Figure 4.1). Here we use an academic article that we wrote.

Let's start on the right-hand side. We can see that there are 6799 words in the text in total and 1314 different words. The word 'token' here means each individual word in the text. The sentence you are now reading has nine tokens. (It contains nine words.) The word 'type' means each unique word. So a phrase like 'the man who bought the dog' has only five types, as the word 'the' is used twice. 'Tokens per type' thus tells us that we used each word, on average, 5.17 times. That may seem like a lot but that includes words such as 'a', 'the', 'or', 'of'. The type–token ratio can be particularly useful with shorter texts. If this is very low it means that you use

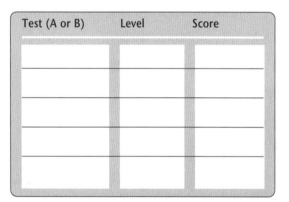

Figure 4.1 VocabProfile website

many of the same words in your text. This could mean your text is boring to read or not specific enough.

Further down on the screen we see various 'onlist' figures. These have to do with the word lists the programme uses to do its analyses. Not all of our words are in the word lists, probably because they are too specialised. But it could also mean that we have made spelling errors and that the programme could not recognise our words. Remember to do a spelling check first!

Moving to the left-hand side of the screen, we get some very valuable information. 'First 500' tells us how many words are within the 500 most common words in English. In our text this is nearly two-thirds of all the words used. And remember that this was an academic article. As you can see, you really need to know your basic words and know them well, as they are so common.

Next we can see that over 73% of all our words are in the most common 1000 words. We further see that 40% are function words and 32% are content words. Function words are words that play a grammatical role but do not have much meaning on their own. Examples are prepositions such as 'at' and 'up', articles like 'the', and pronouns such as 'she'. Content words are words such as 'house' and 'university' or verbs like 'write' and 'check'. As you can see in our example, slightly more words are function words than content words. Of course, the ratio depends on the type of text you are writing. A description of a building will be likely to use more content words.

K2 words are those that are within the list of the 2000 most common words in English. Only 5% fall in this category in our text. AWL stands for 'Academic Word List' and these words are particularly important for you as a student. Even though these are not common words in everyday English use, you can see they make up 11% of the words in our text. If you are writing an essay and you score very low on the number of AWL words you may want to look into this, as your text may sound too informal.

A word list of your writing

If you would like to see a list of all the words you use in your text you can use the website www.lextutor.ca/freq/eng/ (see Figure 4.2)

Using this website you can see which words are the most common in the text. In the example below, the most often used words (apart from the grammatical words such as 'of', 'and', 'or', etc.) are words like 'centre', 'language' and 'self-access' (the topic of the article). Looking at a list like this will help you find any words you use very often. Too much repetition is not good and it may be useful to look up synonyms in a thesaurus (see below, p. 51, for information on how to do that).

Tokens: **6669**
Types: **1440**
Ratio: **0.2159**
Sort: **descending**

RANK	FREQ	COVERAGE		WORD
		individual	cumulative	
1.	439	6.58%	6.58%	THE
2.	289	4.33%	10.91%	OF
3.	223	3.34%	14.25%	AND
4.	194	2.91%	17.16%	IN
5.	165	2.47%	19.63%	A
6.	163	2.44%	22.07%	TO
7.	76	1.14%	23.21%	THAT
8.	71	1.06%	24.27%	SELF-ACCESS
9.	68	1.02%	25.29%	IS
10.	66	0.99%	26.28%	FOR
11.	65	0.97%	27.25%	LEARNING
12.	60	0.90%	28.15%	AS
13.	55	0.82%	28.97%	CENTRES
14.	48	0.72%	29.69%	CENTRE
15.	48	0.72%	30.41%	THEIR
16.	47	0.70%	31.11%	MATERIALS
17.	45	0.67%	31.78%	LANGUAGE
18.	43	0.64%	32.42%	SAC
19.	43	0.64%	33.06%	THIS
20.	41	0.61%	33.67%	ON
21.	41	0.61%	34.28%	THEY
22.	40	0.60%	34.88%	ARE
23.	38	0.57%	35.45%	SUPPORT
24.	38	0.57%	36.02%	WAS
25.	35	0.52%	36.54%	BE
26.	34	0.51%	37.05%	SACS
27.	33	0.49%	37.54%	NOT
28.	32	0.48%	38.02%	BY
29.	32	0.48%	38.50%	ONE
30.	32	0.48%	38.98%	WERE
31.	31	0.46%	39.44%	IT
32.	31	0.46%	39.90%	STUDENTS
33.	29	0.43%	40.33%	AN
34.	29	0.43%	40.76%	MENTIONED
35.	29	0.43%	41.19%	STUDY
36.	28	0.42%	41.61%	&
37.	28	0.42%	42.03%	OR
38.	26	0.39%	42.42%	ALSO
39.	26	0.39%	42.81%	NEW
40.	24	0.36%	43.17%	AT

Figure 4.2 Lextutor website

© Hayo Reinders, Nick Moore and Marilyn Lewis (2008), *The International Student Handbook*, Palgrave Macmillan Ltd

Practising your vocabulary

Now that you know what vocabulary you use, how is this different from a native speaker? Ask a friend if you can analyse his/her essay, and write down the results below. What differences can you find? (If you can't find anyone to give you a copy of their essay, perhaps your teacher has a model essay you could use.)

Another approach is to compare a first draft with a later draft of your own. Do you use more words or more types of words? How about your academic words?

How to learn new words

Having learned another language you will know how important it is to learn vocabulary. It is just as important as learning the grammar of the new language. Some people would even say learning words is more important. But with so many words in the English language, you have to learn smart, not just learn a lot. Focus on the most frequent words first, then the academic words and the words specific to your subject (see above). It is also important to think about how you will learn (and remember!) new words, as there are more and less efficient ways.

Which of these suggestions do you do already?

Students have told us they use many different ways to learn new words. Here are some of them. Do you do these? Put a tick in front of every technique, and at the end add them up.

To find new words . . .

- I highlight or copy words I don't know from my textbook and other readings.

  This is a good idea, but be careful to (at first) choose only words that are quite frequent, as you don't want to spend your energy on words you will not see or use again.

- I try to write new words down during the lecture or tutorial.

  This can work, but be careful: it is difficult enough to follow the lecturer without also having to worry about new vocabulary, so unless a word is repeated again and again, it may be more important to get the overall message, rather than focus on individual words. It may be better to set aside specific time to learn vocabulary.

- I study lists of words and phrases we are provided with.

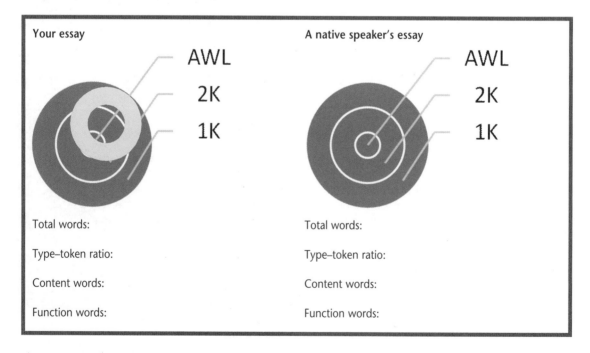

Your essay	A native speaker's essay
AWL	AWL
2K	2K
1K	1K
Total words:	Total words:
Type–token ratio:	Type–token ratio:
Content words:	Content words:
Function words:	Function words:

Words given out by your lecturers (usually in the form of glossaries), or lists of (usually) subject-specific words with a brief definition. These are important to learn as they are very relevant to the subject.

● I use the 1000, 2000 and Academic Word Lists on the internet, and check I know those words well.

This is an excellent strategy. You can find the links to the 1000 and the Academic Word Lists at http://esl.about.com/library/vocabulary/bl1000_list1.htm

To remember new words . . .

● I group words by their meaning.

This works well as it is the same way our brain stores information. Words that go together often are easier to remember together. Figure 4.3 gives an example. You could add many more words.

● I try to create a story with the words I want to remember.

Some students use memory techniques like storytelling, such as this one: 'I am going on holiday and will bring . . . [add the new words here]. Others use the new words to describe a person (especially good with adverbs and adjectives) or a process (good for verbs).

● I classify words.

For example, cats and dogs are both 'animals' so

they can be grouped together. Animals and humans are both 'living creatures', and so on. Remembering words in relation to other words like this can help.

QUESTION

All three examples above are to do with grouping words. How many different ways could you group the words below? Talk with someone else about how you would group them and why.

acute, clinical practice, complain of, complications, diphtheria, doctors, fever, high rates, illness, infected, pain, patients, penicillin, preventable, preventative, rheumatic fever, suffer from, swabs, therapy, treatment

● I link new words with pictures.

Some learners are more visual than others and, for them, associating words with pictures is a good way to remember them. For example: the word 'bumblebee' (an insect).

'The bumblebee sat on the newsreader's nose and read the newspaper.' Or you can simply think of the image of a bumblebee when learning the word.

● I review regularly.

This is probably the most important one. Research has shown that without review we forget up to 75% of new information within ONE DAY (see Chapter 3)! So it is extremely important to

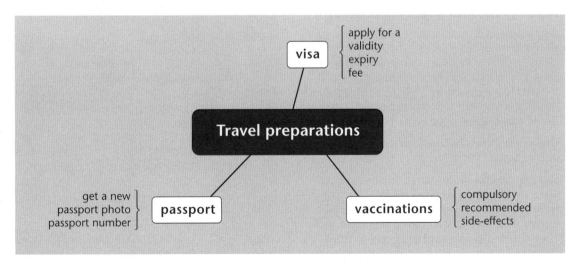

Figure 4.3 Word grouping

have a schedule. This is especially difficult if you are studying hard but the truth is simple: if you don't review them, you may as well not learn new words in the first place. Have a system!

● I use a flashcard system

One of the best ways to learn new vocabulary! See further on in this chapter.

To **use** new words . . .

● I choose five new words in the morning and remind myself to find a way to use them that day.

This works well for many students as there are so many words and you won't be able to start using all of them straightaway. Choose words that you think are important for you to be able to use yourself, rather than to be able to recognise only.

● I keep a list of words near my desk or on my computer so that when I am writing an essay, it reminds me to use those.

Great! And don't forget the glossary your lecturer may have given you.

Did you get 12 out of 12? If so, well done! If your score was lower, try and see if any of these suggestions sound like they might work for you. Perhaps do this with another student, so you can help and remind each other.

Work out the meanings of new words

When you meet new words in context they will always seem difficult but by looking at the meaning, it will be easier to remember the word. Look at this sentence and imagine that **********s is a new word. What might it mean? Write down as many words as possible that would make sense.

The albatross deaths have attracted attention at international **********s.

Look at the end of this paragraph to find the word that was in the actual article. Many of the words you wrote down will have meanings similar or related to that of the original word. They will be like synonyms. Trying to think about the meaning will help you remember the new word. (The word was 'conferences').

Now look at your textbook and find a word you don't know. Try to work it out using these clues:

● How do the words in the rest of the sentence help?
● Do the parts of the word remind you of other related words?
● Take a guess at the possible meaning.
● Use a dictionary as a last resort.

One technique is to look at the different word parts. Many words in English are made up of words from other languages. Sometimes knowing this can help you recognise their meaning.

For example, have you heard people talk about 'the post-modern age'? The word 'post' here comes from Latin and means 'after', so 'post-modern age' refers to a period in history after the modern period. We call 'post' a *prefix* because it comes *before* the word.

Can you recognise the others below? Fill in the empty spaces in the table.

Prefix	English meaning	Example
ante- & pre-		pre-war period
anti-	= against	
auto-		autonomous, autocrat
bi-		bicycle
inter-		interaction
intra-	= inside	
mis-		misinterpreting = interpreting the wrong way
mono-	= one	
multi-	= many	
neo-		neo-colonialism
pan-	= all	
tele-		telephone, television

Check your answers on p. 205.

English also uses many affixes which come at the end of a word. Here are some examples:

Suffix	Meaning	Example
-ance, ence (*noun*)	state of being	residence, permanence
-age (*noun*)	belonging to	percentage, coverage
-ful (*adj*)	with	doubtful, meaningful
-less (*adj*)	without	doubtless, purposeless

Learning academic vocabulary

Above, we talked about different types of vocabulary and discussed the importance of academic vocabulary for your university studies. Here, we look at where to find out which are the most important words and how to learn them.

If your score is not very good, you will want to practise these words. You can use the website below.

TIP

Do you want to practise? Use http://web.uvic.ca/~gluton/awl/ to find dozens of exercises for learning the academic words.

Learning vocabulary with flashcards

Learning words is one thing; remembering them is another. Flashcards (little paper cards) can be of great use as a way of keeping track of words you want to learn. The clever system that you'll learn here also gives you a very effective way to learn them as well. How does it work?

SIDE A	SIDE B
word or expression	Definition Sentence with that word collocation translation pronunciation any other information

TIP

Researchers from New Zealand have created a list of the 570 most frequent words found across different academic fields. You can visit this list, called the Academic Word List, or AWL, here:

http://www.vuw.ac.nz/lals/research/awl/headwords.html

You will notice that the list is called 'headwords'. This means that words such as 'analyse' and 'analysis' are grouped together. The word 'analyse' is the headword from which other, related words can be made.

How many do you know?
Since these words are so important it would be good to download the full list from the website above, and test your understanding of them.

How many, as a percentage, do you know? Write down the date and the percentage here:

Date: Percentage:

On one side of the card you write the new word, expression or sentence you want to remember. On the other side you write a definition, an example of its use (perhaps as you encountered it yourself), a translation, collocations (see p. 51) and any other information you want to remember about that word (e.g., pronunciation, where you heard it, etc.).

The cards should be written in such a way that if you look at them again after a long time, you know what the word means and how to use it.

Here's an example:

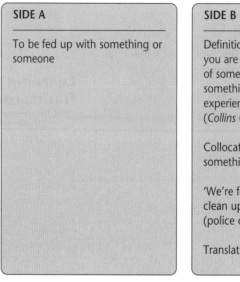

SIDE A	SIDE B
To be fed up with something or someone	Definition: 'If you are fed up, you are unhappy, bored or tired of something, especially of something you've been experiencing for a long time' (*Collins Cobuild*) Collocation: fed up with something or someone 'We're fed up with having to clean up behind the tourists' (police officer on the radio) Translation: ergens zat van zijn

Here's a good system for using the flashcards to help you learn new words.

1 Put all the new flashcards in one pile.
2 The next day, practise them again. Put the ones you know into a new pile, number 2. The ones you don't know stay in pile number 1.
3 The next day, do the same thing. The words you know from 1 one should go into pile number 2, the ones you know from pile 2 should go into a new pile – number 3. Words you don't know stay in their original pile. If you learn any new words in the meantime, put these in pile number 1. Do this until you have five piles.
4 Practise all the words every day until they are all in pile number 5. The good thing about this method is that words that are very difficult take more time to get to pile number five, whereas you don't spend a lot of time on easier words.

TIP *Learning vocabulary through games*

Wordcards are excellent to do vocabulary games with. For example, with a friend you could take 20 cards and test each other. If your partner gets the answer right, he or she gets your card. If not, you keep it. The first person to get all 20 cards is the winner.

5 After a word has arrived at pile number 5 and you still know it, put it into pile number 6. This is a special pile because you only practise it once a month. If you practise these and you still know them, put them into pile number 7. This one you only practise once every six months. If you still know a word then, you will probably remember it forever.

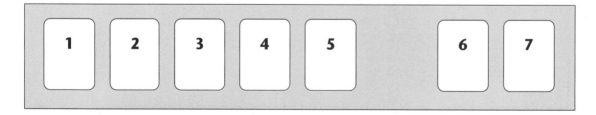

| 1 | 2 | 3 | 4 | 5 | | 6 | 7 |

How to make the most of a dictionary

One tool you will be using a lot is your dictionary. Most people use them to look up the meaning of an individual word but few realise that dictionaries give far more information than that. Before we look at the use of a dictionary, let's see what different types exist:

Translation dictionary

This is the most popular type of dictionary with international students. It is quick and you get an immediate idea of the meaning of a word through your own language. There is nothing wrong with using a translation dictionary, but they are more useful as a practical tool rather than for learning vocabulary.

English–English dictionary

This is where you will find a wealth of information not only about the meaning of a word but also about how it is used in practice. We will look at some examples below. Learners' dictionaries often include study pages, help notes and information on how words are related to other words. A learner's dictionary is not the same as a vocabulary book. A dictionary's main function (even a learner's dictionary) is to help you find out the meaning of words. A vocabulary book's main function is to help you learn words.

Special dictionaries

If you study medicine you will probably want a dictionary that explains all the medical terms you are likely to come across. Luckily, such a dictionary exists and there are others for law, science, and many other subjects. Have a look through your bookshop; having one of these can be very valuable.

Thesaurus or dictionary of synonyms

A thesaurus is a dictionary that gives you a word's synonyms (another word with the same or similar meaning), such as the words 'flat' and 'apartment'. (The opposite of a synonym is an antonym. Examples of antonyms are 'good' and 'bad'). Using a thesaurus is great for when you have to write an essay and can't think of another word to avoid saying the same thing over and over (see below).

Collocations

Collocations are words that go together. So we say that we 'have' an argument, not that we 'do' an argument. Getting collocations right is a difficult task for non-native speakers but not paying attention to them can result in a very different meaning and often makes your speech sound unnatural. There are special 'collocation dictionaries' and they are a great help for your writing.

If we look at a collocations dictionary, we may find the following information for the word 'flower':

Adj.	colourful, fragrant	A fragrant rose
Quant.	bouquet, bunch	A bunch of roses
Verb + flower	have, to produce	The nursery grows roses
Flower + verb	to set seed	Roses set seed after flowering
Flower + noun	petal, stem	A rose can have many petals
Prep. phrases	in flower	The roses are in flower

As you can see, you will find examples of adjectives commonly used with 'flower'. It also shows you which quantifiers we use (so we say 'a bunch of flowers', not 'a group of flowers'). Next, you can see examples of how to combine a verb with the word 'flower', 'flower' with a verb, and 'flower' with a noun. Finally, we learn that the preposition used with 'flower' is 'in', and some common phrases with the word. Very helpful, especially when you are writing an essay.

Phrasal verbs are another difficult area for learners. A phrasal verb is a verb followed by a preposition or adverb:

> bring (something) up
>
> hurry up

These have a specific meaning; for example, 'to bring something up' can literally mean to bring (say, a book) up (for example, to another room in the house). But often it means 'to start a new topic' or 'to mention something in a conversation'. So even though you may know the meaning of the verb ('bring') and the preposition ('up'), if you didn't know the special meaning of 'to bring something up', you probably couldn't guess it.

Another thing to know about phrasal verbs is that some are *transitive* (they can take an object), like our example: 'he brought up *a new topic*' ('a new topic' is the object). Other phrasal verbs are *intransitive*, such as 'to show up' (meaning, 'to arrive'), and do not take an object. There is nothing in the phrasal verbs themselves to tell you if they are transitive or intransitive and you will need a dictionary to tell you.

Similarly, some phrasal verbs are *separable*, which means that the object can come between the verb and the preposition. An example is 'to make up a story'. You can say:

> I made the story up
> but also:
> I made up the story

Again, you will need a dictionary, as for most verbs it is impossible to tell. Several of the major publishers sell phrasal verb dictionaries and workbooks.

TIP

A free website that will help you with phrasal verbs is this one:
www.phrasalverbdemon.com/

What information does a dictionary give?

Have a look at the example in Figure 4.4, and see if you can list the different types of information that are included.

accentuate /ækˈsɛntʃueɪt/ **accentuates, accentuating, accentuated.** To **accentuate** something means to emphasize it or make it more noticeable. *His shaven head accentuates his large round face… The whole air of menace was accentuated by the fact that he was so cordial and soft-voiced.*

◆◇◇◇◇
VERB
=intensify

Vn

Figure 4.4   Dictionary entry

Source: Collins Cobuild.

TIP

You may be tempted sometimes to just write your essay in your own language and have it translated by the computer. Think again! Have a look at the example below. Can you figure out what this song is?

end the eye it led inside the sleigh O'er which is being opened rushing field us inside the middle laughing the inside fun a spirit and it dawned it made and and laughed to go song the bell in the bob tail ring and and and fun tonight song A-sleighing end other the thing, daughter Rang daughter Rang kind of Ohio and daughter Rang daughter Rang kind inside Ohio inside the middle daughter Rang daughter Rang sound are born inside the sleigh which is being opened

It is the Christmas song 'Jingle Bells', translated from English to Korean and back to English!

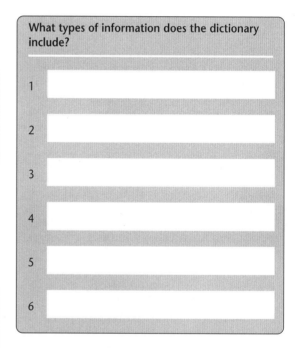

What types of information does the dictionary include?

1
2
3
4
5
6

The answers are at the end of the book.

There are others, but you get the picture: a dictionary gives you a lot of useful information. Some words may have more information, such as different entries for different meanings, phrasal verbs, as well as information about whether the word is formal or informal, spoken language only, offensive, or technical.

Can you find the answers to these questions?

Now that you know how much information a dictionary can give you, see if you can answer these questions. You will need a full-size (not a pocket) dictionary. The answers are at the end of the book on p. 206.

1 Can you say 'the meeting was called by the leader'?

2 Is 'furniture' a countable noun?

3 Is 'darn' an offensive word?

4 What is the difference between the phrasal verbs 'break out' and 'break away'?

5 Where in the word 'legislature' does the accent come?

6 What is a synonym for 'appalling'?

Using a thesaurus successfully

As mentioned above, a thesaurus is a reference book or website that gives lists of words of similar meaning. It can be really useful if you are trying to use a wider and more interesting range of vocabulary; however, a thesaurus needs to be treated with care. Almost no two words can ever be used with exactly the same meaning in exactly the same way all the time. And so it is important to use a dictionary in order to check

the words that your thesaurus throws up at you and find out if they are suitable in the contexts in which you want to use them. The following task takes you through the steps.

Imagine this situation. You have been asked to write an essay about the ways that you have learned vocabulary in another language. You write the following sentence in your essay: 'One of the best **ways** to learn new words is using vocabulary cards.'

However, you realise that you have used the word 'way' many times already and want to use a different word.

You go to an online thesaurus to look for other words for 'way'. Follow these steps:

(a) Go online to the Merriam-Webster Online dictionary, at www.m-w.com/. Enter the word **way** and choose 'Thesaurus'. From the results, there are ten different meanings of **way**. Which one is relevant here? See the answer key at the end of the book (p. 206).

(b) Click on the relevant entry word at the end of this definition. It is a link. It gives the following text:

Start with the synonyms. Which of these look possible in the original sentence in terms of word meaning? You may need to use your dictionary to do this:

Synonyms   approach, fashion, form, manner, strategy, style, system, tack, tactics, technique, way

Related words   mode; blueprint, design, game, ground plan, intrigue, layout, line, plan, plot, program, route, scheme; expedient, move, shift, step; practice (*also* practise), process, routine; project, proposal, proposition; policy

TIP   *Related words*

Often it may be best to stick with the suggested 'synonyms'. The key to using the Related Words is to take a step back and rethink what you are trying to say. They can give you different ideas but they may take you off on a tangent and may not fit in with the point that you are making.

© Hayo Reinders, Nick Moore and Marilyn Lewis (2008),
The International Student Handbook, Palgrave Macmillan Ltd

(c) Now use these words to write alternative sentences. Think about how you might need to change the grammar of the sentence for each of the words.

(d) How is the meaning different in each of these sentences?

Online and mobile tools for vocabulary learning

It's useless having the world's most up-to-date English–English dictionary in your apartment if you need it when you are in a lecture, or meeting your study group in a café or trying to do a bit of reading on the bus – you need your vocabulary reference where you can access it. You can have a dictionary loaded onto your cellphone, your palm top, your notebook, or even your U3 USB storage device. These devices have a lot of advantages over a traditional hard copy dictionary. As an international student, you may already make use of some kind of online or mobile vocabulary device. However, if you are still carrying an enormous paper dictionary around with you, or just thinking of upgrading your electronic vocabulary learning toys, the following task will help you decide what kind of device you need to buy.

Choosing an electronic dictionary

Electronic dictionaries are really expensive. Because they are small, they are easily left on the train, dropped in the sea when fishing, or stolen from your favourite table in the library. So before you buy one, decide whether it's really worth it. You may be able to think of something more important (or fun) to spend your money on. And it might be that a CD rom loaded onto your laptop or even using a dictionary from your cellphone (see below), is enough, rather than buying a very expensive handheld device. The following questions might help you decide what kind of mobile solution you need, to complete your studies

Criteria	Notes	Questions
Quality of language data	The main problem that teachers have with electronic dictionaries is that while the technology is 21st-century, the language data loaded onto the device can be old-fashioned. Learners often come up with bizarre words from electronic dictionaries – some of which don't even exist in English. Make sure your new device is fitted with a decent learners' dictionary from a respected publisher – Macmillan, Longman, Cambridge and Oxford are all good.	• What dictionaries are loaded onto the device? • Is it monolingual (English-English) or bi-lingual (English – your language) or both? (Having both options is ideal.) • Are there example sentences? • Can you hear words spoken? If so – what's the accent like? (Many state-of-the-art e-dictionaries still sound robotic.)
Design	The design of the device or software may affect how easy it is to use.	• How big is the screen/results window size? Can you see all of a word's multiple meanings without scrolling? • How easy are basic search functions? • How easy is it to switch between dictionaries and cross-check words? • If the device has its own keyboard, is it big enough?

Criteria	Notes	Questions
Functions	There are lots of things you can do with mobile devices that you can't do with paper dictionaries. Check what your device can do and decide if you are likely to use these features.	• Can you make a personal database of words that you look up? If so, what information can you save? • Can you export data saved to other software/hardware, e.g. to a printer or a Microsoft® Excel document? • Is there a test function that you can use to test yourself on newly learnt words? • Does it have any other features you need – such as vocabulary games, a diary, a calculator, an address book, an alarm? • How about the battery life?

TIP   *Dictionary CD Roms*

Many English-English dictionaries are sold with a CD Rom. You may be able to just buy the cd rom. It will be a lot cheaper than an electronic dictionary. Load this onto your notebook and leave the paper copy at home! You will have your dictionary with you whenever you are working on your laptop with no need to connect to the Internet.

TIP

Some websites also offer English-language games to play on your cellphone. The BBC is one of them: www.bbc.co.uk/schools/gcsebitesize/mobile/

They have some wonderful games such as the one below. Not all of these can be played on your phone, so check the site.

State of Debate
You are a 'non-adult' living in urban England in the year 2020. JustCo – the one-stop criminal justice system - makes all non-adults' lives hell, by imposing stupid restrictions about what you can do, how you dress and even who you hang around with! Use your quick wit and English-language skills to bluff your way around the law, avoid arrest and help your mates out of sticky situations.

Learning on your cellphone

Several companies now offer dictionaries you can download onto your cellphone. These are not as large as the electronic dictionaries we looked at above and do not include sound. Still, when you quickly need an important word, they can be very helpful.

Using a corpus to learn new words and improve your writing

A corpus is simply a large collection of texts. An English corpus can be a great help to learners to see how the language is used by native speakers in authentic situations, such as in newspapers, in books, in articles, but also in spoken contexts such as in lectures, or on TV. A corpus is different from a dictionary in that it does not give translations or explanations. Instead, it gives you a wealth of information about which words are most common in English and how they are used. The types of questions a corpus can help you answer include:

● What prepositions does 'scared' take in spoken British English?
● Can you say '*X* scared *Y*'?
● When do I use 'scared' and when do I use 'afraid'?

Let's see if we can answer some of these questions.

A free online corpus

The easiest way to see how a corpus works is by using an example. One free website that we recommend is this one: www.lextutor.ca/concordancers/concord_e.html – here you get access to a concordancer, or a programme that lets you search through a corpus.

Let's try and answer the first question above. Go to the website and you will see the screen shown in Figure 4.5.

It may look a bit complicated at first but let's go through it step-by-step. We are interested in the word 'scared', so this is what we type in the first text box. In addition to 'equal to', which looks up only the word you type in, you can choose 'begins with' or 'ends with' or 'contains'. This is helpful when you are interested in finding examples of all words that begin with, say, 'inter', such as 'international' or 'interaction'. You could also look for words that contain, for example, the word 'roll', such as 'enrolling' and 'troll'. In this case we will use 'equal to'.

Next we need to select the corpus we want to use, by clicking on the drop-down box. There are several listed. The most useful ones include:

All of above	This lets you search through all the available corpora.
University Word list	Particularly useful when you are writing an academic essay.
BNC Written	If you are only interested in written language.
BNC Spoken	Likewise, if you are interested in spoken English.

In this case we will use BNC (this stands for British National Corpus) Spoken. If we were interested in US English we could use the US TV Talk corpus, but it is much smaller. This is all the information you need to select, to get started. You can leave the other options as they are and choose 'Get concordance'. Figure 4.6 gives an example of the output.

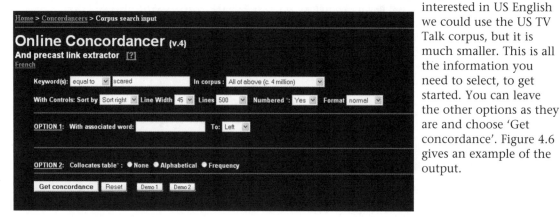

Figure 4.5 Online concordancer

```
Concordances for scared = 21
```

```
1   ough a window and it weren't going. Mum got scared    and he weren't scared    That was, that w
2   even     Yeah.    when I watch it now I get scared, especially the bit when she  goes like that
3   t of fear is a good thing.    Erm, I'm still scared every time I pull away. You know, ji little
4   ian and Roly was giving it  cos you know how scared he was of dogs it was barking at him! And th
5   surprised!   We got four lovely    He'd be scared if he was    Put your leg down!    I got
6   t everybody! Mm, yes you're hard, I'm really scared!    Ma, it's like, it's like   my dad this
7       Go on!    I hate    Right.    Pam! I'm scared now!    Is it dark out!    Yeah.    Good!
8   y the door in case one of them jumped I'm so scared of  spiders I hate them!    I always spot th
9   d Jane to go down to sort her out but Jane's scared  of a fight.    Jane's scared of offending he
10  on her    Yeah.    and, and if she's already scared of his temper and they've not  even lived tog
11  icking one up to get rid of it if you're not scared of it, but  playing with one, keeping it as a
12  out but Jane's scared  of a fight.    Jane's scared of offending her.    I know.    Mind you, I'd
13  it! Gives me the creeps! That's what I'd be scared of otherwise I'd put one. That's it!    Do yo
14   I'd hate to have a load of chop ooh    was scared only children he was scared wasn't he? Tony w
15  n't going. Mum got scared    That was, that was what erm Dempsey done
16  oes like that and he goes aargh I get, I get scared.    That's the end of it, yeah.    Yeah. Rig
17  ? And it was fearsome    Yes    Moses was sc scared    then it says to the, the apostles that the
18  og don't they?    Yeah, but he looks really scared they go, the whole back goes  right up and he
19  two  phones and like, and like I was just so scared to go in there  because I, if you do anything
20   it's come to  the stage where girls are now scared to put their name down to  take home economic
21  chop ooh    was scared only children he was scared wasn't he? Tony was  frightened.    Oh yes th
```

Figure 4.6 Online concordance

WordNet entries for  scared

Each sentence comes from the BNC Spoken corpus. By clicking on the underlined words you can see the whole sentence, but usually it is enough to just look at the part you see on the first screen. The 21 examples only use one preposition: 'of'.

By clicking on WordNet® entries you can see a dictionary definition of the word 'scared'.

You can also search for words used with other words, by typing a word in the 'With associated word' text box. For example, if we search for 'scared' associated with 'of' we find the same 10 examples as we found in the 21 results we got above.

Checking collocation with an online concordancer

Concordancers are also really useful for checking which words go with other words. For example, checking the prepositions that follow some words, e.g.

I am really interested ____ finding out more about music from Cuba.

If you want to check this, follow these instructions:

1 Go online and navigate to www.lextutor.ca/concordancers/concord_e.html
2 In the 'Keyword: equal to' box type 'interested'.
3 In the box that says 'In corpus:' choose 'All of above'.
4 Hit 'Get concordance'.

Look through the list of examples and find those with a similar grammar structure and similar meaning to your sentence. Which preposition follows 'interested' most often?

TIP   *A great resource for vocabulary*

A really good book to help you use effective concordance searches is

J. Thurstun and N. Candlin (1997), *Exploring Academic English: A Workbook for Student Essay Writing* (Sydney Macquarie University).

Your turn!

Now let's see if you can do this. Can you find the answers to the three questions above? The answers are in the key on p. 206.

1   What prepositions does 'scared' take?

2   Can you say 'X scared Y'?

3   When do I use 'to be scared' and when do I use 'to be afraid'?

Use the same procedure to the missing word in the following sentences. These examples are all words from the Academic Word List. Check the answers on p. 206.

(a) The **implication** ____ this theory is that companies should do all they can to keep their staff motivated.

(b) The boom experienced in the mid 1990's **coincided** ____ the fall in the value of the dollar.

(c) They decided to **concentrate** ____ their core markets in the following decade.

TIP   *Sort your concordance search*

Some concordance samplers, such as the one at www.lextutor.ca, allow you to sort your search to the left or right. If you are interested in the word that follows your keyword, order by 'Right'. If you are interested in the word before your search term, order by 'Left'.

Chapter 5

Listening to lectures

CHAPTER OVERVIEW

In this chapter you will learn about:

- students' problems with lectures
- the purpose of a lecture
- lecturing styles that change from country to country
- note-taking tips
- preparing for a lecture
- the parts of a lecture
- the language of the lecturer
- becoming a better listener
- the sorts of questions it is OK to ask in lectures

Introduction

A large part of university life is spent attending lectures. Not only is it difficult enough to understand the lecturers, but you also need to take notes for review later. In this chapter we help you prepare for your classes.

What's the problem?

Here are some of the problems that students report about listening to lectures. In order to see which parts of this chapter you need to look at, try ticking the things that are difficult for you. Then turn to that part of the chapter.

If this sounds like your problem . . .	. . . go to this section of this chapter
• The lecturing style is very different from what I am accustomed to.	'Lecturing styles from one country to another' (see p. 60)
• I find it hard to make sense of the overall shape of the lecture. • I find it hard to know whether a point is important or not. • I can't tell when the lecturer is moving on to the next point.	'The organization and language of lectures' (see p. 67)
• The lecturer talks too fast for me to get everything down. • I can't read my handwriting later when I look back at my notes. • I don't know how to spell the words.	'Note-taking' (see p. 61)

The purpose of a lecture

What's the main purpose?

Respond to each of these statements according to your ideas of whether this is 'probably' or 'probably not' a reason for having lectures. Then check the key at the end of the book.

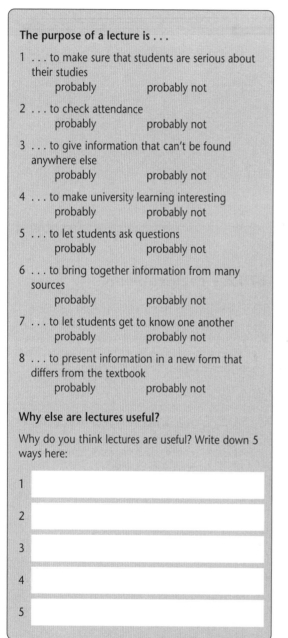

The purpose of a lecture is . . .

1 . . . to make sure that students are serious about their studies

    probably   probably not

2 . . . to check attendance

    probably   probably not

3 . . . to give information that can't be found anywhere else

    probably   probably not

4 . . . to make university learning interesting

    probably   probably not

5 . . . to let students ask questions

    probably   probably not

6 . . . to bring together information from many sources

    probably   probably not

7 . . . to let students get to know one another

    probably   probably not

8 . . . to present information in a new form that differs from the textbook

    probably   probably not

Why else are lectures useful?

Why do you think lectures are useful? Write down 5 ways here:

1

2

3

4

5

Lecturing styles from one country to another

We asked some international students for their experiences of lectures. Here is what they said. For each comment, note down the main difference in lecture style that the student noticed:

Antonina said:

In Italy there were 300 people in a lecture and we couldn't fit in the room so I listened to the lecturer on an intercom in another lecture theatre. We just listened. It was very passive. I was amazed that in lectures in New Zealand, the lecturer liked to be asked questions at any time and she would give us things to talk about.

Ahmed said:

In Saudi Arabia I sometimes feel the lecturer looks down on the students. There is a big distance between 'us' and 'them'. They certainly wouldn't talk to us outside the class. Here in Singapore it is much more open. It is much easier to approach the lecturers.

José said:

In Mexico, my lecturers seemed to make it difficult for us students. They never tried to make things easy or understandable for us and they weren't worried if we didn't get it. In America my lecturers want me to tell them if I don't understand something and they try to make things as clear as possible for us.

As you can see ,there are differences in how lecturers and students interact, in the lecturers' attitude towards students, and also in how approachable they are outside the classroom.

Preparing for a lecture

It's a good idea to spend a few minutes thinking about a lecture before you go in. This is important if the lecture is in your first language, and even more important if you are listening to a lecture in a second language. If you can predict what the lecturer will talk about, you will find it easier to follow the lecture and will get more out of it. You will also have a clearer

© Hayo Reinders, Nick Moore and Marilyn Lewis (2008), *The International Student Handbook*, Palgrave Macmillan Ltd

idea of what information you want to get from the lecture, and that will make listening easier. You can use readings handed out by the lecturer, and lecture titles, to help you prepare.

Predicting from readings

If the lecturer gives recommended readings (either a handout or chapters from a textbook) for you to read before a lecture, make sure you read them – the lecturer will usually talk about the readings in the lecture.

Predicting content from lecture titles

You may also have questions you want answered simply from the title of the lecture. This section looks at lecture titles and encourages you to come up with questions you want answered in a lecture.

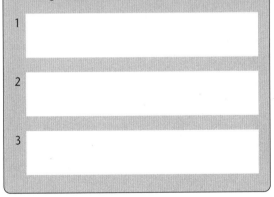

Look at the following lecture title. It is the third lecture in a course on economic development in South-East Asia. Write down three questions you would like answered if you went to this lecture.

Week 3   Wednesday 29th September

Development and Standard of Living in South-East Asia. Accounting for the variation in the region. Challenges for the future.

1

2

3

Now compare your questions with these:

1 How does the lecturer define 'Standard of Living'?
2 How does he/she measure this? What data does the lecturer cite?

3 Which countries have the highest Standard of Living in the region?
4 Which have the poorest quality of life?
5 Why is there such a variation?
6 Which historical factors affect the Standard of Living?
7 What specific challenges will the region face in the 21st century?

Try the same task with the following lecture titles (you may need to look up some of the words). You can check your answers in the key at the end of the book.

1 The Case for Censorship   (journalism)
2 Intermittent Reinforcement   (psychology)
3 The Rise of Social-networking Websites (sociology)
4 Restorative Justice: a Workable Model?   (law)

Summary

It is just as important to become a critical listener as it is to become a critical reader or writer. Being prepared and going into the lecture with clear ideas of what you want to learn is a key part of this.

> **TIP**   *Assignments*
>
> If you have an assignment due in the next few weeks, you may have questions you want answered by the lecture. For example, you may have an idea of what to write in the assignment and want to check in the lecture that you are on the right track.

Note-taking

At first, note-taking in a second language is very hard. It is tempting to write down anything you hear because you are so pleased with yourself that you heard it, whether or not it is important. You think 'OK at least I will be able to look at my notes later and work out what was said!' This is a bad tactic because note-taking has become a brainless task and you have stopped thinking about the content of the lecture. Note-taking is supposed to help you follow the lecture and then remember/think about the content

Try using this worksheet to prepare for a lecture

Thinking about the reading	During the lecture
Is there anything you didn't **understand** from the reading and want explained in the lecture?	I am confused about . . . I want these questions answered: 1 _____? 2 _____? 3 _____?
What do you want **more information** about in the lecture?	I want more details about . . .
Was there anything **controversial** in the readings? Would you like to hear an alternative opinion about this?	I want to hear the lecturer's opinion about . . .
Were there any **problems** with the ideas in the reading? Do you want these expanded in the lecture?	I disagreed with the point about . . . Do other people share my view?
Often textbook readings are **theoretical**. Do you want to hear the lecturer discussing the **application** of an idea?	I want to find out how . . . . . . works in practice.
Sometimes a textbook gives evidence from one **situation** but you may want to hear if this is true in another **situation**.	I want to hear if . . . also applies to/when . . .
Do you need ideas of where to find **further reading** about a topic?	I want more references to read about . . .

© Hayo Reinders, Nick Moore and Marilyn Lewis (2008), *The International Student Handbook*, Palgrave Macmillan Ltd

later. If your notes are not useful, then you are better off concentrating on trying to understand the lecture.

Different ways of organising your notes

Note-taking does get a lot easier with practice. This section gives some examples of how you can organise your notes more effectively. First, we will present some models that you can use.

Then we will list some ways that you can develop your note-taking.

Linear notes

This is when you make notes down the page of the main points in the lecture. It is probably what most students do most of the time.

Look at these notes from the beginning of a lecture about the business side of professional sport. What makes these notes easier to follow? Note down your observations and then check in the answer key at the end of the book.

Professionalism in sport: are footballers worth $X million per week?

last 20 years sport: pastime

big business – entertainment $

– ticket sales (less important now?)
  e.g. Turkish football grounds – ads . . . one side of ground only (cameras from other side)
  Free entry to Wednesday games (Italy)
– TV rights / Satellite TV subs
  pay-per-view boxing
  e.g. highlights on news? <25 seconds – goal / try only (who has TV rights?)
– corporate hospitality (@sports stadium)
– bar sales (in pubs)
  beer / cigarette / junk food advertising $ v. important 4 sport
– advertising – at stadiums / on players / ad. breaks on TV / team – stad. naming rights
  e.g. v. warriors ~ t. clear dome
– shirt / scarf / accessory sales (China – Crystal Palace shirts – 2 Chinese players)

RESULT: Players $$$$$ (celeb. culture) fuel all sales. Commodity?
  – transfer fees
  – wages
  – TV ad contracts – sports shoes / razors / after shave etc.
  – bad (!) autobiographies
  – etc.

(sports media – slaves to business?

lack of critical comment on sport?)

The man the brand. How much does he earn?
  per game?
  per goal?
  per shirt?
  per ad?
  per razor sale?

Using diagrams to organise your notes

Diagrams are often easier to review than linear notes and visual learners find information in a diagram easier to remember in an exam and refer back to when writing assignments. Here are three examples. Use an organisation that fits the lecture content.

Example 1: A simple classification diagram

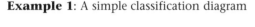

Immigration

Push factor	Pull factors
political / racial / ethnic persecution war poverty / debt unemployment drought / famine	start a new life better standard of living love better climate family reunification better quality of life better standard of living

Example 2: A mind map

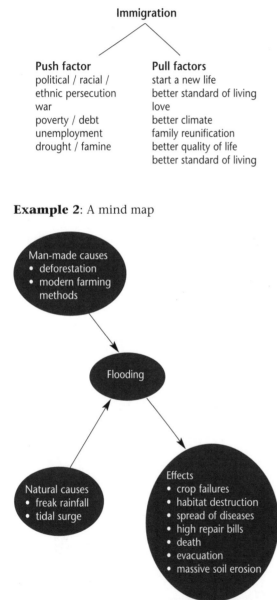

Man-made causes
• deforestation
• modern farming methods

Flooding

Natural causes
• freak rainfall
• tidal surge

Effects
• crop failures
• habitat destruction
• spread of diseases
• high repair bills
• death
• evacuation
• massive soil erosion

Example 3: The Cornell note-taking system

(Adapted from http://lifejacker.com/software/note-taking/geek-to-live--take-studyworthy-lecture-notes-202418.php)

Date of lecture	Topic:
CUES	NOTES
*Main ideas	*Record the lecture here, using
*Questions that link points	• Concise sentences • Shorthand symbols • Abbreviations • Lists
*Diagrams	
*Prompts to help you study	*Skip lots of space between points
WHEN?	WHEN?
After class during review	During class
5 cm	10 cm
SUMMARY	
WHEN? After class during review	*Top level main ideas *For quick reference 4 cm

Explanation

Notes column (right)

Record the lecture here during class, using short sentences and fragments that transcribe the facts you'll need. Eliminate all unnecessary words. Use bulleted lists for easy skimming, and as much shorthand as possible (without sacrificing readability). Develop a vocabulary of abbreviations, like 'e.g.' or 'ex' for 'for example', 'v' for 'very', 'tho' for 'though'.

Cues column (left)

After class, review your notes and jot down questions and memory joggers in this column that help connect ideas listed in the notes section. When you're studying, you'll look at these cues to help you recall the salient facts in your notes.

Summary area (bottom)

After class, while you create cues, sum up the notes on each page in one or two sentences that encapsulate the main ideas, and write them in the bottom area. You'll use the summary section to skim through your notes and find information later.

A summary of good note-taking practice

Here is the script from an excerpt from a seminar on note-taking. First of all, highlight the beginnings of new

'OK. Thank you all for coming. Today our seminar is about good note-taking practice. At the beginning of last year, I did a small study of the note-taking habits of successful students, looking at the techniques they use when taking notes in lectures, and then I asked them for their advice to students who wanted to improve their note-taking. I will present some of the findings of this study and then at the end of this presentation, there will be an opportunity for you to talk about the note-taking strategies that you found the most effective. <u>First of all, let's look at what you should make notes on – I mean the paper – not the topics!</u> Now, lots of students use notebooks for their lecture notes. This is fine, but some students find it easier to use a loose-leaf notebook – that means one that you can take the pages out of – rather than one with fixed pages. This means that you can take the pages out and put them into a folder with your course notes. Then you can collect notes and course readings for each course in one place, in a separate notebook or section of a notebook – write name + date of lecture. Sometimes lecturers give out a handout with the main points from the lectures. You could find it useful to make notes on the handout, in the margins – this will help you organise the notes you make. Also, some lecturers put their own notes on the course website after a lecture. You can print these out and put them in your folder next to your notes. The appearance of your notes is really important too because you will need to refer to them later. If you find yourself making doodles or writing notes to your partner on your lecture notes, remember that not only is this manual activity stopping you from concentrating but it will be annoying and confusing when you look back at your notes – i.e. when you are using them to revise for an exam. It is worth losing a bit of speed in order to write legibly – this saves time in the long run. If you find you don't have time to write neatly, then you are probably writing too much. Note only key words, not every word – and think critically about what you write down. If it is not going to be useful later – don't write! The other thing you can do if you can't keep up is to leave gaps [   ] when the speaker is moving too fast. You can always check with a friend later if you see a gap in your notes. In fact, it's a really good idea to review your notes as soon as possible. You could do this with another student. Read through and improve the organisation as necessary. Looking at the layout of your notes, some students make the mistake of writing all their notes in the top quarter of the page. Leave space between points. Indent. Spread it out. Mark ideas which the lecturer emphasises, with an arrow or some special symbol. Put a box around assignments and suggested books so you can identify them quickly. In terms of developing your listening skills, pay attention to signals for the end of an idea and the beginning of another. If you hear these, they will help you follow the flow of a lecture and lay out your notes logically. Transitions such as 'therefore', 'finally', and 'furthermore' usually signal an important idea. Also, pay attention to the lecturer's voice. The voice will often go down in pitch at the end of a section and then up at the start of a new section. As a final point, often the most interesting and useful things you can gain from lectures are the examples, sketches and illustrations that the lecturer presents. Lecturers often talk about their research in relation to points they make, or tell stories from their experience. You can get the theory from a textbook, but often this experience is unpublished and cannot be got from books. They are often the most interesting parts of lectures and you can use them in your assignments and exams – so although stories may seem off the point, they may be worth noting down.

OK. Now, I'd like you to look back over your notes and . . .'

sections. The first section has been underlined as an example. You can check your answers in the key at the end of the book. Make notes of the main points. You could try to use one of the organising systems above and as much of the advice in the seminar as possible.

Symbols and abbreviations for note-taking

Here is a list of common symbols and abbreviations to use when taking notes.

Symbols			Abbreviations		
@	=	at	e.g.	=	for example
↗	=	rise, increase by, grow to/by	etc.	=	and so on
↘	=	fall, decrease by, decline	i.e.	=	that is
&	=	and	no.	=	number
$	=	money	sth	=	something
$$$	=	lots of money	s.o.	=	someone
~	=	approximately	NB	=	note that
>	=	is more than	ref.	=	reference
<	=	is less than	doz.	=	dozen
∴	=	therefore, so	K	=	thousand (she earns 89K)
∵	=	because	C	=	century (C21st = 21st century)
♂	=	man; men	m.	=	million
♀	=	woman; women	esp.	=	especially
#	=	number (Phone # / Case #)	c.f.	=	compare with/contrast with
/	=	per (Kb/s = Kilobytes per second)	w/	=	with
1980 →	=	since 1980	govt	=	government
← 1980	=	1980 and earlier	w/o	=	without

Ways of developing your note-taking

Here are four ways that you can develop your note-taking.

Method	Details
1 Use published EAP material. (English for Academic Purposes)	There are a number of good EAP textbooks with recorded lectures and note-taking tasks. One is the "Contemporary Topics" series published by Longman. There are three books in this series at Intermediate, Upper Intermediate and Advanced level and they contain graded lectures with tasks. Because the language is graded, they are useful for developing note-taking skills. D. Beglar and N. Murray, *Contemporary Topics, 3* (Longman, 1993).
2 Use lecture scripts from the internet.	Google your subject and the words 'lecture scripts' and you will find lecture scripts on the internet. Use these to practise note-taking.
3 Go to some low-stakes lectures.	You don't want to develop your note-taking with lectures on your course that really count, so why not sit in on some courses that you are not enrolled on. This is great to do if you have not yet started at university. Most lecturers are happy for you to do this so long as you ask first.
4 Record your lectures.	Use an MP3 player to record your lecture and then make notes when you listen back to it. This is much easier because you can stop your recording when you need to.

The organisation and language of lectures

What is the lecturer saying?

When lecturers are speaking, their remarks may be one of the following seven types of talk (see Table 5.1). The left-hand column tells you the words the lecturer is saying. The right-hand column tells you what to expect next. Thus, when you hear the words 'and that leads to . . .' you can expect to hear a new topic next.

Table 5.1   The lecturer's words and their meaning

Listen for these words . . .	In other words . . .
And that leads to . . . We now come to look at . . . Right. Well, if we move on . . . What I'd like to do now is . . . O.K now.. For instance . . . For example . . . One way this works out is . . . Let me give you an illustration.	1 Here's a new topic.
This means . . . According to . . .	2 Here's an example or an explanation.
X would have us believe . . . I think this is . . . The most interesting point here is . . .	3 This is what someone else thinks.
Let me just say in parentheses . . . By the way . . .	4 This is what I think.
I might say here . . . So where was I? Well anyway . . .	5 This is interesting but not important.
To get back on the track . . . So . . .	6 Now I'm getting back to the topic
What I'm saying is . . .	7 Here's a summary.

(Adapted from J. R. Nattinger and J. S. deCarrico, *Lexical Phrases and Language Teaching* (Oxford University Press, 1992).

Table 5.2

These words....	mean
I'd like to talk about . . . What we're doing today is . . . This morning we'll start looking at . . .	
In other words . . . So the question is . . . So . . ./What I'm saying is . . .	
That's not the same as . . . The catch here is . . . That's not what we really mean by . . .	
And that leads to . . . We now come to look at . . . Right. Well, if we move on . . .	
For instance . . .For example . . . One of the ways this works out is . . . Let me give you an illustration . . .	
According to . . . I'm a great believer in . . . X would have us believe . . . The most interesting point here is . . .	
By the way . . . I might say here . . . As a sidelight . . . But I'm getting a little ahead of myself . . . So where was I? Well anyway . . . To get back on the track . . .	
That would go for X as well as for Y . . . Along the same lines . . .	

Here is a three-step task for you.

1 Read the columns in Table 5.1 from left to right.
2 Cover over the right-hand column and see if you can recall what the words mean.
3 Now look at some more examples of what the lecturer means to say in Table 5.2.

Which words mean . . . ?

- Explaining something he or she has just said in a different way
- Giving an illustration of something that's just been said
- This is not part of the main lecture
- This is the same as something
- These are opinions rather than facts
- A new subtopic is coming
- This is different from something else
- Announcing the topic

Check your answers on p. 209.

Hearing signposting language

Effective lecturers use pauses and intonation (changing the pitch of their speech) to signal the transitions in their lecture. Try the following task:

1 Sit in on a lecture and record it.
2 Try to get the main idea about the lecture but don't worry too much about the details. In your notes, write down any of the signposting language that you hear, from the task above.
3 When you listen back to the lecture, listen to the pitch of the lecturer's voice when she uses these signposting expressions. You could indicate pitch change like this:

So . . . what I'm saying is . . .

Try and see what patterns you can find.

A lecture transcript

The following extracts come from a lecture to students on the topic of English language teaching. In the left-hand column you will find the text of the lecture. Try writing your own commentary in the right-hand column. Your commentary should describe what is happening in the lecture at that time. The first four examples have been done for you. Check your answers in the key at the end of the book.

The lecturer's words	The purpose of the words
Today we are going to have some information about how students can help themselves learn a language. In other words, I'll be talking about what we call language-learning strategies. One definition of these strategies is on your handout. Cohen (1998:4) defined them as 'processes which are consciously selected by learners . . .'.	To announce today's topic To introduce a technical term To remind students that they needn't write it down. To define a technical term
In today's lecture I'll be starting by discussing the need for strategies and some definitions of them. I'll be passing on some theories as well as providing you with some examples. Finally there will be some general points about how you might apply the ideas from today's lecture.	**Start from here**
Let's start with a question. Why is this topic important to you? . . .	
We have various categories of learning strategies. These are social strategies, cognitive strategies, organisational strategies and metacognitive strategies . . .	

The lecturer's words	The purpose of the words
Now let's turn to some examples of cognitive strategies for learning vocabulary. You have probably used some of these yourselves. Let's see, how many of you try to remember a word by linking it to another word you know in any language? . . . Another aspect that students say they need to learn better is listening. Think of all the contexts where you need to listen: on the telephone, in a social conversation, at a public place and of course in a lecture like this one. In some of these places you have to practise selective listening. What we mean by this term is that a person decides to block out much of what is said and listen just for some information that they need. Some of the occasions when you might practise selective listening are . . . Etc. etc.	

TIP   *Visuals*

Visuals on overhead projectors and Microsoft PowerPoint® are really helpful – they help you follow the main points in the lecture and often have useful quotations or diagrams. Sit near the front so you can see them. Ask the lecturer to post them on the course website or email them to you so you can download them. Don't waste time copying them down if you can get them later.

Some students bring a camera to class and photograph visuals. Please check with your lecturer first!

Asking questions in lectures

If you have questions to ask of your lecturer, you have different times when this could happen such as:

- One-to-one later with the lecturer (see Chapter 11 on 'Communicating with Staff')
- At the end of the lecture
- During tutorials (see Chapter 6 on 'Small group learning')
- In lectures when the lecturer asks 'Any questions?'

Ranking questions for usefulness

When you think about whether or not a question is worth asking during lectures, you could try running it past a short test. Ask yourself whether the following apply.

A   The question is useful to more than one or two students.
B   It is not about just repeating something the lecturer has just said.
C   It is about the lecture content not something organisational like assignment dates.
D   It refers to what has been said not what is going to be said later.

There are other things to look for as well.

- Has the lecturer just answered a similar question from someone else?
- Has the lecturer invited questions?
- Is he or she looking at the class and waiting for questions to be asked?

Four of the following are questions that probably should not be asked in lectures. Read them and decide which is the good question. For the others, write the correct letter at the end of it to explain why it should not be asked.

1 *Is it OK if we email you about changing the time of handing in the next assignment?*
2 *Excuse me. What was that point again?*
3 *I have a problem with reading your handwriting on the board. My eyesight isn't great.*
4 *Will you be telling us more about that shortly?*
5 *How does this point compare with what you said earlier about . . . ?*

Now check in the key at the end of the book for the answers.

Becoming a better listener

So far in this chapter we have concentrated on telling you about lectures. From here on we have ideas to make you a better listener in general. This should help you in lectures and in many other university tasks.

Overcoming listening problems

Here are some of the problems people report when they are listening to a new language. These problems can make listening to lectures especially difficult. For each problem we suggest some ideas for you to try.

1 I can't work out where one word stops and the next one starts

For example:

Lennonnmcartney;
BondandBond;
Centralafrican Republic;
HeartofMidlothian

What to do

Write down what you think you hear but write a question mark over the word or words you are unsure about. Later ask yourself which words are most likely in this place.

Learn about features of connected speech – e.g., how words run together in fast speech. A good pronunciation book for this is M. Hewings, English Pronunciation in Use Advanced (Cambridge University Press, 2007).

2 For me it's the intonation that's most difficult to recognise. I never know if the lecturers are asking something or telling me something.

What to do

In lectures the difference between a question and a statement is often not very important. Lecturers often ask questions that are more like headings. For example, they may say:

> What do we know about the spread of this virus?

as an announcement of the next topic:

> I'm now going to tell you what we know about the spread of this virus.

The key thing is to notice the transitions in the lecture. For example, the lecturer's voice may go down at the end of a section and go up again when he or she starts the next section. Lecturers also stress really important points with intonation – so listen for these signals.

3 Most of the time there are many words in the lecture that I don't understand.

What to do

Understanding the words that relate to the subject is a very important part of your studies. Your textbook is a good place to find definitions of key topic words.

Often, when lecturers use technical words for the first time they explain them. So, pay attention at times when lecturers give definitions, e.g., '**Photosynthesis** – by this I mean the process by which plants get their energy from the sun.'

4 I understand individual words and phrases but often I can't follow the overall topic of the lecture.

What to do

Prepare yourself for each lecture. How many of these things do you usually do?

- Look at the lecture schedule for the semester.
- Glance at last week's lecture for hints about what will come next.

- Read the relevant chapter in your text book.

During the lecture:

- Record the lecture with an MP3 player or voice recorder. During the lecture just focus on understanding the main ideas. Write down the topics the lecturer covers. Download the recording to your computer. If you need to understand the details about one of the topics the lecturer talked about, listen back to the recording and make notes from that. The advantage of this is that you can listen as many times as you want.

After the lecture:

- Talk to another student about the lecture afterwards. This will help you put the pieces together.

5 The most annoying thing for me is to hear everyone laughing and to know that I have missed a joke again.

What to do

Understanding jokes in another language is very, very difficult. Sometimes the joke depends on knowing what events are in the news or on TV at the moment. At other times the joke depends on cultural references. We don't have any quick suggestions for understanding jokes in a new language. It is probably better to concentrate on what you *can* understand. However, if everyone else laughs and you don't get it, make a note of the joke and ask a native speaker about it afterwards.

Summary of advice

Three types of 'active listening' are important for lectures:

> **TIP** *Keep a journal of your progress with lectures*
>
> After each lecture, reflect on how effectively you listened. You could write about whether you understood the main points; if you got the details; if you were able to understand any jokes; if you asked a question; how well you were able to make notes. This will help you see your progress.

- Listen for the general meaning that you are expecting in today's lecture.
- Listen for details if the lecturer is speaking carefully or with emphasis.
- Listen for answers to questions you expect to be answered for this topic.

Conclusion

To end the chapter we are adding ten tips that students say have helped them. You may already use some of these suggestions. Tick the ones you already use. How high is your score out of 10?

1 Find out what the lecture is on, before you go. Predict what you think the lecture will be about.
2 If there is recommended reading to do before the lecture, make sure you do it.
3 At the beginning of a lecture, lecturers may revise what they said the week before and give an overview of what they are going to talk about. Pay attention to this overview – it will help you follow the lecture.
4 Don't worry if you don't understand everything. Make a note of topics or subjects that you need to read up on. You can always check later.
5 Don't try to write down everything. Often lecturers will post their slides or notes on the course website (especially if you ask them to).
6 Record the lecture with an MP3 player. This allows you to listen for the main idea in the lecture and keep up. You can listen to sections of the lecture that were difficult or very detailed, later.
7 Take a team approach to lectures. Work with a partner. Compare your notes afterwards over a coffee. Talk about the most important parts and any bits that you couldn't understand.
8 If you can't understand a part of the lecture but don't want to ask a question, write to your lecturer afterwards and ask.
9 Often lecturers say what the next lecture is going to be about at the end of a lecture. They may tell you what to read to prepare for next week.
10 You don't have time to use your dictionary. If there are words you do not understand, do your best and check them later.

Chapter 6

Small-group learning

CHAPTER OVERVIEW

This chapter will help you to:

- understand the purpose of tutorials
- consider reasons why some people don't attend tutorials
- hear ideas from other students about how to act in tutorials
- plan for tutorials
- build up your vocabulary of phrases for joining in discussions
- note ways of getting a turn to talk
- think about cultural differences in tutorials

Introduction

When you have started attending lectures you will probably be given the outline of the course for the semester. In the outline you may notice that some tutorials are listed. What are tutorials? What happens in them? Let's find out in this chapter.

Why have tutorials?

Tutorials or seminars are a really important part of university life. They are different from lectures in that the class size is much smaller (usually no more than 20 students) and students have different roles. In lectures, students are relatively passive – they listen and take notes. The way of learning is different too – in tutorials students learn by talking about ideas, asking questions and doing tasks in small groups. So in tutorials, lecturers expect students to be much more active and contribute much more than they do in lectures. Students are often unsure about their role in tutorials.

What is the purpose of tutorials?

This section looks at the reasons why tutorials are a good idea.

Think about your experiences of tutorials. To what extent do you agree with the following ideas about tutorials? Add up your score and see what this says about your attitude to tutorials.

1 Talking helps students clarify their own ideas.

    agree . . . . disagree

      1   2   3   4   5

2 In tutorials you can learn about other students' ideas.

    agree . . . . disagree

      1   2   3   4   5

3 Students make contact with other students they can meet outside class.

    agree . . . . disagree

      1   2   3   4   5

4 Tutorials give you a chance to use in context the new technical terms you have learned from the lecture or the course book.

> agree . . . . disagree
>
> 1 2 3 4 5

5 Students can find out what others think of their ideas.

> agree . . . . disagree
>
> 1 2 3 4 5

6 Tutorials often require students to contribute, so everyone gets a chance to practise talking and thinking about the ideas.

> agree . . . . disagree
>
> 1 2 3 4 5

Reasons students give for not attending, and for attending

We interviewed a number of international students about their attitudes towards tutorials and the following themes came up:

1 Understanding the point of tutorials
2 Personal learning style
3 Confidence about language
4 Confidence about subject knowledge
5 Feelings about the tutor
6 Feelings about other students

The following task will help you to analyse your attitudes towards each of these themes. Place yourself on the scale for how positively you feel about each one. For each theme, some suggestions are given.

1 Understanding the point of tutorials		Suggestions from students:
+	–	
'I think they are useful. Talking about something is a good way to learn about it.'	'I can't see the point' 'I'd rather go to the lecture and get information from staff, not from other students.'	• Keep trying. They will never be useful if you don't go. • Prepare well and go in with questions. (See next section.) • Try to say more each week. • Remember WIIFM (What's In It For Me) – Make them relevant. • Talk to your tutor about how you feel.
YOUR ATTITUDE? ◄───────────►		

2 Personal learning style		Suggestions from students:
+	–	
'I learn well by talking and listening to other ideas on a subject. This helps me to think about something.'	'I learn best by reading or listening so they are a waste of time.'	• Even if you are not learning a lot about the subject, they are great language practice. • I use tutorials to try out ideas I am not sure about. It's better to do this in tutorials than in assignments. • You can ask questions about things you don't understand.
YOUR ATTITUDE? ◄───────────►		

3 Confidence about language

+	−
'I've always enjoyed having a go at speaking other languages. Even as a child I'd try and talk with some of my parents' friends in their own languages.'	'I feel quite shy about how bad my English is.'

YOUR ATTITUDE?

◄─────────────────►

- Try thinking about other students in the class who are also shy.
- When you start speaking, look straight at the tutor and (we hope!) he or she will give you some encouragement.

4 Confidence about subject matter

Suggestions from students:

+	−
'Some of the subjects I'm studying for my degree I studied to a high level at high school, so I feel reasonably confident that I know what people are talking about.'	'My only reason for taking this subject is that it's compulsory. I just know I'm not going to do well at it.'

YOUR ATTITUDE?

◄─────────────────►

- Prepare by your tutorial by reading over the lecture notes.
- Start by listening and then start speaking when you know even a little bit about the topic they are on at that moment.

5 Feelings about the tutor

Suggestions from students:

+	−
'The tutor is the main reason I attend. She can make quite difficult ideas sound easy.'	'To be honest, nobody likes this tutor. I've heard lots of students say that's the reason they don't attend.'

YOUR ATTITUDE?

◄─────────────────►

- My older brother started work last year after he graduated. He's told me that having to work with people you don't like is good preparation for the workplace.
- I try not to think about my personal feelings for or against the tutor while I'm sitting there. I try to pretend she's someone else.

6 Feelings about other students		Suggestions from students:
+	–	
'Tutorials are a great place to meet other students socially.'	'Most of the people in my tutorial are as bad as I am at the subject. We are all there because we didn't fill in our names fast enough to get to a tutorial at a good time.'	• Think of a tutorial as doing many things: it's a time for learning, and for socialising and (occasionally!) for relaxing and having fun!). • Sit in a different spot each week so as to get to know more people.

YOUR ATTITUDE?

← →

TIP   *Give tutorials a try*

They are an important learning opportunity. If you don't participate, you may miss something important.

Planning for tutorials

Sometimes it is difficult for native speakers to talk in tutorials. It can be even more difficult for international students. If you are finding it difficult to contribute in tutorials, then a good way to start is to be well prepared and go in with your own agenda – just like if you were going to a business meeting. If you go to a business meeting you think about what you are going to say in advance and what you want to

get out of the meeting. This section gives you ideas of ways to prepare for a tutorial.

Goal-setting for tutorials

Tutorials are predictable. Lecturers advertise them in advance – they have titles which tell you what they will be about. Often a tutorial follows on from a lecture and is a chance for students to ask about issues that came up in the lecture. Sometimes tutors give readings that they expect students to do before a tutorial. At other times they may use the tutorial to set up an assignment. If you want to participate in the tutorial, make sure you have done the reading, been to the lecture and thought about the assignment task beforehand! Bring your lecture notes and the reading texts to the tutorial.

Use this template to set your own goals for the tutorial each week:

Tutorial title

Tutorial date

Preparation	What do I want to find out about/learn about in the tutorial? (write your questions here)	In the tutorial, did you find out what you wanted? (if you do, tick in this column)

Lecture title and date	I want to check my understanding of these points . . .

Reading details (author/text/ pages)	I don't agree with these points . . .

I would like some examples of these ideas . . .

Assignment	• Check these points about the instructions for the assignment . . . • Talk through my ideas about . . . • Get more ideas from other students/the tutor about . . .

Phrases for starting a conversation or discussion, and for asking someone's opinion
- I'd like to know . . .
- I'm interested in . . .
- Could I ask . . . ?   [formal]
- Could you tell me . . . ?   [formal]
- Perhaps you could tell . . .   [formal]
- What do you think of . . . ?

Phrases for interrupting
- Excuse me . . .
- Sorry, but . . .
- Excuse me for interrupting, but . . .   [formal]
- May I interrupt for a moment?   [formal]
- Just a second . . .   [informal]
- Can I add something?
- Can I say something here?
- I'd like to say something, if I may.   [formal]
- Can I ask a question?
- May I ask a question?   [formal]

Phrases to use when you are explaining your opinion
- First of all, . . .
- The main reason is . . .
- The main thing is . . .
- The most important thing is . . .
- Secondly, . . .
- The other reason is . . .
- Another reason is . . .
- Besides that, . . .
- And on top of that, . . .
- And finally, . . .

Phrases to use when you want to refer to a point in someone's argument
- The trouble is . . .
- The problem is . . .
- The trouble with . . .
- The problem with . . .
- The point is . . .
- Don't forget that . . .

Phrases to use when you want to say something you think is new information
- Do you realise that . . .
- Believe it or not, . . .
- You may not believe it, but . . .
- It may sound strange, but . . .
- The surprising thing is . . .

- Surprisingly, . . .
- Oddly enough, . . .
- Funnily enough, . . .   [informal]

Phrases to use when what you are going to say may surprise or shock
- Actually, . . .
- The only thing is . . .
- To tell you the truth, . . .
- To be honest, . . .
- Frankly, . . .

Phrases to use when you want to change the subject
- Talking of . . .
- That reminds me . . .
- By the way, . . .   [informal]
- Oh, before I forget, . . .
- Why don't we move on to the next point . . .

Phrases to use when giving your opinion, but when you are not certain
- I think . . .
- I suppose . . .
- I suspect that . . .
- I'm pretty sure that . . .
- I'm fairly certain that . . .
- I wonder if . . .

Phrases to use when you are certain of your opinion
- I'm certain that . . .
- I'm sure that . . .
- It's my opinion that . . .
- I'm convinced that . . .
- I honestly believe that . . .
- I strongly believe that . . .
- Without a doubt . . .
- I'm positive . . .
- I'm absolutely certain that . . .

Phrases to use when you want to emphasise that what you are going to say is your own opinion
- In my opinion, . . .
- I personally believe . . .
- I personally think . . .
- I personally feel . . .
- Not everyone will agree with me, but . . .
- From my point of view, . . .
- Well, personally, . . .
- In my case . . .

Notes

- It is really important to make notes of what you want to find out and take these to the tutorial. This will help you keep track of what's happening if you feel lost.
- If you find out what you want from the tutorial, then great. If you don't, you may need to think about how you can ask extra questions (see later in the chapter).
- At the end of each tutorial, the tutor may say something to introduce what they are going to do in the next tutorial. She may say something like 'Next week, we're going to discuss the question of . . .' Or she may give out a reading for the following week. Bring next week's template along and fill it in as she talks.

How to talk in tutorials

Having discussions in tutorials can be daunting. Often people speak fast and interrupt each other and it can be difficult for second-language speakers to get a word in. Remember though, often lecturers set up group work or pairwork, which can be easier than in whole class discussions. By practising and memorising the language below, you will be able to participate better.

TIP *Trying out new expressions*

Each time you go to a tutorial, set yourself the goal of trying out a few of these expressions. At the end of the tutorial, evaluate whether you used the expressions successfully.

The language of discussions: taking the lead

Look at the list of useful phrases for joining in and being proactive in tutorials (on the previous page). These phrases will help you direct the discussion. Discussions are much easier to follow if you are in charge! Tick the phrases you would use already. Put a star [*] beside some that you could start to use.

Building discussions: reacting to what people say

Often international students find that group discussions are dominated by confident native speakers and they find themselves having to respond rather than lead. As well as agreeing or disagreeing, you can steer the discussion.

When you respond to something someone else has said, you have these choices: you can . . .

1 Check the meaning of what they have said.
2 Fully agree with them.
3 Draw conclusions from what they are saying.
4 Partly agree with them.
5 Disagree with them.
6 Add your opinion.
7 Not give an opinion.
8 Ask for other people's opinions.
9 Refocus the discussion.

Look at the following expressions. They are in groups that have a similar purpose. Give each group a heading from the list above. The first one has been done for you as an example. Check your answers in the key at the end of the book.

(a) 8 Ask for other people's opinions

What do you think about . . . ?
How do you feel about . . . ?
Do you agree with . . . ?
You haven't said much about this. What do you think?
Are you opposed to . . . ?
I think . . . What is your opinion?

(b)

What do you think/feel about . . . ?
Would you agree/say that . . . ?
John, what is your opinion on/about . . . ?

(c)

I'd just like to say (that) . . .
I think/believe/feel that . . .
It seems to me (that) . . .
I am convinced (that) . . .

(d)

I just don't know.
I don't feel strongly either way.
I'm not sure.
Actually I can see both points of view/both sides.
Maybe. (Who knows?).

(e)

In my opinion, the main thing is . . .
As I see it, the most important point is . . .
I feel that the most important consideration is . . .
I believe that the highest priority here is . . .

(f)

Let's move on to the next point.
OK. We've talked about . . . what about . . . ?

(g)

Yes, I agree.
Yes, I see what you mean.
That's for sure.
That's a good point.
Absolutely!

(h)

I don't agree . . .
I don't think so . . .
Yes, but I think . . .
Yes, but don't you think . . .
I agree to some extent but . . .
I'm afraid, I must disagree with you.

(i)

It could be that . . .
Maybe it is the case that . . .
One option would be that . . .
I partly agree . . .
Probably you're right . . .

(j)

OK. So that means . . .
That relates back to what we were saying about . . .
The logical extension of that is that . . .

(k)

I'm sorry, I didn't catch that . . .
Sorry, what was that again?
Do you mean that . . . ?
Are you saying that . . . ?
. . . Is that what you mean?
In other words, . . .
To put it another way, . . .

TIP   *Note all the ways of clarifying understanding above*

When you don't hear something or don't understand, it is really important to try to check your understanding. You can either get the speaker to say the same thing again, or ask for confirmation by rephrasing what the speaker said. If you don't check the meaning, you will miss a learning opportunity.

Getting a turn

Tutorial groups are fascinating places for people-watching. If you understand how students and lecturers behave in tutorials, then you will find it easier to get a turn. Look at Figure 6.1. This is a diagram showing a typical university tutorial. The tutor is sitting at the head and the 15 students are around the table.

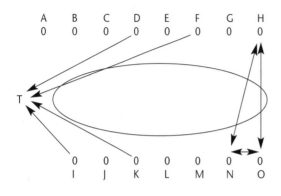

Figure 6.1 A university tutorial

We'll look at the students' behaviour first. The following are descriptions of the way students typically behave in tutorial groups. If you haven't been to a tutorial yet, then this will warn you about what often happens in them. If you have experience of a tutorial group, then as you are reading the descriptions, think which people fit the descriptions in your tutorials.

1 *Three students know one another very well. They are quite outgoing. If one of them puts forward an opinion, then the other two argue together.*
2 *Four of the students never say anything unless the tutor asks them directly.*
3 *Another four students like asking the tutor questions but they are not very interested in what their fellow students say.*
4 *Two of the students hardly ever say anything and even the tutor ignores them.*
5 *Three students will speak occasionally to another student but never seem to answer the tutor's questions.*

Accounting for this behaviour
Now read the following explanations (a–e) of

these students' behaviour and match them to the types of students (1–5) above.

(a) For students like these, the teacher is the most important person in the room and the focus of their learning in the room. They may not see the point of talking to other students or the point of doing tasks in smaller groups, because they want the right answer from the teacher.
(b) These students may not feel confident and may be worried about speaking up in front of the whole class. They may be worried about their English language level or their subject knowledge.
(c) These students do not seem to be participating actively in the class. They respond when they have to, but are not really involved.
(d) These students are actively involved. They may be interested in the tutorial but are completely passive in the class. Maybe they are unfamiliar with this style of learning. Or maybe they are demotivated.
(e) These students are fully involved in the ideas in the class but only communicate with their friends.

Summary
All of these students are missing out in some way in the learning opportunities offered by the tutorial. They may be missing:

● the fact that tutorial learning should be active (i.e., you should be asking questions and testing out ideas);
● the fact that you can learn from talking to everyone in the group, not just the tutor or a couple of other students;
● the point of group work.

The tutor's view
You may be interested to know that tutors, as well as students, give thought to interaction in small groups. For example, here is what one person said about her reasons for certain patterns.

I use pair work if the group seems very shy. They talk about ideas with just one other person first and then they seem to find it easier to report to the whole group afterwards. As for the choice

Your participation: a reflection task

Try this reflection task after a tutorial if you find it difficult to participate. Use it to help you set goals for your next tutorial.

Tutorial date:

Tutorial topic:

Today, I was . . . (*mark your position on the arrow below, in terms of your participation*).

passive ←————————————————————————————————→ active

I was happy with the way I . . . (*tick the list below*)

- [ ] understood the lecturer
- [ ] understood other students
- [ ] participated in pair work
- [ ] participated in small group work
- [ ] participated in whole class discussions
- [ ] was understood by other students
- [ ] was understood by the lecturer
- [ ] asked questions
- [ ] answered questions

I want to improve the way I . . . (*choose an aspect of tutorial performance above that you want to improve*)

To do this, I'm going to . . . (*here, think about how you can solve the problem you have chosen above – what can you do differently?*)

between group work versus the whole-class discussion, I find that often I will plan for one but then change to the other. I choose group work because it involves more people talking so it makes the class more active. I especially like using group work if each group has a different task. Maybe each group is looking at a different aspect of the same problem. This means that when groups report, there is more interest. The biggest problem I have with group work is that often students don't seem to know how to work together. I sometimes give them roles in their groups – for example, I might suggest that one person makes notes for the whole group and one person is the spokesperson who has to report back. The other problem with group work is that it can be slow and so sometimes I decide to go back to full class to speed things up.

What sort of questions can I ask?

If you ask questions, try and make them interesting and think about how much discussion the question will generate.

Look at these two questions. Which will generate the most amount of talk?

1 *Don't you agree X is terrible?*

2 *Why do you think X is terrible?*

The problem with the first question is that it really has only two possible answers:

EITHER: Yes I do.

OR: No I don't.

Although often people do say a lot more than 'yes' or 'no'! (See transcript, below.) Open questions, like the second one, ask for longer answers.

On the other hand, to answer the second question a person has to do more thinking.

Sometimes, especially if English is not your first language, you may want to keep things simple and ask several closed questions. The answers to such questions are often predictable and short, making them easier to understand, but can build up to more talk.

Look at this example of a tutor (T) talking to a student (S) about how the student has revised his writing. Notice how the tutor encourages the student to talk by using a combination of closed questions and open questions.

Transcript	question types
T: OK. So have you made many changes since we last met?	closed
S: Yes – a few. Mainly I have worked on the links between sections.	
T: Great. Like we talked about?	closed
S: Yes.	
T: OK. And when you made changes, can you tell me about the process you went through?	closed
What were you trying to do differently?	open

Here are some more questions that would encourage more than just a short answer:

● Why do you think that?
● Can you explain that to me more clearly please?
● What proof can you put forward for that viewpoint?

Questions are also different depending on how much they make people think. We talk about this more in Chapter 10, the assessment chapter.

Types of question

First, let's look at types of question, ranging from the simplest to the type that makes everyone think. In the left-hand column there are examples of students' questions. In the other column is a list of their functions. Match them up and check your answers in the key at the end of the book.

Students' questions	Type of question
(a) Could you please tell us what . . . means?	summarising
(b) What would happen if someone . . . ?	predicting
(c) What if . . . had been written in a different century?	evaluating
(d) Is this similar to the point you made last week about . . . ?	defining
(e) Reading between the lines, is it true that the poet is trying to say . . . ?	making an inference
(f) Can we sum this up by saying . . . ?	comparing and contrasting
(g) In your opinion, what would be the most likely cause of . . . ?	hypothesising

TIP *Try out different types of questions*

. . . and check out the responses

Culture and tutorials

We asked some experienced international students to tell us what surprised them about tutorials. This is what they came up with. Are there any that you are surprised by?

Sunny (from Korea): 'I was surprised that different cultures' body language was so different when I started at university. At that time I found this strange. Students from some countries are very expressive in tutorials. They use eye contact and wave their hands around much more than Korean students in particular, to interrupt. I copied what they did and that helped, but I still find it difficult to keep eye contact through discussions.'

Nikolay (from Russia): 'I enjoyed tutorials. In Russia, everybody is very serious in university tutorials. If you smile too much people will think that you are strange. But here (Australia) I found that people made jokes and laughed – even the lecturer sometimes made jokes.'

Lu Lu (from Taiwan): 'I found it very difficult at first to give my opinion all the time. I was uncomfortable – especially when I had to give my opinion to older men and the tutor. I got used to it. I couldn't believe how direct the native speaker students were with the tutor. To me it felt quite rude.'

Ahmed (from UAE): 'I liked the oral learning style in tutorials. Sometimes the tutor gave us papers to read and this was good. I read them and could then talk about them with other students. And it was good you can ask any question you like. I also like the active learning style. It is more interesting for me than reading or lectures.'

Before you start at university, talk to other students from your country who have experienced tutorials in an English-speaking university culture. Ask them what they noticed. When you start your tutorials, be aware that attitudes towards eye contact, body language, laughter, learning style, and giving your opinion, may be different from what you are used to.

Conclusion

We hope that, after reading this chapter, when you start tutorials on your university course you will have more idea of what you are getting into and can make the most of your opportunities. Like other aspects of university life, if you prepare well for them and have a clear idea of what you can get out of them, then you can participate and make them work for you.

Reading

Introduction

One thing is guaranteed – whatever course you decide to do, you will need to read a lot. Reading in your own language takes time and reading in a second language can take over your life if you let it. The important thing is to be smart about what you read and the techniques you use when reading.

Case studies – learning from other students' experiences

We interviewed a number of international students about reading at university. We asked them what they had learnt about reading. This is what they said. For each answer, underline the key problem. In the column on the right, make your own notes about these problems. The first one has been done for you. Then decide what the main thing is that the speaker has learned about reading. Check your answers in the key at the end of the book.

Christophe says	You say
'At the start of most of my courses, the lecturer gives out a list of the topic of each lecture and a reading list. They usually have one set or prescribed reading which is really important and some suggested extra readings. I find it really helps me understand the lecture if I have done at least the set reading. The lecturer expects us to have read the set reading and so if I haven't, I can't understand the lecture. Often I don't get time to read the extra readings before the lecture. They are often more difficult than the set readings – often though if I just read the first two or three paragraphs or if it's a research article, the abstract, then at least I know what the lecturer is talking about when he mentions them. I read them afterwards if I'm interested enough. Some lecturers put these reading lists online and I can download or print them.'	Christophe needs either to find the time somehow or to stop worrying about it. Christophe may be doing the best he can with the time available.

What did Christophe learn?

Marie says	You say
'At first I didn't understand the point of textbooks – especially introductory ones. They seemed really boring and obvious. Then I realised how important they are – they define key words for my course. Often the course is organised around the same content as the book. They often have key ideas or theories explained, so if I didn't understand an idea in a lecture, I could find an explanation in the textbook. Then at the end of my first semester we had an exam which was 33% of the course mark and basically all the answers were in the textbook. We asked the tutor what would be in the exam. He said what we have done in lectures and in the textbook. If I hadn't read the textbook, I would have failed.'	

What did Marie learn?

George says	You say
'I studied communication studies. On my course, we needed to read so much. Our lecturer used to give comments on essays saying – "You must read more widely." When I started at university I read everything the same way. I wasted a lot of time looking for the books in the library, then photocopying and then I read each article very carefully with my dictionary. It was terrible. One of the other students asked me to join their study group. This was great. There were four of us. We got the reading list from the lecturer and then divided up the reading between our group. Each week, we read one article or book chapter and then met and talked about our different articles. We had 10 minutes each to summarise our article. We saved so much time and energy. When we talked about the articles we could decide if we needed to read them ourselves. We also saved money. One of us bought the book for each course and then we shared it.'	

What did George learn?

Rose says	You say
'When I got feedback on my writing, my tutor said I needed to read more critically. I didn't know what this meant. He explained that I needed to read and think these things through for myself. I had to challenge what is said and what is not said in the article I was reading. I found this very difficult. At first, I struggled just to understand the words on the page, but critical reading means understanding the words and then assessing them against everything else I knew and had read before, and deciding for myself if it was right or if I agreed or if the ideas made sense. I think I used to read in a very passive way. I just accepted what I read – I had been successful in this way in my country. I learnt that I needed to be a much more active reader.'	

What did Rose learn?

Andrea says	You say
'When I did my Master's I realised that I needed to read in different ways again. I had to understand other people's research in order to plan my research. My problem was that I couldn't see how one person's research fitted in with what other people had said before and other things I had read that were the result of research findings after the article I was reading was written! I was reading 25 years of research and all the time, the ideas and theories were changing so I had to keep the big picture in mind – for each piece of research I had to think . . . "OK. Now this guy had seen this other research so he thought this, but later we found out that that was not the case!" The literature review section of each article was so important. One of my lecturers told me about "State of the Art" articles. These were really useful. They look at one area of research and just review what researchers have found to show where the research is up to now. From these, I made a timeline in my head and fitted other reading and research onto this.'	

What did Andrea learn?

Khaled says	You say
'I found my English got so much better the more I read. I found that once I had read one type of text, e.g. a research article, once and understood the point of different parts of it, I could read the next one much more quickly. When I started, I didn't even know how to use an index to find the parts of a book that I needed to read or the Contents page to find the relevant sections. I wasted so much time getting lost in texts.'	

What did Khaled learn?

Why university students read

Reasons for reading

Here are some of the reasons why students read at university. Read the list and, for each of the reasons, think of something you have read recently with that purpose.

- to find out important information for your course / university
- to learn something new
- for pleasure / enjoyment / interest
- to improve your English
- to prepare for an exam / assignment

Whenever you are reading an article or section of a book on your course, the first step to reading efficiently is to think about this question:

Why am I reading this?

If you can answer this question, then you can think about the best way to read the article or book.

For example, if you are reading a text to learn words that you can use when you are writing essays, then you would read in the following way:

1 Read the text to understand the main ideas.
2 Notice vocabulary in the text that you think you can use when you are writing.

3 Read the sections where those words are used in detail.
4 Look these words up in your dictionary to check what they mean and how you can use them.

If you can't answer the question, you are wasting your time. Do something more useful!

What university students read

Types of academic text

It is also important to know what type of text you are reading. The task below will help you sort out the meaning of the names of some common academic text types.

Match the list of text types on the left to the descriptions on the right. Check your answers in the key at the end of the book.

Text types	Description
Prescribed texts or recommended books	(a) All the chapters in these books are written by the same writer or writers. They often report the writer's own work or summarise the work of many people.
Edited books	(b) Presenters at a conference may be asked to write an article on what they said. These may be edited and then published so that people can read about what was talked about at the conference.
Single-author books	(c) These are journal articles that sum up current research in a particular academic field. They are usually written by a very established researcher or writer and will talk about the work of many researchers.
Journal articles	(d) These books are chosen by the lecturer or department as really important for a particular course. All students should have a copy of them. They will usually be listed on a course reading list or your lecturer will tell you about them in a lecture.
State-of-the-art articles	(e) These appear in journals, which are academic magazines that are important for your subject. You can read about current research in them. They are published in hard copy and often on the Internet, every year or several times a year.
Research reports	(f) While journal articles often have a word limit fixed by the journal, these will go into a lot more detail about the methodology used by the researchers. This means that they will say exactly how the research was done. They may be written by a research company or a government department.
Theses	(g) These books have chapters that are all written by different authors on a similar topic. They are collected by an editor or editors, who usually also write the introduction and final chapter in the book. On the cover you will see ed. or eds. after the person's name. This is short for *editor* and *editors*.
Conference proceedings	(h) These are research reports that are written by students at your university. They will be kept in your university's library.

Reading different types of academic texts

The good thing about academic texts is that they are usually predictable and so, when you understand how each type of text is organised, reading other examples of the same text type will be easier and quicker. For example, when you have seen and understood one thesis, you will find that other theses have similar organisation (although this may be different from theses in your language or in other subjects).

Understanding the organisation will help you see the main point of each section. Recognising text organisation will also help you when you have to write different types of text. This section looks at one type of academic text – research articles. You can apply this kind of analysis to common text types in your subject. For example, if you are a science student and need to read a lot of experimental write-ups, work out how they are commonly organised.

The organisation of research articles

Usually research articles have the sections shown in Figure 7.1, and in that order.

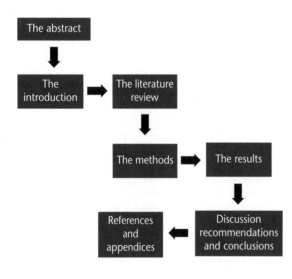

Figure 7.1 Sections that make up a research article.

Find examples of research reports in your field of study or on a topic you are interested in. To do this, go to a university library and look in some research journals for examples of studies in your field. Or Google some key words related to your area of interest: e.g., to find a study about air pollution levels, type **2003** (for example) **air pollution study**. (*Note*: You are more likely to find free reports you can access if you enter an earlier year than the current one as your search term.)

Now look at the following list of questions and decide in which part of the research article you will find the answers. Check your answers in the key at the end of the book.

1 How was the study planned?
2 What do the results mean?
3 Who is interested in the results?
4 What was the study about?
5 Why is the topic important?
6 What did the researcher want to find out?
7 What was the main finding of the research?
8 Where was the research carried out?
9 What did the researchers find out?
10 What research instruments were used?
11 Who else has studied this topic?
12 What have other researchers found out about this topic?
13 How does this piece of research fit in with what other researchers have previously found out?
14 Where are the full titles of the books and articles referred to in the article?

Planning your university reading

At the beginning of a course or when you are writing a research proposal it can seem that you are facing a mountain of reading. This can be depressing – especially as all the books are in your second language! There are two approaches you can take when it comes to your reading.

1 Panic, go to the library, find as many books as you can on your class reading list and frantically try to make some progress.

or:

2 Take a more strategic approach and plan your reading week-by-week.

Remember, you are looking at a whole semester's reading . . . or two if you are writing a thesis. If you are training to run a marathon, you need to do a lot of kilometres over the months before your race. It would be difficult to attempt this without a training schedule. The same is true with your university reading. If you take a step back and take a strategic approach to your reading, things begin to look more manageable.

Three steps to keeping on top of your university reading.

This task will help you plan your reading and stay on top of it week by week.

Step 1: Get a list of readings for your courses

You can usually get a reading list from your lecturers for each course that you are doing. Sometimes these are published before the course starts or posted on the course webpage. Sometimes they are handed out at the first lecture. They are usually organised so that they tie in with lectures or classes.

Alternatively, the course librarian in your university's library may be able to help you with readings for a particular course.

If you are writing a dissertation or thesis, you will have to find your own readings to a certain extent. Find a 'state-of-the-art article' or a book that summarises the previous work of lots of researchers on the topic of your research.

Make a provisional list and show this to your supervisor.

Step 2: Plan your weekly reading schedule

As soon as you get your timetable, work out when in the week you are going to do your reading for each lecture, each week. For example, if you are a business student and have Marketing lectures on Monday, you need to do your reading for this lecture during the weekend at the latest – earlier if you want to meet another student to talk about it. Likewise, if you have Personnel Management classes on Wednesdays, then you will need to get your reading for those classes finished on Tuesday at the latest.

If you are involved in a study group, set a regular day each week when you can meet and discuss the week's readings.

You also need one day per week to get to the library to find texts. Many students plan to go to the library once a week only, to find texts for all their classes. This saves time and so is better than going to the library for each course you are taking.

Step 3: Staying on top of things

You will probably not have time to read everything for every one of the courses you are taking. So, start with the most essential texts and then read optional texts if you have time left. You can decide which texts are the most important by:

- Checking the course reading list. This may mark texts as 'essential', 'set' or 'extra reading'.
- Checking with students who took the course the year before.
- Looking at the assessment schedule for the course and seeing which texts directly feed into assignments and exams. Remember, exams often test students on the topics of the set text – so make sure you read it!
- Deciding which of the readings look the most interesting.

Lecturers often talk about what reading you should do for the following week, at the start or end of a lecture. They may confirm the information in the course outline or explain how one piece of reading has a higher priority than others. Pay attention and adapt your plan if necessary.

Summary

It is important that you try and stagger your reading across the course – don't leave it all until the week your assignment has to be handed in or when you are trying to revise for an exam. Early on in a course, there are usually fewer assessment dates so you should try to get the bulk of your term's reading done then. Try to get into a weekly pattern with regular reading slots for each subject and a regular time in the week when you go to the library.

Finding reading texts

Once you have decided what you need to read, you need to find the texts. For some courses, there may be one textbook that the lecturer will refer to constantly throughout the semester. You may decide to buy this. Buying books can be expensive but it can be really useful having your own copy. Here are the options.

Your campus bookstore

This will probably be the most convenient option. It will have lists of books recommended for each course at the university. Remember, you can always share the cost of a textbook with classmates.

Visit your campus bookstore. Find out:

- new prices for prescribed texts or recommended reading for your course;
- if they offer a student discount;
- if they buy back textbooks from students and sell them second-hand. (If so, at what cost, and at what time of year?)

Other places to buy books

Ask some current students on your course how they found their textbooks. Find out:

- if there is a notice board in your department or union building where students advertise books for sale;
- if there is a good second-hand book store that sells university texts;
- the address of an internet auction site, e.g. www.ebay.com, where people buy and sell books.

And the university library

See next section.

Using the library

Libraries are still an important part of student life. They have large physical collections of books and resources. They also have large digital collections of e-journals, e-books and databases of resources available around the world in other universities. There could be significant differences between the way your university library operates and the methods of other libraries you have used before. This section will help you get the most out of your library.

Getting the most out of your library orientation

At the start of each semester at university and maybe at other times during the semester as well, your library will run orientation seminars. Make sure you go – although they may not sound like much fun, one hour in a library seminar could save you a lot of time later in the semester. Take a list of books or references that you need to find. This will help keep things concrete. For example, if the librarian starts talking about finding journal articles, you can ask about one of the journal articles that you need to find.

Here is a checklist of things to find out about at the library orientation. Take it with you and tick the things that you find out about.

Category	Questions	Tick here!
General services	Opening hours?	☐
	● during term time (incl. weekends)	☐
	● in holidays	☐
	Rules – e.g. no cell phones?	☐
	Library seminar times?	☐
	Extra services offered, e.g. binding?	☐
	Study rooms that you can book?	☐
Finding your way around	How many sites?	☐
	What's in each one?	☐
	Which site is most useful for you?	☐
	What's on each floor?	☐
	How are the shelves organised?	☐
Finding books	How does the catalogue work?	☐
	Who can help you?	☐
	Who is your subject librarian?	☐
	Which database will be useful?	☐
	Interlibrary loans?	☐
Borrowing books	Which books can be borrowed?	☐
	Which books can't be borrowed?	☐
	Which books are on short loan?	☐
	How many books?	☐
	How long can you borrow them for?	☐
	How much are the fines?	☐
	Where can you take books?	☐
Photocopying	Where are the machines?	☐
	How do photocopy accounts work?	☐
	How much does photocopying cost?	☐
Computer/online resources	How can you access the library catalogue from home?	☐
	Databases you can access.	☐
	Where can you print?	☐
	Internet access.	☐
	E-books you can read.	☐

A mini-glossary of library words

Libraries have their own vocabulary of technical terms that you need to know if you are going to use them effectively. Here is a mini-glossary of library words.

author	A person who wrote the book.
binding	If you write a thesis or dissertation, you will need to get it bound. Your department will have information about this. Your library may be able to help.
call number	The number or code that the library gives the book, e.g. 664.805652.McD.
e-book	An electronic book that is stored on a library server and can be downloaded.
interlibrary loans	When your library doesn't have books that you want, but other libraries may have them, you can request these books from another library. You may have to pay a fee.
isbn number	This is a number written just above the barcode on the back cover of a book. It is unique to that book. e.g. ISBN 978-0230-54519-9. It is a common way of identifying books, and is used by librarians and book shops.
key word	An important word in the subject/title of a book, journal or journal article.
overdue notice	If you get an overdue notice, it means your book is late being returned. If you ignore these, you will probably be fined.
periodical	Another name for a journal.
recall notice	If a book you want to read has been lent out to another student, you can request that they bring it back to the library. If you get a recall notice, you may have to return a book quickly (e.g. within 24 hours) or pay a fine.
reference material	Dictionaries, atlases etc. Usually these can't be borrowed.
short loan	These books may be borrowed for a short time (sometimes only 2 or 3 hours). You have to pay big fines if you are late returning these books. There is usually a short-loan desk.
special collections	Your library may have a section of rare books, for example, sixteenth-century poetry or early maps and records. You may have to make an appointment to see them.
subject librarian	A librarian who has special knowledge about a particular subject, such as law, literature, history, agricultural studies. These people will have detailed knowledge of your area and will be able to help you.
title	The name of a book or journal. Sometimes you can search for journals separately.

Getting help in the library

Look at the following dialogues between an international student and a librarian. Which one is the most successful? How do you think the student felt in each? How do you think the librarian felt? Check your answers in the key at the end of the book.

Dialogue 1

A busy Wednesday afternoon in the library. The librarian is sitting next to a sign that says 'Ask me for help.' She has lots of jobs she is trying to do but there is a queue of students.

Librarian   Yes? (*rising intonation*)
International student   I need this book. (*pointing at a piece of paper with the name of a book written on it*)
Librarian   What's the call number?
International student   . . . what?
Librarian   OK. I'll check it in the database . . .

Dialogue 2

A busy Wednesday afternoon in the library. The librarian is sitting next to a sign that says 'Ask me for help.' She has lots of jobs she is trying to do but there is a queue of students.

International student   Hi, Lynn, how are you? I'm having trouble finding this book. I looked it up on the database and found the call number, but I couldn't find it on the shelf. (*pointing at a piece of paper with the name of a book written on it*)
Librarian   Can you tell me the call number?
International student   It's 919 67TS.67.
Librarian   OK. I'll check it in the database . . .

You never know when you will need the help of a librarian. It is important that you do ask them for help if you need it. If you don't approach them and ask, they won't know that you need help and you can waste a lot of time. Here are seven important things to remember that will help you keep librarians happy. Tick the ones that you think are worth trying.

1   Use their names. (They often have name badges.)

2   Ask them how they are before you ask them to do something for you.

3   Frame any requests by explaining briefly what you are trying to do.

4   Show them that you have done some of the work for yourself – e.g., you have tried to find the book in the database.

5   Follow library rules – especially about cellphone use, eating, drinking and talking loudly in the library.

6   Don't wait until just before the library closes if you want help or want to borrow books.

7   Respect the books (don't write in them, treat them with care).

Using your library catalogue

Your university library will give you access to its catalogue. Library catalogues list the resources stored in that particular library. You will probably be able to access the library catalogue off-campus (from home). This is really useful because you can check whether the library has what you want without having to waste time and actually go to the library.

You can search by:

> **Title** (name of book or article)
>
> **Journal or serial title** (name of journal)
>
> **Author** (writer or writers)
>
> **Call number** (the number the library gives the book)
>
> **Keyword** (this is useful if you only know one word in the title.)
>
> **Subject heading** (your topic)

You can find out:

● if your library has the books you need;
● which library site they are stored in;
● where in the library they are located (i.e. which shelf);
● if the books are there (or if they are loaned out);
● if the books can be borrowed;

Try out a library catalogue search online

If you know the address of your library catalogue already, enter that in your web browser. Otherwise, you choose a library from http://sunsite.berkeley.edu/Libweb/

Try out these searches:

SEARCH 1

Look up the **title** of this book, *The International Student Handbook*, and find out if your library has a copy.

Don't use **a / an / the** in your title search.

SEARCH 2

Look up a **journal title** that is relevant to your subject, to find out if the library subscribes to it. Find out if you can access it online or not.

TIP   To find a list of electronic journals for different subjects, go to these sites:

http://www.e-journals.org
http://gort.ucsd.edu/newjour/

SEARCH 3

Do a 'keyword' search. These are useful if you don't know the full title of a book or journal. For this book, try '**international student**'.

TIP 1   If you want to broaden this search, try **stud*** rather than **student** – **stud*** will give results for **student / studies / students / study / studious** etc.

TIP 2   You can use **AND, OR, NOT** to narrow your keyword search. For example you can search for '**international AND student NOT business**' to get titles with the words **international** and **student** but exclude those with the word **business**.

SEARCH 4

Search for books by a particular **author**. You may know of an author whose books you want to search for. If not, try searching for books by one of the authors of this book – **Lewis, Reinders** or **Moore**.

TIP   Often, if you search by authors with common names, such as Smith, you will get thousands of results! Narrow your author search by entering the author's initials, e.g. 'M N', or combining the author search with a 'keyword' search.

SEARCH 5

Try a subject search for resources in a topic you want to study. You could try the title of one of your papers, or the words '**study skills**'.

TIP   Ask a librarian for suitable search terms.

Finding readings on the internet and in databases

The internet is a great place to find readings for your course and information about being a student. Sometimes you find whole texts that you can access for free. Often you find references for articles and books which you can then search for in your library catalogue. You can find:

● Research articles on topics that you are studying at university.
● Articles that you can borrow from the library.
● People who are interested in the same subjects as you.
● Information that you can use in assignments.

Some essential searches to try out

1 Basic searches with a search engine
Usually, it is best to start with a search engine – e.g., www.google.com or www.yahoo.com

Sometimes a basic search is all you need, especially if you know what you want.

TASK

Go to www.google.com and enter the name of the university you want to go to and the words international student office to find the webpage of your university's international student office.

e.g. '**university of Illinois international student office**'.

2   Advanced search
Both Google and Yahoo have an advanced search function, which is really helpful as you can make your search as specific as you need. For example, you can search for pages only in your language, or pages only in html.

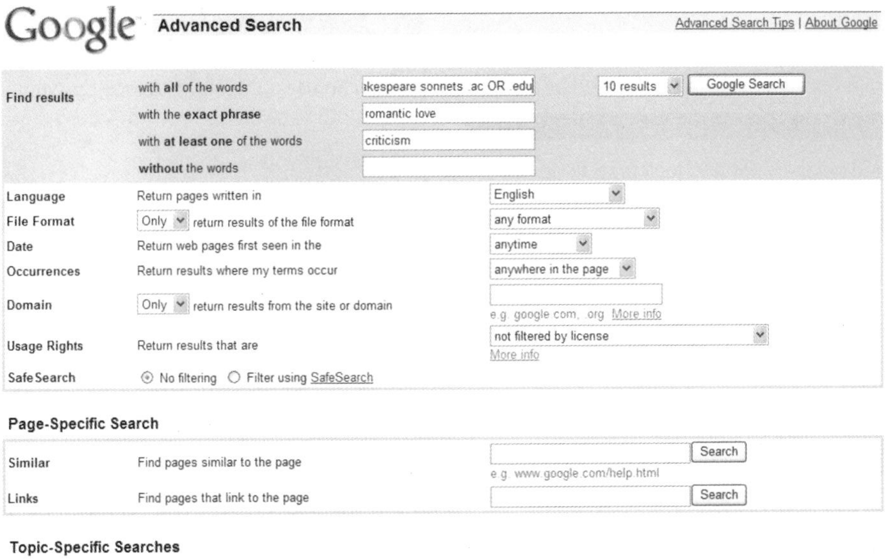

Figure 7.1 An advanced Google search for pages of literary criticism on Shakespeare's sonnets which contain the exact phrase "romantic love". All the pages will be from universities (".ac" or ".edu")

TASK

Go to www.yahoo.com. and click on 'Advanced Web Search'. Try to find some research articles done in the country in which you want to study.

3 Yahoo Directory http://dir.yahoo.com/

This is great if you don't know exactly what you are searching for. For example you are interested in early Egyptian history. Click on 'Arts & Humanities' then 'History' then 'By Region' then 'Countries' then 'Egypt'. At this stage, there are some interesting links to check out but they are still quite general. You can keep going clicking on the links to make your search as specific as you need.

TASK

Go to http://dir.yahoo.com

Find your subject area in the menu on the left of the page.

Follow the pages to find a text on an area you are interested in.

4 Google scholar

This is a website that lets you search academic papers, theses, and even full-text books. It is a great tool, especially if you don't have access to your university library.

TASK

Go to Google Scholar (http://scholar.google.com)

Search for the name of a famous researcher/writer in your subject area.

Go to the Google Scholar Help and find out what the results mean.

5 Wikipedia

This is an online encyclopedia created by web users. Anyone can add an article to Wikipedia – they do not have to be an expert but if their information is wrong, then other users will correct it. It has articles in many languages and is a great place to go to learn some basic facts and definitions. The articles are good for language learners because they contain many explanations of common words. But be critical of the information you find. Because *anyone* can add and edit the information, it may not be accurate. Wikipedia is convenient to find new information quickly but other sources are more reliable.

Databases

In addition to the internet, the many databases are another important resource for students and researchers containing references to new articles that have come out (often from dozens or even hundreds of journals), abstracts of those articles, sometimes full articles, conference proceedings, theses, and much more. A *subject-specific* database is a database that contains information about one subject, and because it has so much and such carefully selected information in one place, it can be one of the most powerful tools you will use during your studies. Most libraries have a website with links to the different subject-specific databases they have access to, so look under your faculty or subject for the ones that are most relevant for you.

You can search most databases in a variety of ways, for example by 'keyword', or by year of publication, or by author, of by a combination of these. One of the difficulties that students have is that they search for a certain word (using the 'keyword' option) and there are no results. This does not mean that there really are no useful resources, but perhaps that you need to search using a different word. For example, the terms 'finance' and 'economy' are closely related but searching for only one of them may not show the results for the other. In other words, think of synonyms!

So, if you find nothing for 'problems', try 'issues'. If you find nothing for 'elderly', try 'geriatric'.

Another problem is that many students search for the wrong keywords. For example, if you are interested in Impressionism, the nineteenth-century art movement, you could look for 'painting' but the information would be too general to be helpful. Similarly, you could look for information on 'Monet' or 'Renoir', two of its famous painters, but the results might be too specific. Think about what terms will give you the information that you want. Let's look at an example. Say you are interested in finding information on the topic 'care for the elderly in New Zealand in the 1950s'. This is a very specific search because you are looking not only for one, specific topic (care for the elderly), but also for information on that topic limited to one country (New Zealand) and one period (the 1950s). The best way to structure your search is as follows:

1 Search for the exact information you want to find. Type in 'care for the elderly in New Zealand in the 1950s'. You never know, there may be a resource with that exact title or on that exact topic!

2 If you can't find anything, try looking for synonyms. Try 'geriatric' instead of 'elderly' and try 'healthcare' instead of 'care'.

3 If you still can't find anything, try broadening your search. Perhaps you could leave out 'New Zealand' or '1950s'.

4 One way to make your searches more powerful is to use *operators*. Operators are search terms such as AND, OR, and NOT, that help to make your search more specific. Other examples include '?', which you can use, for example, when searching for both 'woman' and 'women' by typing 'wom?n', and '*', which you can use to show results such as 'car', 'cars', and 'cardealer' by typing 'car*'. Not all databases and library catalogues use the same operators but here is a list of operators used by several of them: www.library.ubc.ca/hss/qso.html

Here is a list of operators that work in Google: www.googleguide.com/advanced_operators. html – these are well worth practising as it can save you a lot of time.

Searching for readings online – key skills

The following strategies will help you avoid wasting time on the Internet searching for readings.

- Make your search as specific as possible. Use advanced search functions. You can waste a lot of time if you don't know what you want to find out.
- Give yourself a time limit to find reading texts and stick to it.

And then once you find a text to read . . . read critically. Remember that everything on the internet has been written by someone with their own agenda, for their own purpose. Question what you are reading on screen as you would any other text. Ask yourself questions like the following when you are reading onscreen:

1 Is this true? Is it fact or opinion?
2 Who wrote it? Who is paying them? Are they qualified to say that?
3 Do conclusions given fit in with other texts I have read and things I have been told in my lectures?
5 What are the problems with what is being claimed?
6 What evidence is given?
7 Are there other ways of seeing this evidence?

Remember that you need to cite any information that you find on the internet and use in an assignment, so keep a record of searches that you do. Store any successful searches in 'Favourites' on your computer or save internet addresses in a text file.

You should also check out the section 'reading online' that appears later in this chapter (p. 111).

Becoming a more efficient reader

How not to read

Sometimes when you are in the university library looking for a reference, you find a book which is covered with underlinings, translations and notes in the margin, and looks as if it has been analysed word by word. Please don't do this to library books – it makes the book impossible to read for other students, and the librarian will make you buy the book if they catch you!

Imagine the reading process this student used. What's the problem here? Why do some international students fall into this trap? Check your answer in the key at the end of the book.

1 Open the book.
2 Start on page 1.
3 Get to third word.
4 Get out dictionary.
5 Check translation of word in dictionary.
6 Write translation in margin.
7 Go back to beginning. Read again.
8 Underline a difficult bit.
9 Stop at next difficult word.
10 Scratch head.
11 Go back to 5 and repeat for next 3 hours.
12 Collapse exhausted.

Getting it right

If you find you are getting frustrated with all your university reading, this section will give you some ideas about how to get on top of things again. One of the key first steps is to be really clear about your reason for reading. Before you start reading a text, make sure you are clear about why you are reading – what you want to find out. If you know this, then you can decide how to read and how long it will take you.

Coming up with your own reading questions

Look at the following situations and decide what questions you would want to find the answers to when you read. Check your answers in the key at the end of the book.

	situation	text
1	You are going to a conference on your subject in another city an hour away by train	The conference programme.
2	You are about to hand in your first written assignment.	Your department's submission guidelines for assignments. (This tells you what you need to do when you hand in an assignment).
3	You need to design a practical science experiment to do yourself.	Experimental write ups from similar experiments.
4	You are doing background reading for an essay about the dangers of nuclear power.	Newspaper clippings that contain reports of nuclear accidents
5	You are going to a lecture about public health policy in South Africa.	Three journal articles that report studies of public health policy in South Africa (recommended reading).

It's really important to have a clear reading question when you approach a text, so that you can decide . . .

1 . . . if it is actually worth reading

2 . . . how long to allow yourself to read the text

3 . . . what you should focus on in the text and which sections you can skip over

4 . . . what information you need from the text

5 . . . an effective reading process to use (see next section)

6 . . . what notes to make

and so that you are able to take a critical stance, i.e. you are using the text for your purpose and assessing its usefulness/value rather than accepting what it says.

Use this table to help you plan your reading. You will find this useful if, for example, you need to do background reading for an assignment.

An example is given based on a text from the *British Medical Journal* reporting medical research about the health benefits of playing a didgeridoo.*

Topic:

Deadline to complete background reading by:

Text	Time	My questions
1 Didgeridoo playing as alternative treatment for obstructive sleep apnoea syndrome: randomised controlled trial.	(20)	• Why did they decide to study didgeridoo players? • Is it an effective treatment? If so, why? • Is it suitable for everyone? • What about other instruments – e.g. the trombone?
2		
3		

* a didgeridoo is a long, wooden, aboriginal Australian wind instrument. You can read this text in full and try to find answers to the questions at: www.bmj.com/cgi/content/full/332/7536/266

Critical reading

In English-speaking cultures, critical thinking skills are highly valued and lecturers will often say that 'good' students are those who can think critically. It is important, when reading, not only to be able to understand the meaning of a text but also to be able to assess its value. Is it fact or opinion? What is the opinion of the writer? What is the purpose of the text – to inform, to persuade, to raise questions? Is it supported by evidence? Do you trust that evidence? Is it possible to come to conclusions other than those that the writer has given? Asking these kinds of questions when you are reading will help you develop your own critical voice when you are writing and speaking at university. This means that you will question what people tell you and find problems when things seem too simple. When you are reading in a second language, of course, this is difficult because you have to go beyond the meaning of the words on the page, but you can train yourself to do this.

What does this mean? Looking beyond the text

A key first step in critical reading is to be able to tell FACT from OPINION. Sometimes this is easy, when the writer is explicitly giving her opinion. For example, in a magazine column, a writer argues against the law that makes helmets compulsory for cyclists: 'I will simply add my voice to those who think the law requiring all cyclists to wear helmets is draconian.'

Definition *draconian*

= harsh; related to Draco, a lawmaker from Athens in the seventh century, who wrote a code of laws which prescribed death for almost every crime.

However, at other times, it is harder to spot which is opinion and which is fact, especially when the opinion is written as if it were fact.

Fact or opinion?

Look at the following list of statements about the artist Salvador Dalí and decide whether they are probably facts or opinions:

1 *Salvador Dalí was a Spanish (Catalan) artist and one of the most important painters of the twentieth century.*
2 *He completed his best-known work, 'The Persistence of Memory' in 1931.*
3 *Dalí had an interesting life and liked doing unusual things to draw attention to himself.*
4 *Sometimes his behaviour caused more public recognition than his artwork.*
5 *Dalí should not have drunk so much.*
6 *Dalí experimented with Dada, which influenced his work throughout his life.*
7 *He met the poet Federico García Lorca and it was rumoured by some that they were lovers.*
8 *After the death of his wife, Gala, Dalí lost much of his will to live and deliberately dehydrated himself – possibly as a suicide attempt, possibly in an attempt to put himself into a state of suspended animation, as he had read that some microorganisms could do.*
9 *Dalí's work reflects his powerful imagination and idiosyncratic view of life.*

Looking at these statements, you can see that they are all opinion to some extent. Even the second statement "his best known work" is someone's interpretation and therefore opinion. When assessing the value of something that you are reading, look out for the following:

Look out for . . .	Examples
general statements that you cannot check or that are not supported by evidence	'one of the most important painters of the twentieth century' 'Dalí lost much of his will to live'
words that contain a value judgement	'should not have drunk so much
words that sound good but are vague	'rumoured by some'
words that sound impressively complex but do not mean much	'his powerful imagination and idiosyncratic view of life'

Applying this to your university reading

A criticism of some students at university is that they accept what they read and do not work hard enough to understand the meaning of a text critically. They see reading like this:

The passive sponge-like reader

The critical reader

The critical reader asks himself/herself:

- The writer's purpose/world view? The writer's reason for writing it?
- Other things I know/have read? My purpose in reading it? My ideas? My opinion? My experience?
- How does it all fit together? How does this text fit with what I already understand

Developing your critical reading: a Q U E S T analysis

One useful way of putting this into practice and engaging with the ideas of the text rather than just the surface meaning of the words is to try a Q U E S T analysis. Take an article or a chapter in a book on the reading list of one of your courses and try it out. Compare your Q U E S T analysis with another student's. You will probably find that you have quite different responses to the same text.

Q	Questions	After reading the chapter/article, what questions do you still have? Is there any part of it that you feel you need more information on or that was not explained thoroughly enough? Does the article talk about any concepts that you do not understand and so need to read more on, to find an answer? If the writer had presented his article as a lecture, what would you ask him?
U	Unhappy	Is there anything in the article or chapter that you are unhappy with? Is there anything in the article that does not fit with your ideas on the topic? For example, you may feel that a particular opinion was not supported by evidence, or that the writer takes a position that you do not agree with. You may feel that the article or chapter was badly written in places or simply difficult to read. You may simply feel confused by the article. (Much academic writing can be extremely confusing.)
E	Excited	What excites you or makes you think differently about the themes? What have you learnt by reading the article/chapter? Maybe the article introduces some new research that helps you to understand a concept better. Maybe the article summarises an idea in a way that is helpful for you.
S	Strengths	What do you feel are the strengths of the article? Is it well written? Is it easy to read? Does it use helpful examples to illustrate the points it makes? Does it have a useful literature review? Are the definitions helpful? Is it well supported by evidence?
T	Themes	What are the main themes in the chapter/article? What ideas does it talk about? If someone asked you what it was about, how could you answer, e.g. 'It's an article that looks at . . .'

- Read the article through quickly first of all and identify themes, then read it again and look for the other parts.
- Read the article or chapter and use a different colour to highlight Questions, Unhappy, Excited, Strengths and Themes.
- Try to identify at least one part of the text for each section.

Other ways of developing your critical reading skills

Becoming a critical reader in a second language can be fun and challenging. Here are some ways of developing your critical reading skills that will be particularly useful before you apply to do your course. Remember that if you are looking for the meaning beyond the text, first you do need to understand the words on the page.

Text types	What to look for and what to do
Magazine adverts	Look at a range of advertisements from magazines. First work out what product is being sold. Then, look for the ways in which the writer tries to persuade the reader to buy the product. You may find: • complex scientific-sounding language that gives evidence for why that product is the best • comparison with other products • statements that you cannot check • over-the-top language, e.g. lots of adjectives that sound impressive
Song lyrics	Song lyrics are useful because often they are short and often there is a 'message' behind the poem or the song. Your job as a critical reader is first to understand the meaning of the words and secondly to understand the message. What is the song-writer saying about themselves or their world? If there are any cultural or musical references that you do not understand, look these up or ask someone about them.
News in brief	Often newspapers have a section where they summarise stories from around the world in short articles of about 50 words. This means that lots of details, facts and background are left out. • First work out why the story is newsworthy. • Secondly, write the questions that you want answering about the story. • If you want, you could go to a news site on the internet, e.g. www.bbc.co.uk or http://cnn.com and research the story to find out what is missing.
Letters to the editor	Newspapers have a page or section in which readers can write their opinions and send them to the editor of the newspaper. They are great for analysing the writer's stance on an issue and spotting holes in the letter-writer's logical argument. • First, work out whether the writer agrees or disagrees with what was said in the newspaper. • Decide how well the letter-writer justifies their opinion. • Spot any holes in their argument or gaps in their logic.
Satire/comedy	Satire is when writers or comedians hold a mirror to society by making jokes about people or institutions in the news. Trying to understand why a story is funny is a good way to develop critical reading. 'The Onion' (www.theonion.com/content/) is an American website that looks at stories about US celebrities, politicians and events. There are probably blogs or websites about news in your country. • First, understand the story. You may need to do some research if you are looking at a site from another country, like 'The Onion'. • Then decide why it is funny.

Source: First task adapted from F. Grellet (1981) *Developing Reading Skills* (Cambridge: Cambridge University Press).

Ways of reading

How do university students read?

Here are some different ways of reading. Which of these are you good at?

- **Reading for the big picture/for gist** Reading something quickly to understand the main ideas of a text.
- **Reading intensively** Reading a section of text really carefully and understanding every word.
- **Scan reading** Searching in a text for a particular detail that you want to find out more about.
- **Skim reading** Looking quickly over a text to decide on the topic.
- **Reading between the lines** Reading critically to evaluate a text for yourself, and working out the meaning that is not written.

The reading process that you decide to use will depend on your reason for reading, they type of text you are reading and the questions you want answered. Now, look at these typical reading tasks and decide what reading processes you might use. Check your answers in the key at the end of the book.

Reading tasks	Reading process?
1 Looking through the 'References' section of an essay for the name of a particular text.	
2 Reading a research article to find out what the research study was about and the main findings.	
3 Reading a particular book that your lecturer tells you would be good background reading, to get a quick idea of what it's about.	
4 Reading an exam question before you start an essay.	
5 Reading a literature review and deciding on the viewpoint of the writer.	

Improving your reading

This section has tasks that you can try out to get better at reading for gist, scan reading and reading intensively.

Reading for gist

Reading for gist is about reading a text quickly and getting a rough idea about its meaning.

Make sure you know why you are reading. Predict the information that you think will be in the text and then read quickly to see if your guesses were correct.

Try this:

Find a text from your course that you want to read. Choose an article that looks interesting and is not too long. Alternatively, you could try this with a magazine or newspaper article.

⬇

1 Look quickly at the title, any illustrations and any subheadings in the article. Use your dictionary if necessary at this stage.

⬇

2 Write down five things that you think the article will say or that you want to find out from the article.

⬇

3 Read the first paragraph and check the predictions that you wrote down in stage 2. Revise your predictions if necessary.

⬇

4 Give yourself a time limit. You could start with two minutes for every page of the article. Quickly skim-read the article and make notes against any of your predictions that are mentioned in the text.

⬇

5 Tell a friend about the main points from the article. Talk from your notes and speak for no more than a minute.

Tips for reading for gist

● Don't try to understand everything. Remember, you can always read again if you want more information.
● Skim-reading means looking through an article and getting an overview of the text. If you find yourself looking at individual words and trying to figure it out, stop – this is not gist reading. Move faster and think about the

meaning of the text, not the meaning of words.
● The first line of every paragraph is often really important and explains what the paragraph is going to be about. Spend a little more time on these lines.
● Don't use your dictionary when reading for gist. It will slow you down. Skip over words you don't understand at this stage.

TIP *Read lots of fiction in English*

Reading fiction is good practice for gist reading. There are large series of graded readers published by Cambridge University Press, Oxford University Press, Longman and Palgrave Macmillan with titles that are graded (simplified) for language learners. They use only the most common words in English, so you can concentrate on the story (and by doing so you can improve your gist reading) without worrying too much about vocabulary. If you can read this book without too much difficulty, choose the highest level or try to read easier 'ungraded' fiction.

Scan reading

Scan reading is when you are looking at a text and looking for particular words or numbers. It is a bit like the 'Ctrl + F' (FIND) function of a computer.

Scan reading is a really useful technique for situations when you know exactly what word you want to find – for example:

● You are looking a word up in the index of a book.
● You get a page reference and then look at that page and look for the word.
● You are looking for an idea in the Contents page of the book.
● You are writing an essay and need to check a fact or a quote.
● You look for a name or date in an article.

Try this:

Find a chapter in an introductory university textbook for your subject. Choose the type of book that gives lots of definitions of key terms for your subject.

1 Find the index at the back of the book.

↓

2 Look up the name of an important researcher in your subject. Choose someone you have heard about in a lecture but that you don't know much about. The index is arranged A–Z.

↓

3 Note down page numbers.

↓

4 Find those pages. Look quickly over the page and spot the name of the researcher.

↓

5 Read around the names you have found.

Tips for scan reading

● Do it at speed.
● Have a number of search terms in mind. Don't just look for one word, like 'earth-moving', but also look for 'earth-shifting', 'landscaping' and 'excavating'.
● When you are finding a word, you do not need to read the other words on the page.

Reading intensively

Reading intensively means reading something to understand it in detail. It is slow . . . so make sure the section of text is really worth reading intensively. An example of a text that you should read intensively is an essay question in an exam! You need to make sure you understand it fully.

First read the passage for gist. After you have read something for gist, ask yourself these questions:

● Do I need to read this again?
● If so, which parts of the text?
● What information do I need?

If the answer to the first question is 'no', go on to the next text. If you feel that you need to understand something in the text in more detail you may need to read it intensively.

Try this:

Find a chapter in an introductory university textbook for your subject. Choose a text that explains key terms for you subject.

1 Choose a term that you don't understand. Suitable terms might be **osmosis**, if you are studying biology, or **depth of field**, if you are studying photography.

↓

2 Scan the index of the book to find the pages where the words are explained. Scan those pages to find the definitions and explanations.

↓

3 Decide what you think the words mean, and read the explanations quickly to check whether the explanations match your idea.

↓

4 Read the explanations intensively and note down any differences from what you understood.

To test if you really understand a concept or a procedure, try explaining it to someone else. If you can teach them, you have probably read intensively enough. If they have lots of questions, you should go back and try again.

Tips for reading intensively:

● Make sure you read for gist first.
● Work out the meaning from word to word, but don't forget the meaning of the text as a whole.
● It's slow and takes a lot of brain processing so don't do too much.
● Use a dictionary at this stage if necessary. You need the exact meaning of words.
● Read critically. Test the meaning against your previous knowledge and look for connections within the text.

Increasing your reading speed

How to read faster

Students often ask how they can learn to read faster. There is no easy answer to this. The key to becoming an efficient reader is partly to read strategically and work out when to read for gist and when you need to read in more detail. You can also train your eyes and brain to process text more efficiently. This section has seven ideas you can try out that will help you to read faster. How many of these do you already do?

1 Set a time limit

Always set yourself an appropriate time limit. Look at how long the article is and think about how important it is for your studies. It may be useful to give yourself 10 minutes. Then ask yourself the question again: Do I still think it is important? Have I got enough out of the text? Do I need to keep going?

2 Be happy with 'good enough'

Read well enough to answer your questions . . . you do not need to understand EVERYTHING in a text and you don't have time to! The next time you read something – aim to get 60 per cent of the meaning, and set a time limit that is half what you would normally allow for a text of that length.

3 Read in a team

Think about forming a study group to share out your course readings.

4 Analyse your dictionary use

Some international students are very dictionary-dependent. Looking up lots of words in a dictionary is slow and you may lose track of your reading. However, sometimes it can be important to look up the meaning of a few key words, for example in the abstract of an article. At other times, either skip over words you don't know or try guessing the meaning from the context. You may not guess the meaning 100 per cent, but your guess will probably be good enough.

5 Chunk it

Read chunks of three or four words at a time rather than individual words.

Don't read . . .

> THE + MOST + IMPORTANT + CONCEPT + IN + SPEED + READING + IS + . . .

but read . . .

> THE MOST IMPORTANT CONCEPT + IN SPEED READING IS + . . .

Train yourself to do this by marking meaningful chunks of words together in one of your textbooks.

6 Read down, not along

Slow readers move their eyes along the line of text from left to right. More efficient readers move their eyes down a text. Focus on the middle of the line and place your finger in the middle. Move your finger down and follow it with your eyes. This takes practice and is easiest with texts that are written in narrow columns, like newspaper articles and magazine articles.

7 Notice the direction of the text

When you are reading, don't get bogged down in the details. Look out for discourse markers that show the argument or direction in a text. Look out for words like:

In addition **Moreover** **A further point in relation to X is . . .**	*To add another point*
Thus **Therefore** **However, . . .**	*To show a logical next step*
On the other hand	*To introduce a contrast*
In order to illustrate X, take . . . **Another example of this is . . .**	*To introduce an example*
To sum up **In conclusion**	*To introduce a conclusion*

Reading strategies

There are many reading strategies that can help you to become a more effective university reader. The following task will help you to think about the strategies that you currently use when you are reading and those that are worth trying.

A reading strategy checklist

Check the strategies that you use against this checklist. Give yourself a point for each of the strategies that you use. Check your score in the answer key at the end of the book to find out whether you are a strategic reader.

Before reading

- Use the Contents page and the index of a book to locate sections that are most likely to be useful.
- Scan a chapter for key words that are relevant to your studies and be prepared to not read.
- Think about what you know about the topic from lectures and other readings.
- Make predictions about the content of the text.
- Ask yourself questions that you think might be answered in the text and then read to check these.
- Research the writer. Find out when they were writing, what their position is on the subject and who maybe influenced their ideas.
- Make use of the title, abstract, introductory paragraph and any illustrations in order to predict the content of the text.
- Quickly look over the text and decide if it is worth reading before going on.

Text genre/organisation

- Think about other texts that you have read that aim to do the same as the current text you are reading (e.g. other research articles or other introductory texts that define a lot of technical terms), for clues to the texts' organisation.
- Look for general patterns within texts – e.g. claim–counterclaim; general–specific; theory–example.

- Use these text patterns to predict what is coming next.
- Notice signposting language, e.g. -Another example of . . is . . .', so that you can think of the text as a map.
- Look for useful topic sentences as a clue to the content of each paragraph.

First reading

- Read for gist (general understanding) before reading for detail.
- Answer a gist question (e.g. What did the researcher find out?) when reading for the first time.
- Set yourself a time limit when reading for gist.
- Live with a little confusion – don't try to understand everything.
- Only use your dictionary to look up really key words that you don't understand.
- Ignore most of the words that you don't understand – try to make sense of the text without them.
- Use skimming (looking over the whole text for main ideas) and scanning (looking for key words/numbers/dates).
- Note sections that look really important and think about questions for a second reading.
- Keep testing the ideas in the text against your experiences and other things that you have read/learnt about that topic.

Second reading

- Think carefully about your purpose in reading for detail – why do you need a detailed understanding of parts of this text?
- Set yourself detailed questions about different sections of the text and answer them as you read.
- Set yourself a time limit for the second reading.
- Use highlighter pens and Post-it® notes to identify key areas of the text.
- Test the text against your world knowledge and other texts that you have read.
- Make notes as you read using a note-taking summary sheet or your own system.
- Note down questions that you have about the text, which you need to investigate further.

After reading

- Tell someone who hasn't read the text about it so that they get a rough idea of what it is about.
- Talk through the ideas in the text with someone else who has read it.
- Turn the text over and try writing a very short summary (a single paragraph) of the main points in the text.
- Follow up on key questions that you had when reading – either with your lecturer or classmates or through further reading.
- Make notes of nice expressions in the text that you can use when you are writing yourself.

Keeping track of your reading

It is frustrating when it comes to writing an essay or revising for an exam, when you need some information or a quotation and you are sure that you have read something relevant but you can't quite remember what it was or where you found the quote! Even more frustrating is to go searching for a reference in the library, find it and then realise that you've already read the article! It is amazingly easy over a year to waste a lot of time looking for things you have read earlier on. The trick is to keep track of your reading and adopt some kind of system to store your notes. It is important to keep notes of texts that you have read, even if you decide when you read them that they are not really relevant.

What information do you need to store from your reading?

All readings:

Full reference (including title, year, author, publisher)
Essential if you want to find the text again or include the reading in an assignment.

Overall summary (main themes)
What was it about?

A rating of how useful/relevant/interesting the text is
How important is this likely to be for your assignment/course? Some readings will be essential. Others more marginal.

Date read
This at least gives you a sense that you are making progress, and will allow you to look back and see what you have read.

These will depend a little on the nature of your study and the reason you decided to read this text but may include:

> useful definitions;
> other references to check out;
> useful summary of other research;
> key theories explained;
> good description of methodology;
> key research findings;
> questions that you had when you read the text;
> usable quotes.

Different ways of keeping a record of your reading

There are a number of ways of keeping a record of your reading. The one you choose will depend as much on your own preference as anything else. There are five methods on the next page to try out.

TIP *Experiment with different storage strategies*

Talk to other students about how they organise their notes and try a range of different approaches until you find a way that works for you and your course.

Storage method	Notes
A paper record in a folder or notebook	• Low-tech. No need for a computer. • Easy to add to and access in tutorials and lectures. • Easy to incorporate with readings that your lecturer may hand out. • You can keep all your readings for a particular assignment or paper together. • Think about using a template like the one at the end of this section as a cover sheet for each reading (see p. 109).
Computer files	• No special software necessary – just use your normal word processing application. • Useful if you work onscreen a lot and access a lot of readings from online journals. • Again, you can sort readings into folders by author, theme, date or paper name. • As above: set up a template on a word processing document for each reading.
OneNote®	• This software is produced by Microsoft® and can be downloaded from the internet. You can download a trial version for free. Type 'OneNote download' into your search engine and try it out. • It is quite easy to use. • It is aimed at students and business people and has the advantage that you can use it to keep track of multimedia input . . . not just text onscreen. • Useful, for example, if you have accessed diagrams online and want to incorporate them into your notes, or want to include photos or voice recordings as well as written notes.
Free note-taking software	• There are dozens of free alternatives to OneNote® to help you to take notes. A very popular programme at the moment is www.evernote.com – This programme also lets you share your notes online with friends and classmates.
EndNote	• www.endnote.com • Software application basically designed for keeping track of and formatting references, but could be used to keep short summaries of readings. • Can be launched from Microsoft Word®, and allows you to cite as you type. (Very handy.) • Build up your own library of references for a course. You will need to store summaries under the authors' names. • A bit tricky to use at first but worth learning – many university libraries will run short courses. • Once you have learnt it, you may as well use it to store notes on readings as well, rather than learning to use a new software application such as OneNote®.

Reading and note-taking cover-sheet: a photocopiable resource:

Short title: (Give the article a name that is meaningful for you)

Interest rating:
(Give a mark out of 5.
5 = very interesting.
1 = terribly dull.)

Date read:
(When did you
read it?)

Full reference: (Include: author, date, full title, publisher, journal, page numbers etc.)

Relevance rating: (Give the article a mark out of 5 for relevance/importance in relation to your course: 5 = essential reading; 1 = non-essential wider reading.)

Main themes: (Include: purpose of writing, i.e. to inform, or to report on research, or to summarise research; also a brief indication of topics covered.)

Content notes: (Here you may include: useful definitions, a useful summary of other research, key theories explained; a good description of methodology, key research findings, questions that you had when you read the text, usable quotes, diagrams etc.)

Action: (Note down anything you need to do as a result of reading this article, e.g. check out more references or re-read something; add a paragraph to your assignment; ask your lecturer to explain something.)

An example of a completed reading record (NB: This was completed by a student studying an English literature course.)

Short title:	Interest rating:	Date read:
Shakespeare's sonnets	+++++	17 May 2007

Full reference:	Relevance rating:
The Sonnets, William Shakespeare, Everyman edition, published 1993	+++++ (assignment 3)

Main themes:

definition of nature of romantic/poetic love compared with act of writing/poetry ...
time and aging + death + decay (youth + idealism vs. experience + learning)
darkness + beauty
the stars/destiny vs. individual choice?
love — misery — comedy
The Dark Lady?

Content notes:

Key sonnets for assignment 3:
116 (Let me not to the marriage of true minds ...)
130 (My mistress's eyes are nothing like the sun ...)
18 (Shall I compare thee ...)
73 Note sonnet structure ...
range of sonnet structures

Introduction (by M. R. Ridley)
    difficulties/problems with the sonnets
    Are they a sequence? What's the order?
    Who was Shakespeare writing to?
    Who was the Dark Lady?

Action:

close analysis of sonnets above
further reading on sonnet structures

Reading online

Quite a lot of the reading you will do at university will be online (on a computer screen). This section looks at some of the similarities and differences between reading online and reading paper-based texts and also some specific 'online' reading activities that you will need to do as part of your course.

Reading online vs. reading paper-based texts: same or different?

There are a lot of similarities between reading online and reading paper-based texts. Look at the following and decide to what extent you feel these statements are true. Read the discussion in the answer key at the end of the book and compare your ideas.

1 You still need to read critically.

2 You can use the same reading strategies (skimming, scanning, reading intensively etc.) when reading online.

3 It's easier to get distracted and waste time when reading online.

4 It's worse for your eyes.

5 You find the same text types online.

6 It's better for the planet.

Some cool things about reading online

As well as being able to find lots of texts and information online and run advanced searches (see the section on finding readings on the internet), there are many more things that you can do with computers that make reading easier and save you time. Here are some for you to try.

1 Find on page

Use 'CTRL + F' on your keyboard to bring up this search box. This is a really useful tool for scanning a document or webpage. You can use it to help you decide whether an article is worth reading and then which parts of the article are worth reading intensively. For example, you are interested in air pollution in the USA from industry. You find an article online about air pollution in the USA. Now find out how often the word 'industry' is mentioned. If it doesn't mention industry, you could go to the next article. If it does, you probably don't need to read the whole article. Just read just those sections of the text where the word 'industry' is used.

2 Save your favourites

If you find useful articles, you can either download them and save them on your computer or save the URL (internet address) as a 'favourite' or 'bookmark'. This means that you can get back to it really quickly. Many students use online tools such as http://del.icio.us to share their bookmarks with other students and to find interesting new websites.

3 Links to reference materials

When you are reading online, you can have an online dictionary or subject glossary open at the same time so that you check the meaning of words online. If you use Firefox® as your browser you can download 'extensions', which let you do things like click on a word to get a translation or a synonym. Check out: https://addons.mozilla.org/

4 Tabs/windows

Right click on links that you are not sure about and they open in a new window. This is useful because you do not navigate away from the page you were first looking at. It's like opening a new book while keeping the one you are reading open rather than closing the book and putting it away and opening the new one.

5 Copy and paste direct quotes

You no longer need to copy out direct quotes that you want to use in essays. If you are reading literature for an essay, keep a Microsoft Word® document open, in which you can store quotes for your essay and copy and paste as you read. Remember you also need to keep a record of where you got the quotes from, so that you can reference them properly in the text of your essay and in your bibliography.

Reading online: looking after your eyes

Reading online can be really bad for your eyesight. Look at how many computer programmers wear glasses!

We interviewed an international student (Jason) about reading online. Read the interview and note down what he should do differently to protect his eyesight.

Interviewer: So you say your eyesight is deteriorating. Tell us about how you read. Do you read much from your computer?

Jason: Yep. Most of my reading is from the screen. My lecturer scans readings for us and so it is easy to access them onscreen in my flat. I spend 2 to 3 hours reading onscreen every day. We also have to do online discussions on the course webpage.

Interviewer: Do you read continuously for 2 to 3 hours or do you take breaks.

Jason: I often take breaks. I check my emails or watch some video clips online to relax my eyes.

Interviewer: Tell us about your computer set-up.

Jason: Well, I use a laptop. It's great – I can even read lying down in bed with the laptop on my knees. The lighting's not good but it's really comfortable.

Interviewer: And how do you set up your browser. What settings do you use?

Jason: I like to see as much as I can at once – so I have the text quite small. It's not a very big screen. . . .

Look after your eyesight. Look at the following advice on reading online. Which of these do you do already?

Do you do this?	How?
Give your eyes frequent breaks	• Have a clock next to your computer and give yourself a time limit. • Have a break at least every 15 minutes. • Make sure you do something in your break that doesn't involve looking at a monitor. (Walk around and have a stretch. Don't check your emails or watch videos on YouTube.com in your break!)
Use your printer	Print out articles you need to read intensively and those you will probably need to re-read.
Room set-up	• Make sure you have good lighting • Position your monitor so that you can easily focus on something in the distance. If possible, use a height-adjustable chair.
Computer set-up	• Turn down the screen brightness. This control is usually on your monitor and has a small 'sun' icon. • Make sure your monitor is not too high.
Notebooks/ laptops	If you are reading a lot online on a notebook, think about buying a monitor to plug your laptop into. Second-hand monitors can be bought very cheaply.
Zoom in	• Magnify your screen so that the words on the screen are bigger. You can do this in Microsoft Word® by clicking on **View** and then choosing **Zoom**. • Turn off any unnecessary toolbars so you reduce clutter on your screen.

Conclusion

In this chapter we have tried to show that by thinking about why you are reading and by choosing appropriate techniques you can become a more active and more efficient reader. Often students only get feedback on their 'reading' when they write assignments. Students get comments such as: 'Your writing shows that you are reading widely,' 'You have clearly researched this topic thoroughly,' or 'You make good use of the sources you cite.'

This may be all the positive feedback you get about your reading. Keep track of these comments as well as more negative comments you may get in your writing feedback as they will give you an indication of whether you are doing enough. For example:

'You have only cited two articles for this essay.'

'At this level you are expected to show that you have read more widely than this.'

'You need to read more critically and show in the essay what you think about the readings rather than just report them.'

It may be hard for you to work out how much you should be reading as it may be different from your previous educational experiences and may also vary depending on the subject or the lecturer's expectations. If these expectations are not clear to you, you should talk to someone in your department or seek advice from an academic advisor.

Chapter 8

Essays at university

CHAPTER OVERVIEW

In this chapter you will meet tasks to help you understand:

- some common questions that students ask about written assignments
- ways of interpreting essay questions
- types of assignment you can expect
- ways of making the essay topic easier to understand
- how to gather your information

As you will see, although we mention many types of writing, we give most space to essay writing. At the end of the book, you will find references to more specialised academic writing books that are designed for students writing for particular subjects.

In the next chapter you will practise putting the material together in a good order.

Introduction

Each department at each university asks for different types of writing. The departments also prepare guidelines for students. These can be found in handbooks or on websites. Here are some examples to look for.

- Essays that present arguments for and against a point.
- Essays that summarise research articles.
- Research papers (especially for senior students).
- Proposals (before you do major research).
- Reports (especially in subjects that have laboratory or field work).
- Responses to case studies.
- Text analysis (in literature and language classes).
- Critiques (an evaluation of a text).

In this chapter we will mainly look at the first two of these but a lot of the information also applies to the other types of writing.

What bothers students?

Here are some common problems mentioned by students. If these apply to you, look up the sections below that deal with these points.

1 If I understood the question then I'd be halfway there in my essay writing.

_____ a big problem for me

_____ worries me sometimes

_____ not a problem for me

(See the section below on 'Understanding essay questions'.)

2 Lecturers say we should work out what type of writing to do in different parts of the essay but I have no idea how to do that.

_____ a big problem for me

_____ worries me sometimes

_____ not a problem for me

(See the section below on 'Types of writing'.)

3 I don't know where to find the material I should be reading.

_____ a big problem for me

_____ worries me sometimes

_____ not a problem for me

(See the section below on 'Collecting ideas for your essay'.)

4 I keep hearing people talking about an 'argument' essay but for me an argument is something angry. I feel much safer just reporting things.

_____ a big problem for me

_____ worries me sometimes

_____ not a problem for me

5 When someone asks questions during a lecture or tutorial then I can understand them. Why are essay questions given such difficult wording?

_____ a big problem for me

_____ worries me sometimes

_____ not a problem for me

(See the section below on 'Rephrase the question'.)

6 For my last essay the marker wrote something about not having enough variety in my writing style. What does that mean?

_____ a big problem for me

_____ worries me sometimes

_____ not a problem for me

(See the section below on 'Types of writing'.)

Understanding essay questions

One reason students often lose marks unnecessarily is because they misunderstand the question. Let's try and simplify the process of understanding the question. First, you need to know that there are three types of essay questions:

Speaking very generally, an expository essay explains points, an argument essay shows two or more viewpoints on the same topic and an analytical essay looks at all the details of something and shows how they fit together.

Let's see if you can figure out what essay types the following questions are:

1 *Choose a TV advertisement. Through an analysis of the camera effects used, explain how these techniques contribute to the success of the advert.*

   EXPOSITORY   ARGUMENT   ANALYTICAL

2 *Describe the types of public housing built between 1920 and 1950 in Moscow.*

   EXPOSITORY   ARGUMENT   ANALYTICAL

3 *The type of housing children grow up in has a considerable effect on their quality of life. Discuss.*

   EXPOSITORY   ARGUMENT   ANALYTICAL

4 *Describe the alternative ways that national roading projects can be funded and say which model is the fairest towards lower socioeconomic groups.*

   EXPOSITORY   ARGUMENT   ANALYTICAL

5 *Through a close analysis of Shakespeare's sonnets, discuss the poems' treatment of the notion of romantic love.*

   EXPOSITORY   ARGUMENT   ANALYTICAL

6 *'Austen's novels are truly radical when you look at what is unsaid.' Analyse three key passages in* Pride and Prejudice *and say to what extent you feel this opinion is justified.*

   EXPOSITORY   ARGUMENT   ANALYTICAL

Check your answers in the key at the end of the book.

© Hayo Reinders, Nick Moore and Marilyn Lewis (2008),
The International Student Handbook, Palgrave Macmillan Ltd

Simplifying the essay topic

One reason why essay questions are often difficult to understand is because they use difficult language and are quite 'dense', meaning that there are a lot of important words in a small amount of text. In spoken English we usually use simpler language. So one tip is to try and 'translate' the essay question into a spoken question. Start by asking yourself which of these questions best matches the essay question.

Who?

Why?

What?

When?

Where?

How?

Let's try this with a few practice sentences. Read the following typical essay starters below (A) and match them with the spoken questions (B). Turn to the end of the book for the key.

Typical essay starters	Spoken questions
1 Discuss the role of . . .	What is . . . like? What is similar about . . . ?
2 Give an account of . . .	Why is . . . important? What happened . . . ?
3 Explain/Discuss the reasons for . . .	What was the result of . . . ?
4 Explain/Discuss the significance of . . .	What is the purpose of . . . ?
5 Distinguish between . . .	Why should . . . ? What is the difference
6 Account for the popularity of . . .	between . . . ? What causes . . . ?
7 Describe the characteristics of . . .	Why did . . . happen? Why . . . ?
8 Make the case for . . .	
9 Draw some parallels between . . .	
10 Outline the effects of . . .	

Rephrase the question

You have just matched essay questions with topics. This next task is harder. You are going to try turning the following essay topics into your own words. The first example has been done for you. The answers are in the key at the end of the book.

Essay question	Simple spoken questions
Discuss, with reference to specific examples, the role of the messenger in ancient tragedy. (Classical Studies)	What did the messenger do? Which plays used messengers? How are they important to the plays' story?
Give an account of the war of . . . against . . . , including . . . In what ways is this war unlike the . . . War? (Classical Studies)	
Discuss the ways in which . . . derived influence from . . . ? (Physics)	
What, according to . . . , is the relationship between . . . and . . . ? (Physics)	
Examine the significance of . . . (Physics)	

© Hayo Reinders, Nick Moore and Marilyn Lewis (2008), *The International Student Handbook*, Palgrave Macmillan Ltd

Types of writing

Here are some types of writing which you need to do for an essay. In the right-hand column is a definition of each. When you have read this table, try the task that follows.

Type of writing	
Process	A 'process' describes things that happen, step by step, in order.
Classification	Classifying things means putting all the same things together.
Exemplification	To help make something clear, you give examples or illustrations.
Comparison/ contrast	Show how things are similar to one another but have some differences.
Cause/effect	Often there is a chain of events, with one thing happening because another happened.
Problem/ solution	What went wrong? How was it put right?
Definition	Explain the meaning of something, using different words.
Analysis	Look at all the details of a situation and draw some conclusion from those details.

Now look at the following essay questions and see what types of writing they call for. Choose your answer from the list in the table and then check with the answer key at the end of the book.

(a) *With reference to Toronto, describe the steps that are taken to treat waste water before it is pumped out to sea.*

(b) *Outline the main causes of soil erosion in an agricultural system that you have studied and put forward some possible solutions.*

(c) *Describe the factors that led to the collapse of Enron and describe the consequences of this business failure for stakeholders.*

(d) *Compare and contrast the practices of Chinese medicine and 'evidence-based' medicine.*

(e) *Identify the main varieties of fern growing in the southern hemisphere.*

(f) *Define the term 'eco-tourism' and provide some examples of how eco-tourism ventures live up to their name.*

(g) *Through an analysis of Martin Luther King's speech, describe the literary effects that he uses in order to persuade.*

Collecting ideas for your essay

Imagine you are asked to write an essay on this topic:

> What services does the University have to help students learn English? How suitable are these services for someone of your language level and needs?"

Step one: Decide what type of essay this is?

Answer: Like many essay questions, this one is a mixture. It is mostly **expository** (explaining the University's services) but you also need to **evaluate** the success of the services and **argue** to what extent they meet students' needs.

Step two: Collect your ideas.

The main ways to collect ideas for your essay are:

● Design a questionnaire, which you give to someone to complete.
● Brainstorm with your peers.
● Practise your arguments with a friend, to hear other viewpoints.

We now look in detail at these three ideas. Of course there are other ways of getting ideas, such as using reference books, reading your lecture notes and textbooks, asking to borrow assignments from last year's students.

Design a questionnaire

Part of your answer could be based on a survey. Conducting a survey involves designing a good questionnaire and then asking people to respond to it. Plan a questionnaire to investigate the second part of the assignment.

(a) What questions could you ask, to find others of your language level and needs?

(b) Once you have identified these people, what questions could you ask, to survey their opinions?

Now use the questionnaire to collect data. There are some suggested questions in the answer key at the end of this book.

Brainstorming to collect ideas

Another way to collect ideas is by brainstorming. These are the steps to follow:

1 Get a large piece of paper or a tape recorder.

2 Write down or record everything you think of related to the topic, even if it seems silly at first.

3 Do this as quickly as you can. Give yourself no more than a few minutes. Just write words/draw pictures, arrows etc. Don't write full sentences at this stage – it's too slow.

Afterwards you can try and group ideas that seem related, for example by using colours.

A good way to help you in your brainstorming is to use the P P P P P system. In this system you try to come up with ideas by looking at different or opposite sides of a topic. Here are some examples:

Extend and sort out your ideas by looking at opposite sides of each topic	
Practical reasons	Abstract reasons
Personal reasons	Reasons affecting society
Permanent reasons	Short-term reasons
Proven reasons	Hypothetical (possible) reasons
People-related reasons	Financial reasons

Let's try these prompts out with the following topic.

Learning a foreign language should be compulsory in all high schools.

Here are some notes you could brainstorm under each of the headings.

Practical reasons	Abstract reasons
helps trade	any different type of learning develops the brain
Personal reasons	**Reasons affecting society**
students could travel, earn money and get better jobs	countries could understand one another better
Permanent reasons	**Short-term reasons**
it will develop students' thinking skills	it may motivate students
Proven reasons	**Hypothetical (possible) reasons**
societies with multilingual populations are said to survive longer	maybe helps world peace
People-related reasons	**Financial reasons**
being able to understand another language helps us to develop better relations	a multilingual society can trade more easily and be more successful financially

Try out this next topic with the same P P P P P categories.

Cities would be better off if cars were banned.

Leave the list for a day and then come back to it. Can you think of new ideas to add?

Argue with a friend

Here is a task we have called 'the tennis match'. The purpose is to collect three types of examples that you need for an argument essay, namely:

Here are some examples to give you an idea of what these terms mean for the following essay:

Poverty in any country is the responsibility of all countries

The idea is to go backwards and forwards with the arguments.

ARGUMENT

(a) an argument

Today's world has been referred to as 'a global village'. Just as, in a village, everyone is responsible for caring for anyone who is poor, so in the world today, richer countries must look after the poorer ones.

COUNTER-ARGUMENT

(b) a counter-argument

The comparison with a village is an attractive one. However, we could argue that with better planning the poorer countries would not have become poor. In other words, it is their fault.

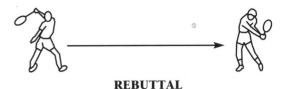

REBUTTAL

(c) a rebuttal

Most belief systems around the world acknowledge that some people are better at looking after themselves than others and that the better organised are not necessarily better people. Neither are the poorer people necessarily to blame for their poverty. As in a family, we need to look after those who, for whatever reason, find it hard to look after their own needs.

So an **argument** is like an opinion, a **counter-argument** is an alternative to that opinion, and a **rebuttal** is a response to the counter-argument.

Good essays don't just present one side of a topic but usually also consider other viewpoints. Being able to weigh up the benefits and drawbacks of different arguments is a key aspect of critical thinking (see Chapter 12). By doing the task below, you will probably come up with a lot of ideas for your essay. You could do this task alone but it works better if you do it with a friend. Your task is to find three types of statement: an argument, a counter-argument and a rebuttal.

Each counter-argument and rebuttal MUST refer to the previous statement. We have given an example above. Now think of arguments, counter-arguments and rebuttals for the following essay questions:

This university should have better . . . for students.

People in country x have a better life today than they did one hundred years ago.

The elderly/the young are the worst car drivers.

We can't give you an answer in the key without looking at your ideas. This is a task which it is best that you do with another student. If you can also find an 'umpire', as in a tennis match, you will get some good feedback on your points.

Conclusion

In this chapter we have tried to help you to get started with your writing. We have looked at what different types of essay questions mean and how to start gathering and organising your ideas. In the next chapter, you will read more about the process of actually writing your essay. As we said in the introduction to this chapter, we have focused mainly on essay writing here, but there are a number of more specialist academic writing books available that will give you more help with other types of university writing.

Chapter 9

The essay writing process

CHAPTER OVERVIEW

This chapter will help you to:

- develop the essay topic into an essay thesis
- write an essay introduction
- develop an essay thesis into paragraph-topic sentences
- develop topic sentences into paragraphs
- make a paragraph read smoothly
- link ideas together in a variety of ways
- acknowledge your sources (referencing)
- make all the essay parts fit together into a readable whole
- edit and proofread your draft essay

Introduction

In the last chapter you tried out tasks for understanding the essay question and gathering ideas. In this chapter you move to the next stage, which is actually writing the essay. As with the other chapters, you will see a mixture of examples and tasks for you to try. One difference with this chapter is that we take a spiral approach to the topic of essay writing. This means that we come back to some aspects of the topic in increasingly difficult ways.

From essay topic to essay thesis

What's the difference?

What is the difference between an essay topic and an essay thesis? Look at these two examples.

This is an essay topic:

Discuss the role of advertising with specific reference to one medium.

This is a thesis sentence:

Advertising is mainly for the benefit of the sellers

As you can see, the thesis sentence states the main point which the essay writer plans to build on. It tells the reader what the critical stance of the writer is towards the topic. Here is another example.

Topic:

Through the ages and from one society to another, views have varied on the extent to which children should be protected from the world around them. Discuss this issue with reference to two 21st-century societies.

Thesis sentence:

Most societies agree that little children should be sheltered from some of the most frightening world events.

Practise writing thesis sentences:

1 Read the topics below.

2 Think about the angle you would take if you were going to write the essay. What position would you take?

3 Talk to a friend about what you would say.

4 Write a thesis sentence that contains your argument.

5 Read our suggestions in the answer key at the end of the book.

Topic 1

'Companies selling tobacco products and marketing alcoholic drinks should not be allowed to sponsor sports events.' Discuss.

Topic 2

Immunisation against common diseases is a contentious issue in many countries. Looking at an illness you have studied, evaluate the arguments for and against mass immunisation programmes.

Topic 3

Describe the effects of tourism on an area that you have studied. Evaluate the extent to which it has benefited the area.

Topic 4

The standard of training of waiting staff in restaurants is critical to the success of a restaurant. Discuss with reference to case studies you have looked at.

Investigate
One important way to become more critical is to read lots of opinions and reactions and think about how the writers are positioning themselves in relation to the topic they are writing about. A good place to find these is your local newspaper.

Letters to the editor of a newspaper are often similar to mini-argument essays. They take one side of a topic and argue for that. They also argue against the other side.

Here is a letter to the editor of a newspaper or magazine. The style of letters is different from the style of essays. For one thing, letter-writers often word their messages quite indirectly. For example, read this letter and then decide on a title for the letter and the main thesis.

Dear Sir/Madam,

As a responsible dog owner I would like to add my response to your recent article 'Dog attack victim speaks out'. Let's keep things in perspective. While I understand how the victim feels, it would be crazy to introduce the type of dog control legislation that he advocates. Dogs bite people. Unfortunately it's a fact of life. Bees sting people. People get hurt in road accidents. Will legislation stop people being stung by bees? Can legislation alone stop people being hurt by cars?

And another fact of life. Some dog owners are irresponsible. We already have rules about registering dogs, keeping them on leads, where you can let them off the lead and where you can't. According to your article, the dog in question was neither registered nor on a lead. Surely the most appropriate response to this 'dog attack' is to prosecute the irresponsible dog owner in question rather than make it even more difficult for responsible dog owners to enjoy having a pet in the city.

Yours

Mrs D. Oglover

St Kilda, Melbourne

Now look at the answer key at the end of the book.

Investigate
Go to your local newspaper, choose a 'letter to the editor' and check two things.

1 The title of the letter supplied by the editor

2 The thesis sentence to the letter. This is usually (but not always) the first sentence in the letter. How well do you think the two match?

TIP *For more practice, go to this site*

http://news.bbc.co.uk/1/hi/talking_point/default.stm

Find a story that you are interested in and write a thesis statement for three of the postings. Try posting your opinion on one of the stories. You might get published!

Developing your critical stance

Many international students find it hard to find a critical voice when writing essays and feel they have nothing original to say. If you have this problem and cannot decide your stance on an issue, you may try to think in these ways:

1 Look for problems involved in the topic.

2 Question what is understood and not said.

3 Look at the words used, think about their definitions and challenge the way they are used.

4 Challenge the evidence for the topic.

5 Apply the topic to different situations – is it still unproblematic?

6 Think of the implications of the topic.

7 Think about your own personal experiences with the topic. Does your experience support the views expressed?

For example, take another look at the first of the topics from the last exercise:

'Companies selling tobacco products and marketing alcoholic drinks should not be allowed to sponsor sports events.' Discuss.

Here are some ways to approach this topic in a critical way.

Question these words and aspects of the topic	Ask these questions
'not be allowed'	• Who allows them? The government? The Society? The sporting organisation? • Do they have the right to make decisions like this? • Who would have to ban them? • How could this be done? • How could a ban be enforced? By police?
'companies selling tobacco products and marketing alcohol drinks'	• Which companies are these? • What about larger conglomerates that happen to own a company that sells alcoholic drinks?
'tobacco products and alcoholic drinks'	• If no advertising is allowed, is smoking allowed at the sports ground? • Is beer for sale? • When the team wins a competition, are they allowed to open a bottle of champagne? • What about other products that are dangerous to health, like junk food – should they be banned too? How can anyone draw the line? • What about companies that cause environmental damage? Should they be banned from sponsoring sport too?
'sponsor'	• If these companies are not allowed to sponsor, how will the sports organisations cope with the missed income? • If they are not allowed to sponsor events, are TV companies allowed to show advertisements for alcohol or tobacco in ad breaks on the TV when they are broadcasting the events?
personal experience	Does seeing alcohol advertising at a sports ground make me think that drinking alcohol is healthy?
evidence	Is there evidence from other countries that cutting out tobacco and alcohol advertising reduces smoking and alcoholism?

Practice this way of thinking by looking at another topic. The more you do, the easier it will get. You may also want to read about critical thinking in Chapter 12.

Writing an essay introduction

The parts of the introduction

Let's look at one introduction to an essay on whether schooling should be compulsory. First of all, decide what you think about this topic. Do you think there should or shouldn't be a compulsory curriculum? What would be your thesis statement? Now read the introduction below, and decide if the writer agrees. Check your answer in the key (p. 215).

Below, we have listed some of the purposes of the sentences. For each purpose, add the number of the sentence. Your introduction may do these things:

Introduce the topic of your essay.

Make a generalisation.

Ask a rhetorical question.

Introduce your thesis statement (i.e. your position on the topic).

Tell the reader about the organisation of your essay.

The thesis sentence is underlined as an example. You can find the other answers at the end of this book.

The order of the introduction

Now look in detail at another topic: 'the experience of studying overseas'. You will look at an introduction to a student's essay. The sentences are in the wrong order.

Organise the following sentences into the best order. (Check your answer in the key at the end of the book.)

While many people clearly benefit from the experience of studying at university in another country, for some students the experience is far less positive.

It is becoming increasingly important for individuals to experience life in another country to make them more employable in a world job market.

The case studies also suggest that for some individuals, the sacrifice made for an overseas education may not ultimately be worth it.

By looking at a series of individual case studies, this essay will outline the ways in which young people can benefit from study overseas.

With the movement towards globalisation in recent decades, both business and education have become more international.

Example of an essay introduction	Purpose of the different sentences	
(1) Ideas about when and whether children should have compulsory education have varied through the ages and from country to country. (2) In some countries the choice has been left to individuals and in others the government has made one rule for everyone. (3) Most countries of the world now have compulsory schooling between certain ages but the form of the schooling may vary between institutions. (4) Variety may sound like a democratic idea but in practice how does it work out? (5) In this essay the case will be made for national education to include certain fixed areas of learning. (6) The reasons will be explained in terms of equity for individuals and the good of the nation.	1 2 3 4 5 Thesis statement 6	

Check your introduction

You could now try to write an introduction based on one of the essay topics you wrote thesis statements for earlier. You could also look at an introduction for an essay you are studying for your course. Use the following checklist to edit an introduction that you have written.

	Questions	OK or rewrite?
Topic introduction	• Does it tell you what the topic of the essay is? • Does it sound interesting?	
Thesis statement	• Is your opinion clear? • Is your critical stance on the topic clear? • Is it clear how you will argue this?	
Signposting	• Have you indicated how the essay is organised?	
Organisation	• Is the introduction organised in a logical way, e.g. topic introduction, then thesis statement, then signposting?	

From essay thesis to topic sentences

The next step is to plan your paragraph-topic sentences. These are usually the first sentence in a paragraph. What do you want to write as the main point of each paragraph?

Coming up with topic sentences

An essay has one thesis sentence but many topic sentences, one for each paragraph, as you will see in the examples on the next page. We have shown you the skeleton of an essay, with the start of topic sentences underlined.

Practise writing topic sentences

Stage 1: Brainstorm the points you want to make
If you wanted to say why you believe that competing in the Olympic Games is a difficult challenge, you might want to make these points:

1 It takes a long time to get that good.

2 It is necessary to sacrifice career, friends, family.

3 Need to have natural ability. Wrong genes?

4 Need for expert coaching and facilities – not always available?

5 Need to care.

6 Need of funding/sponsorship.

7 Need to meet qualification times/schedules

8 Risks – sickness/lack of form/injury

9 Need to peak at the right time. The Olympics happens only every 4 years.

Stage 2: Reorganise the points you want to make
At this stage, look at your list and decide which points are not necessary or could be combined. (And Points 7, 8 and 9 could be combined – they are both about reasons why you may not compete at your best level.)

Working out a logical order:

● Points 1 and 2 are about build-up and ambition and commitment.
● Point 5 is about ambition.
● Point 6 seems to follow on from sacrificing career (Point 2).
● Points 3 and 4 are about natural ability and coaching – could go together.
● Points 7, 8 and 9 are all linked. They are all about the selection process.

So . . . a suitable paragraph order might be:

1 then 2, then 5, then 6, then 3 and 4, and finally 7, 8, 9.

Stage 3: Write each as a topic sentence
So you know the points you want to make and the order. Write each one as a topic sentence that could introduce a paragraph in your essay.

Sentences from the essay	The purpose of the sentence
In an academic writing class students are asked to do a number of activities such as . . . and. . . . Sometimes they see the point of each activity; on other occasions they don't even think about the purpose.	To give the background
Does it matter if students do things for which they see no point?	To address the question
This essay states the case that . . .	To state the essay's thesis
The reasons, counter-arguments and rebuttals are based on a class discussion in one academic writing class.	To explain the source of the ideas
One important reason [why/for]	To support the thesis
For example	To support the reason
Some people say	To state the opposite view
However, this view	To counter that view
Another point in support of the case that . . . is	To introduce a 2nd reason
It has been said that". . ." (xxxxx, 2001:13)	To support the 2nd reason
This point too has its critics. People say/ask	To state the opposite view
This claim may be partly true, but	To counter that view
Perhaps the most important reason of all for (not) . . .	To introduce a third reason
Studying in class is like . . .	To support the 3rd reason
Some claim that there is a problem with this argument. They say that . . .	To state the opposite view
The answer to this point is . . .	To counter the opposite view
Conclusion	

Each one is like a mini-thesis-statement for the paragraph. It should give the main idea of the paragraph. The first one has been done for you.

1 It takes many years of training and competition for athletes to get to a standard where they can be considered for a country's Olympic team.

2 _____

_____

5 _____

_____

6 _____

_____

3 _____

_____

4 _____

_____

7/8 _____

_____

9 _____

_____

Now check with our examples below.

How about these?

2 For some champions the prize comes at a cost to friends and family.

5 Others miss out from lack of drive.

6 Many potential champions miss out because of lack of financial support.

3 Finally, nothing would bring results if a certain basic talent were not there.

4 To get to a standard where athletes can compete at the Games, they need specialist coaching and facilities.

7/8 In order to compete at the Games, athletes first need to qualify. There are many physical reasons why athletes may miss qualification.

9 Then there is the tricky matter of timing. People who peak during the four years between Games will miss out on the prize.

Further practice:

Use a similar procedure to the above to practise writing topic sentences. You can use some of the thesis sentences from the section 'From essay topic to essay thesis' at the start of the chapter or if you have essays to write on your course, start with one of the thesis statements for those.

From topic sentence to paragraph

There are many ways to develop your topic sentence into a paragraph. The topic sentence starts the paragraph but further sentences are needed to complete it.

Now you have your sentences. All of them are on the subject of becoming an Olympic champion. For each of the sentences you have chosen, try to develop it by adding to it in one of the following ways.

Here are some examples:

1 Add detail.

2 Compare or contrast.

3 Give examples.

4 Refer to a source.

5 Add a viewpoint at the end.

In this table we take apart a paragraph on the topic *The world is a better place than it was a century ago*.

What to write	Example
1 A topic sentence	The options for entertainment in the early twenty-first century are enormous.
2 More about the topic sentence	Performers from one country can travel by air to amuse audiences in a distant part of the world and be home again in a matter of days. We can flick on the television and be entertained by plays, musical events and of course sports matches from all over the world.
3 Compare or contrast	All this is a far cry from the world of our great-grandparents.
4 Give examples	In their day entertainment was more likely to be provided by people they knew.
5 Refer to a source	According to . . . (2001) . . .
6 Add a viewpoint	It seems that the world of the twenty-first century would be scarcely recognisable to people from the past.

Now you try. Find a topic you have been asked to write about in class and complete the table below. We can't provide an 'answer' here, because the idea is to try writing from a topic you have been given in your subject. If you are working with a friend you could agree on a topic sentence, write one paragraph each and then compare notes.

What to write	Example
A thesis sentence	
More about the topic sentence	
One of the ways of adding to a topic sentence	
More on the last point	
A final sentence	

Referencing in an essay

As we mention more than once in this book, it is really, really important to let your readers know whether what you are writing is your idea or whether you have used ideas from other sources. We call these other sources your references.

Find out about plagiarism

> **TIP** *Go to this website*
>
> www.cite.auckland.ac.nz/
>
> It is useful because you can watch videos of students and lecturers from different cultures talking about the importance of referencing by talking about their culture.
> 1 Find a definition of 'plagiarism'.
> 2 Watch the videos of the students and staff talking. Whose ideas match your own about plagiarism?
> 3 Find out how to reference electronic material correctly.
> 4 Read some of the postings from website users about plagiarism.
> 5 As you look at the website, note any differences between ideas about referencing and plagiarism in your country and on this website.

Is it or isn't it?

Here are some scenarios where students describe how they presented material in their essays. When you have decided whether each one is, or is not, plagiarism, turn to the key at the end of the book.

1 *I had good long quotes, sometimes half a page long, but I always acknowledged where they came from at the end of the essay.*

2 *Every time I used someone else's ideas I used quotation marks and their name and date.*

3 *I think it's safest not to quote. You could plagiarise without knowing.*

4 *I take ideas from the text book but I always change the words.*

5 *If I take ideas from a book, I always say whose ideas they are. The Internet is so huge, I can easily cut and paste and get away with it.*

Find out about plagiarism in your university department

If you are studying in another country or even in a different university, you need to check out the rules about plagiarism. In many universities, if you are caught plagiarising, you will fail your assignment. You also risk failing your course. Your department or faculty will have written guidelines for assignment submission. These may be in a booklet or on the department website. Read them and find the answers to these questions:

1 What are the penalties for plagiarism?

2 Which referencing system (e.g. APA) does your department/faculty use?

3 How should you reference direct quotes in the text of your assignment?

4 How should you refer to other people's ideas?

5 What are the rules for referencing from internet sources?

6 How should you lay out your References section?

Putting it all together

When it comes to putting your essay together, it is a good idea to have an outline. An outline helps you organise your essay and your own thinking. Figure 9.1 shows one example you can use for an argument essay.

The whole essay

Read the argument essay on the next page (you met a version of one of its paragraphs earlier in the chapter). What *type* of information is missing at each point? Then look at the answer key (p. 216) and see if you agree.

Is the world a better place today?

One hundred years ago the car and the aeroplane had only recently been invented, world travel meant months at sea, and the horizons of many people were the limits of their own village or town. Today, cars and aeroplanes are taken for granted as travellers cross the world for weddings and even for funerals, but has life really improved? It seems that despite technological advances the world is not a better place. This argument will be supported with examples from family life, entertainment, transport and health.

One hundred years ago families spent time together on shared tasks involved with maintaining the home and property. As they did these tasks there were chances to talk. By contrast, these days many household tasks are completed by machines. Furthermore, non-stop television and the ever-ringing telephone prevent people from having conversations with others even when they are in the same house. Some family members spend longer talking on the 'phone to people in other places than to those around them in the house. According to Smith (1999), national manager of a telephone company,

[a] _____

It could be argued, therefore, that

[b] _____

One hundred years ago entertainment meant

[c] _____

The options for entertainment in the early twenty-first century are enormous. Performers from one country can travel by air to amuse audiences in a distant part of the world and be home again in a matter of days. We can flick on the television and be entertained by plays, musical events and of course sports matches from all over the world. Does this make the world a better place? It could be argued that much of today's entertainment makes people more passive.

This change seems more like a step backwards than forwards.

In the area of transport, it is true that these days

[d] _____

but these advances have brought extra pressures. For instance, people are expected to fly from all over the world to attend every momentous event in the lives of their families and friends. By contrast, a century ago when a relative was getting married in a different part of the world

[e] _____

It seems that [f] _____

Advances in public health are often given as examples of progress. People point to advances in surgery and to the fact that many former diseases such as tuberculosis and leprosy no longer occur on a large scale. This may be the case, but what has taken their place? Today people die just as frequently but of different causes such as

[g] _____

If the only change is the cause of death, where is the progress?

In a word

[h] *despite* _____

Perhaps we should define what we mean by 'better' before saying that everything in the world has improved. For many people 'better' could mean

[i] _____

© Hayo Reinders, Nick Moore and Marilyn Lewis (2008), *The International Student Handbook*, Palgrave Macmillan Ltd

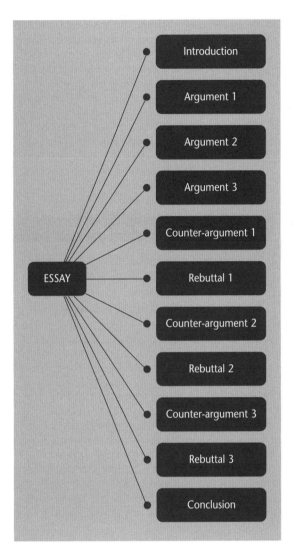

Figure 9.1   An essay outline

You have seen one example. Now use the same pattern to practise writing a real argument essay that you have to do for your course.

Joining ideas in a paragraph

A sentence or a paragraph or an essay is more than a whole lot of words and phrases. When we talk we make connections with what has gone before. We say things like:

That reminds me

Yes, but . . .

And another thing

When we write formally we also join ideas up but in different ways. We call the ways we join ideas together, cohesion. You need three kinds of cohesion

Sentence-level cohesion
By this we mean that the sentence reads like one thought, not several just stuck together anyhow. Words like *and*, or, *but* are the most common links but there are many more.

Paragraph-level cohesion
This is about how paragraphs fit together.

Essay-level cohesion
This refers to how the whole text fits together.

Below you will find some words and phrases. Decide which of the purposes in the right-hand column best match these words. You can find the answers at the end of the book.

These words . . .	Are used . . .
Furthermore	to say the same thing another way
On the other hand	to refer to someone's published view
Conversely	to give an opposite view
Similarly	to make things clearer
As an example	to concede a point but then rebut it
In other words	to illustrate a point
Even though	to say more on the same point
Despite the fact that	to agree slightly (to concede a point)
This is not the same as saying	
This point is also made by . . .	

Proofreading

Sometimes, especially as deadlines approach and you have had a few late nights, you don't see the errors . . . until after you have handed in your assignment – when it is too late. Using a computer can make proofreading even more difficult. It is harder to spot errors onscreen than on paper, and while editing onscreen you can easily add or delete a sentence, which can cause additional problems further down the screen.

Types of errors

There are four types of errors relevant to writing:

- **Typos**. These happen when you mean to write one thing but actually write something else, like typing 'progrmme' when you mean to write 'programme'. Use a spell checker to catch these before you hand in your assignment.
- **Grammatical errors**. Here is an example: can you fill in the missing word? 'One of the most significant problems facing international students ... that they do not have many friends in the beginning.' The missing word should be 'is', not 'are' because the head word ('one') is singular.
- **Vocabulary errors**. For example, one of our students wrote: 'The children had many air balls at their party.' We later found out that she meant 'balloons'.
- **Cohesion errors**. These errors happen when two or more sentences are not connected properly. For example you use 'because', when you mean 'despite of'..

How serious are errors?

Dr Lumley on linguistic errors:

Language errors vary in severity. Sometimes they can be quite superfical and simply annoy me. Spelling mistakes often fall into this category (type 1). At other times it causes me temporary confusion and I need to re-read a section of an essay to understand what the student is trying to say (type 2). However, errors may actually mean that I can't understand your writing at all and will give up in despair (type 3). Even type 1 errors will have a negative effect on me – especially if there are a lot of them and your essay is number 30 in a pile of 50 assignments that I have to grade. I very quick become obsessed with language errors and stop taking the ideas in the essay seriously. Then my mind wonders and I start thinking about university entry requirements and how standards are slipping and how it was better in the old days. On the other hand, when you do get an essay that reads well – it stands out. It's well worth taking the time to keep markers happy.

> **TIP**   *Be careful with cohesive errors*
>
> These are often the most serious type of errors and can seriously affect understanding. When you write a text, always keep the reader in mind and make the text organization as easy as possible to understand.

Spot the errors

Re-read the text above under the heading 'How serious are errors?' In it, there are four errors – one is a typo (he has hit the wrong key when typing), one grammatical (he has made a grammar mistake – tense/singular/plural etc.), one is about vocabulary (he has used the wrong word) and one is about cohesion (e.g. about the organisation or flow). Identify the four errors and decide how serious they are, according to Dr Lumley's categories.

Type of error	Example	How serious is it?
typo		type . . .
grammatical		type . . .
vocabulary		type . . .
cohesion		type . . .

Check your answer in the key at the end of the book.

© Hayo Reinders, Nick Moore and Marilyn Lewis (2008), *The International Student Handbook*, Palgrave Macmillan Ltd

As a student of the English language you probably own a grammar reference book. Use it! Don't stop improving your English. Look things up when you are unsure. Don't forget to turn on the spell check and the grammar check in your word processor and always get someone else to proofread for you.

Keep an error log

Read about the way this student monitored her written language. Do you think it could help you?

I found at the beginning of my studies that I kept on making the same mistakes. I had a problem with word order, especially with adverbs in English and also with punctuation. Every time I got feedback from my writing, I made notes of the errors in a notebook and then as I checked my next piece of writing, I checked all the things that I had had feedback on before. Soon I found I was able to cross things out of my notebook because I wasn't making those mistakes any more.

Peer-feedback

In addition to checking your essay yourself or having a teacher check it for you, other students can also be helpful. By using the worksheet below you can give and receive feedback before handing in your work. Here are some reasons why this is a good idea:

1 Instead of getting feedback from just one person (your teacher), you get comments from several.

2 Dealing with feedback and learning from others' comments is a key skill you will need in the workplace.

3 By helping others with their writing, you have to read critically. This way you also learn to read your own work better.

4 By writing down your comments or talking about someone else's essay, you can improve the way you express yourself.

Working together with another student in this way is a win–win situation. Of course, you will

Names	Notes (strengths and weaknesses)
e.g. *Freda (ex-landlady)*	+ *native speaker.* + *uni ed.* – *finished uni 20 years ago!* + *good at details but not so good at the bigger picture* – *slow!* + *I could baby sit for her or help her fix her car.* + *she's a good cook.*

not be able to find all the mistakes a teacher might, or get the same amount of feedback, but knowing if a non-expert can easily understand your essay, and if not, why not, is very valuable.

How to find a good proofreader

1 Write a list of everyone you can think of who you might be able to use to proofread your work. First of all just write their names in the left hand column.

2 Now, think about the following questions and make notes on the people you have named. (You may wish to keep this secret.)

What's their academic English like?
You don't need to be a native speaker to be an effective proofreader but it is important that you trust the person's basic language proficiency. It might be a good idea to get someone who speaks a different first language, for a different perspective.

What's their subject knowledge like?
Sometimes when you get someone to proofread your work, it is helpful to find someone who knows about your subject (e.g. someone on your course) to give you feedback on your *ideas*. Sometimes it might be better to get someone with no knowledge of the subject and just get them to check your *language*.

What can you do for them?
Maybe you can do a deal with them and agree to proofread their essays too. Maybe you can help them in some other way. You may need to pay them!

How easy is it to get work to them and feedback in return?
Maybe you'll be able to meet over a coffee. Maybe your proofreader is in another country and so you will need to email them and wait for feedback. This could be slower if you are working in different time zones, although it could work really well.

How busy are they? How organised are they? What are their deadlines like? How much notice will they need? How much time do you have?
These practical considerations may be really important.

TIP *Talk it through beforehand*

It's really important to talk through the kind of feedback you want from a proofreader. You may have particular questions you want them to think about or you may be happy to accept anything from them, but remember, it's much easier to give feedback if you have an idea of what the other person wants.

A peer-feedback worksheet

Peer-feedback is most useful when you look at different aspects of the text, not just the language. The worksheet (p. 135) has some ideas of what to look for.

How to give feedback

When giving feedback to someone, there are some things to keep in mind to make your comments as helpful as possible.

1 Focus on strong points as well as on weak points. It is easier for others to accept your comments if you start on a positive note. Ask yourself: what do I like about this text? What is really good about it (e.g. good use of vocabulary, good sentences, logically presented argument).

2 Focus on the content first before moving on to the language. Focus on one point at a time.

3 Your feedback is on the writing, not on the right or wrong of the author's opinions. (However, if an argument is not logically presented, you should point that out.)

4 It usually takes more than one round to give feedback on a piece of writing. It is important to talk about the points that you didn't understand. Try to find out what the author meant and suggest ways to make it clearer.

5 Be patient and be careful with your comments. Even if the text is not perfect, it may have taken the author a long time and a lot of effort to write it.

Peer-feedback worksheet

Organisation   Is the text organised well? Is it clear which part talks about what topic? Does the organisation match the requirements for this type of writing? For example, a laboratory report would look very different from an essay. Ask your teacher for some examples.

Introduction   1 Does the introduction clearly state the topic?
2 Does it state the importance of the topic?
3 Is there any background or general information about the topic?
4 Does it look at what other people have said about the topic?
5 Does it clearly say what problem or questions related to the topic it will cover?
6 (In the case of an argument essay) are the two (or more) sides of the argument presented in the introduction?
7 Does the introduction present what will be covered in the rest of the text?
8 Does the introduction progress from general to specific?

Text structure   1 Is it clear what the main point of this text is?
2 Is the main point followed by supporting ideas?
3 Are the ideas presented in the text clear and meaningfully related to each other?
4. Are the ideas described clearly?
5 Do the ideas progress in a logical way (for example: does the cause precede the effect – does the result of something come after what causes it)?
6. Related questions are: Does the author make use of paragraphs? Does each paragraph focus on one point? Is it clear what that point is?

Conclusion   In academic writing, this part usually summarises the whole article. That is, it repeats what has been said before. Ask yourself if the author has repeated the important points/findings from the text clearly and convincingly.

Relevance   1 Is the topic really important?
2 Is the text interesting?
3 Does it add anything to what you didn't know before, or does it talk about the topic in a new way?
4 Is the language used appropriate for the people it was written for? For example, if it is for people who are not likely to know much about the topic then it shouldn't be too specific and technical.

Language   The other point to look out for is the language of the text. This covers areas you usually probably check for, such as grammar, vocabulary and spelling. You can use the separate worksheet at the end of this section if you want.

How to get feedback

When someone gives you feedback, keep the following points in mind:

1 Try to see why your fellow student gave you feedback on a particular point. You may disagree with him or her, or maybe the feedback is simply wrong. But try to see their point and learn from it. Even if they misunderstood what you wrote, this could mean that you need to rewrite your text to be clearer.

2 If you don't understand why your friend commented on a certain point, then ask!

3 Don't forget: you don't have to agree with everything others say. Don't be put off if they have negative comments. You can learn from these as well!

Checking for grammar

Check that . . .	Example Wrong (or not good)	Correct
• Each sentence is complete.	<u>Fail the test</u>, I will be sad.	<u>If I fail the test</u>, I will be sad.
• The subject and verb agree in each sentence.	<u>Smoking *are*</u> bad for you.	<u>Smoking *is*</u> bad for you.
• The verb tense is consistent.	For me, loyalty <u>is</u> an important part of friendship. A loyal friend <u>*was*</u> true and faithful to me.	For me, loyalty <u>is</u> an important part of friendship. A loyal friend <u>*is*</u> true and faithful to me.
• Capital letters are used in the correct places.	I will see you on <u>*wednesday*</u>.	I will see you on *Wednesday*.
• The punctuation is correct.	<u>Look</u> he is coming.	<u>Look!</u> He is coming.
• The meaning of a sentence is clear.	<u>Arriving at the party, *it was crowded*</u> and Mary was standing alone. (Note. This sentence is not clear: '<u>?It</u> arrived at the party and . . .')	Arriving at the party, <u>we saw</u> Mary standing alone. (Note. This sentence is clear: 'We arrived at the party and saw Mary standing alone.')
• Particular words are not repeated too often.	Speaking and writing are *<u>important</u>* for a student who studies at school. Writing is an *<u>important</u>* skill for a person in modern society.	Speaking and writing are important for a student who studies at school. Writing is an <u>essential</u> skill for a person in modern society.
• The expression is succinct or concise.	<u>I decided to study</u> Spanish in high school, <u>and later</u> to pursue a Bachelor of Arts degree in Spanish literature. <u>I realised to become proficient in Spanish I would have to eventually go to a Spanish country. So, I was determined to save enough money by not going shopping so often and could spend the summer in Guatemala</u>	<u>After studying</u> Spanish in high school, <u>I decided</u> to pursue a Bachelor of Arts degree in Spanish literature. <u>Determined to go to a Spanish-speaking country, I worked all year at San Francisco State University to save enough money to spend the summer in Guatemala City, Guatemala.</u>

Check that . . .	Example Wrong (or not good)	Correct
	<u>City, Guatemala. After working all year</u> <u>at San Francisco State University's</u> <u>cafeteria, I was prepared to venture to</u> <u>Guatemala.</u>	
• Sentence structures are varied.	Mary was ill for two months. She was sacked by her boss. The boss's wife offered her a wonderful job.	Mary was ill for two months; *and unfortunately*, she was sacked by her <u>merciless</u> boss. <u>Interestingly enough,</u> the boss's wife offered her a wonderful job.
• The spelling is correct.	The hotel is really *felthy* and I am not *exeggerating*.	The hotel is really *filthy* and I am not *exaggerating*.
• Sources are used correctly.	In learning a second language (L2), vocabulary knowledge is fundamental to the development of L2 proficiency (Harley, 1996). *Hwang and Nation (1989) looked at the effect on repetition of reading follow-up newspaper stories on the same topic.*	In learning a second language (L2), vocabulary knowledge is fundamental to the development of L2 proficiency (Harley, 1996). <u>Even if an L2 learner can</u> <u>master grammatical aspects and</u> <u>phonological proficiency in the language,</u> <u>without words to express a wide range of</u> <u>meanings, the learner cannot</u> <u>communicate in the L2 in any meaningful</u> <u>way (McCarthy, 1990).</u>
• Reference details are given correctly.	<u>Fox and some people</u> say that red hair results from a deficiency in melanin, a condition which also means the skin of red-haired people burns faster.	Red hair results from a deficiency in melanin, a condition which also means the skin of red-haired people burns faster <u>(Fox, Wolfe & Reece, 1975).</u>

Punctuation

The icing on the cake for an essay is the punctuation. You have three ways to attend to the punctuation of your essay:

● Ask someone else to proofread it at the end.
● Use a computer programme which highlights mistakes.
● Learn about punctuation.

Let's sum up a few points for you to learn about this topic.

Learn about punctuation

Punctuation in writing is like using your voice in interesting ways as you speak. Listen to an interview and pay attention to the voice of the speaker. How many of these can you hear?

A short pause.

A long pause.

The voice is lowered.

The voice is raised again.

Each of these is done for a purpose and has a parallel in punctuation.

A short pause

This is usually indicated by a comma:

The factors affecting this outbreak included poor hygiene, lack of flowing water and little public education.

A long pause

This is usually indicated by a full stop (as at the end of the sentence above) although sometimes it means that it's time to start a new paragraph. There is another kind of pause used in writing, which is called a semi-colon. It looks like this [;]. Although you will see it in your reading, it is becoming less common in students' essays.

The voice is lowered

Did you notice the brackets (. . .) in the sentence above? Anything you write between brackets can be left out and the sentence will still make sense. In the paragraph above, the part between brackets simply gave the reader an example.

Sometimes instead of brackets you can use a comma before and after the extra part that could be missed out. For example:

Some people recommend bonding the wound and even, although we wouldn't recommend it, leaving Nature to heal the wound itself.

In this case, the part between brackets is an opinion put forward by the writer, rather than a general statement.

The voice is raised again

When you end the brackets, or add the second comma, that is like raising your voice again when you have lowered it in speech.

Learn more about punctuation

The key to punctuation, as you have seen above, is to link it to the meaning of what you write. A great way to practise this is to listen to a formal speech (speeches are usually more formal than conversation and therefore nearer in style to your essays) while reading the subtitles. DVDs let you use the subtitles and TVs with teletext often let you view the subtitles also. Try and pay attention to the intonation of the speaker and the punctuation used in the text.

Conclusion

In this chapter we may have made it sound as if there is just one order in which to do the essay stages. That is not the case. Some students simply start writing and then rearrange the material later. This is, of course, much easier using a computer. The only trick with moving material round too much is that you can easily forget cohesion. (See the section above.)

Other students say they like to write the conclusion first. Why not, if you know how your line of thought is likely to go. On the other hand, be prepared to change it later to fit what you have actually said in the body of the essay. Essay writing is like any other craft you may know, such as playing or even creating music. You cannot do it to a formula.

Chapter 10

Assessment

CHAPTER OVERVIEW

This chapter will help you to:

- understand various ways that universities assess students
- note some assessment criteria and ways of using them to your advantage
- learn from feedback
- prepare for exams
- succeed in presentations, portfolios and other forms of assessment

Introduction

You may have been a very successful student in your own country and have passed all your exams. You may have previously felt that not getting an A grade was 'shameful'. The truth is, it is quite common for international students to fail some assessments, especially early on in a course. This chapter answers the question, 'How can I pass this course?'.

Understanding assessment for your course

Difficulties with language, adjusting to a new country and adapting to new ways of teaching and learning all play a role. One way to help yourself is by understanding as much as you can about assessment on your course.

Specifically, try to find out:

- How many 'points' do you need in total to get your qualification?

- What is the pass-mark for each assessment?

- Do you need to pass all assessments in order to pass the paper – or can you fail one assignment and still pass overall?

- What happens if you are sick during the course and miss an assessment?

- Can you re-sit exams or do you have to take the whole paper again?

- How many exams are you allowed to re-sit?

- Is there any penalty if you need to re-sit an exam? For example, do you need to attend summer school or extra catch-up classes? As an international student, will you need to pay more fees to do this?

- Can you re-submit assignments? If so, how many times and is there a penalty (e.g. a lower grade) if you do re-submit?

The answers to these questions will be written in a policy document (maybe on the department website or in your department's handbook).

Types of assessment

Lecturers assess you to see if you are learning what they are trying to teach. There are lots of ways in which you can be assessed during university courses and some of these may be very different from how you have been assessed before, especially if you have studied in a country where critical thinking is not valued so highly. You can find out how you will be assessed when you choose a course, or you may find out in the first lecture. It is important to understand how you are assessed when you start the course so that you can plan how to prepare for the assessment part of the course.

Ways in which you may be assessed

Look at the ways of assessing students, listed in the following box. How many have you done before? Match them to the definitions listed below. Check your answers in the key at the end of the book.

(a) continuous assessment/portfolios
(b) essay exams
(c) short-answer tests
(d) multiple choice quizzes
(e) practicals
(f) oral presentations
(g) open-book exams
(h) assignments
(i) online discussion
(j) learning journal/narrative
(k) take-home exam
(l) exam-questions known

Definitions:

1 Students are observed doing something, for example, teaching a class on a teaching course, making jewellery on a jewellery course or improvising on a performance course. They are graded on their performance.

2 Students are assessed throughout the course and have to prepare a folder of short pieces of work that shows what they have been learning throughout their course.

3 Students need to write a reflective diary or series of stories to show that they are thinking about the content of the course and learning from it.

4 Students have to do an exam in which they write answers of one or two paragraphs. These might be definitions or check key ideas on the course.

5 This is an exam which students are allowed to do at home. They have a time limit of a week or two weeks from the time the exam is set. This is a

common assessment for business courses as the deadline is realistic.

6 This is an exam but you are allowed to bring in your notes and some reference materials.

7 A week or two before this type of exam, you will be given a list of maybe six questions. Three of these will be included in the exam. The aim is that you review the right parts of the course.

8 These are long essays that are set throughout the course. You do them at home. Each is set up by the lecturer and has a deadline.

9 Students have to write a number of essays in a set time (e.g. 3 hours).

10 Students have to give a short talk to other students on the course. They may have to lead a discussion after the talk.

11 This is an exam. Students have to choose the best answer for each question. There may be 60 questions.

12 This is common for distance courses. Students have to visit the course website and contribute to a discussion, which is usually started by the lecturer.

In some courses you may be assessed by a combination of these methods. Find out how important each of these is for your course. For example, 10% of your overall mark may be for an oral presentation, 30% may be for coursework and 60% may be for a final exam. Use this information to decide how much time you are going to spend preparing for each assessment. If the oral presentation is only for 10% of the course grades, do not spend too long preparing for it!

TIP *Put assessment dates in your calendar*

When you find out how you are going to be assessed, write the deadlines or exam dates in your calendar and mark the points in the course when you can expect to be under more stress. This will help you plan your work on the course and your social life around assessments.

Which assessment method is best for you?

Some courses will be compulsory (i.e. you have to do them) so you will have to complete the assessment chosen by the lecturer. Sometimes, however, you will have a choice of courses and it may be that you choose one course over the other because it is continuously assessed (i.e. with coursework and assignments throughout the semester) rather than assessed with exams. For some international students this decision may be very important. If you don't work well under stress you may want to avoid the exam option, at least in the first year until you get more control over your studies.

Look at the table below to see some of the differences between the requirements in exams and in assignments. Which ones suit you better?

Exams	Assignments
• Short word limits	• Long word limits (more than 1000 words).
• Large percentage of course marks in one day	• Often, small percentage of course marks over several days' or weeks' work
• Writing under intense time pressure	• Time to plan, write and edit your writing
• High stress for a few days leading up to an exam	• Lower stress levels but over longer periods of time on the course. Deadlines can be extremely stressful.
• Individual performance in exam (can revise with colleagues)	• Can discuss assignments with other students but final version still need to be individual
• Often can't use dictionaries/reference books	• Can consult dictionaries/reference books
• Markers may be more understanding of inaccuracies if you are writing under time pressure	• High level of language accuracy expected
• You may only find out if you have passed, after the exam	• You know how you are doing throughout the course
• You may never see your marked exam papers or find out why you did well or badly	• You get feedback on assignments, which might help you to improve your writing

Find out what it's really like

Here are some ways to find out what university assessment on your course is really like.

1 **Interview** another international student who is studying or has studied your course. Ask them:

- what types of assessment they have experienced;
- if there were any differences between assessment in their country and in the country where they studied;
- how they prepared for the assessment;
- how they coped with their English in exams;
- if they have any advice for international students starting out like yourself.

2 **Find out** about assessment on your course. There may be information on the department website. You may be able to see old exam papers in the library.

Understanding assessment criteria

When assignments are set, the lecturer will often hand out assessment criteria at the same time. Assessment criteria are statements that the lecturer uses to grade your assignment.

An example of assessment criteria

In the box on the right we give the assessment criteria for a group oral presentation for students studying philosophy at University of Hertfordshire in the UK. The oral presentation was for 30% of the paper's marks.

Read the assessment criteria and decide which of the points below refer to . . .

● your preparation for the presentation (reading and research)
● the content of your talk (what you talked about)
● the way you talked in the presentation (how you talked)

Also, answer these questions about the University of Hertfordshire criteria:

1 You are assessed on three parts in your talk. What are they?

2 What does the lecturer clearly value most when marking your presentation?

Check your answers in the key at the end of the book.

How you can use assessment criteria

Make sure you understand the assessment criteria. If you don't, you should ask your lecturer.

The criteria for an assignment . . .

● tell you what you have to write about/speak about.

Assessment criteria

In assessing presentations, the primary emphasis will be on academic content and quality of argument/analysis. Thus the focus will be on:

● use of literature;
● quality of arguments;
● integration of theory and case study;
● careful reading;
● use of primary literature in relation to secondary sources;
● imagination in interpretation;
● conclusions drawn.

In relation to these aspects you will be expected to:

● set out clearly the problem or position to be discussed;
● select what you consider to be the most important aspects of it and to explain why;
● consider different ways of approaching it;
● answer questions from the other students or your lecturer about your chosen topic;
● explain and clarify points in the subsequent *discussion*.

The following factors will also play a role in assessment:

● Delivery
  – organisation of time;
  – audibility;
  – structure and signposting;
  – use of overheads or handouts.
● Discussion
  – encouragement and involvement in discussion;
  – awareness of wider issues raised (including the ability to recognise and stick to the main issue);
  – coherence of response to questions;
  – use of the imagination in interpreting and understanding questions posed to the group.

© University of Hertfordshire
http://perseus.herts.ac.uk/uhinfo/schools/hum/subject/phil/current/presentation-assessment-criteria.cfm

---

● tell you what aspect of the question the lecturer sees as the most important and which carries the most marks.

- are a guide you can use when you are writing. For each point in the criteria, ask yourself if you have done it yet.
- help you critically evaluate your work so that you can improve it before you hand it in.
- help you understand your grade when you get feedback. You can look back at the criteria, and the lecturer's comments may make more sense.

Learning from feedback

When an assignment or an exam paper is returned to you, it will have a mark (e.g. 55%) or a grade (e.g. B–) on it as well as comments. These comments will answer the following questions:

- How good is this essay?
- Did you do what the lecturer wanted?
- How could you improve?

This section will help you understand grades and lecturers' written comments.

Understanding your mark

When you get your essay or assignment back, don't panic. The mark may be lower than marks you are used to. Take time to understand the lecturer's comments and think them through. Follow these steps:

1 Look at the grade and decide if you have passed or failed. Usually grades A to C are pass marks. Grades D or lower are fails. Check this against your department's assessment guidelines. You may have a percentage rather than a grade. Again, find out if this is a pass or fail.

2 Check your grade with a class average. You may have a grade which you think is low, but this may be normal for the course or for your particular department. Your lecturer can't tell you the grades of other students but some will be happy to tell you, if you are open about your marks.

3 Read the comments the lecturer has made. Decide which ones are positive and which are negative. You may not understand the comments at this stage. (See next section.)

4 Re-read the assignment and see if you can understand the comments now.

5 If you still don't understand, then you can make an appointment with your lecturer and you can ask them about your mark.

6 In your journal, make a note of useful feedback that will help you in future assignments or exams.

Understanding written comments: decoding feedback

Hopefully, comments from lecturers will be clear (you can understand them) and relevant (you can see how they are useful). They may follow this pattern:

1 General comment on your performance

2 Detailed comments (may refer to key words in the criteria) on how you did, including ways you could improve

3 A rounding-off final comment.

In this way, 'negative' feedback may be 'sandwiched' between more positive general statements. Often tutors use this strategy when they give oral feedback as well:

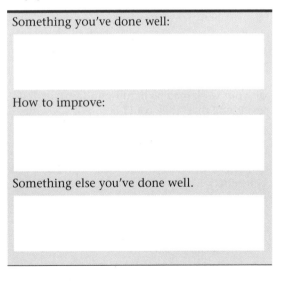

Something you've done well:

How to improve:

Something else you've done well.

Task: Text patterns in essay feedback
1. Identify the positive comments, detailed comments with criticisms, and final positive comment in the following essay feedback:

© Hayo Reinders, Nick Moore and Marilyn Lewis (2008), *The International Student Handbook*, Palgrave Macmillan Ltd

You have presented a competent discussion of the article with an analytical approach that conveys aspects of the researcher's work in a systematic way. The section that needed more consideration was the final part, in which I would like to have seen a fuller account of the practical implications of the study. Mostly the essay is well written; however, at times, I found it difficult to follow your argument and had to re-read sections to understand your logic. I felt that more signposting would have helped me with this. Overall though, the assignment was a balanced critique of the issues that arose from the research and it was good to see that you mentioned many of the limitations of this kind of research that we have discussed in class. Well done.

Grade B–

2 If you got the feedback given above, what would be the two main areas you should try to improve in the next essay?

Check your answers in the key at the end of the book.

Unclear feedback
In the example above, it is quite clear what the student did well and what they need to do to improve. Here are some reasons why comments on your work may be hard to understand and less useful than they could be:

1 The lecturer does not want to be rude and does not clearly explain what is wrong.

2 The lecturer may not be used to giving feedback to non-native speakers so may use indirect or confusing language.

3 They may only mention that there is a problem but not tell you what the problem is or what caused it.

4 You may not be able to read their handwriting.

5 They may comment on the aspects that are easy to give feedback on (e.g. your ideas) but not on more difficult aspects of your language.

If you don't understand the feedback, then make an appointment with the lecturer and ask them about it.

Task: Spot the criticism
Read the examples of essay feedback below and work out what aspect of each assignment the lecturer is criticising. Check your answers in the key at the end of the book.

(a) 'Your argument was clear in most parts of the essay. A statement that previews the structure of the assignment might have helped me navigate through the essay.'

(b) 'While you mostly followed the recommended referencing conventions, at times this was not the case and I was unsure whether you were referring to sources or claiming these ideas as your own.'

(c) 'This is a well-researched assignment. However, I feel it could have benefited from more time spent proof reading before submission.'

(d) 'Make sure that you answer all parts of the question.'

(e) 'This assignment is evidence that you have synthesised information from a number of sources. At times, though, I struggled to hear your voice coming through.'

(f) 'Your literature review is based almost entirely on two sources.'

(g) 'While parts of the essay read well and you make some valid points, the essay as a whole fails to read as a coherent whole.'

(h) 'This is an excellent description of the process. Your writing is clearly signposted and paragraphs flow seamlessly from one to the next. You follow academic conventions well, and clearly have a good grasp of this topic.'

A mini-glossary of common writing problems that lecturers might signal

Sometimes the language that lecturers use when giving feedback on writing is quite specialised.

This table will help you work out what aspect of your writing lecturers are commenting on. Remember, if you don't understand their comments, you should ask them.

If lecturers use these words . . .	they mean . . .
awkward syntax	Bad grammar.
coherence	Overall organisation – introduction/paragraphs/conclusion.
cohesion	The way one idea/sentence follows from the one before and leads to the next.
inconsistent argument	Your thesis statement does not match the conclusion that you have come to in your writing.
inconsistent tone	Writing sounds too 'spoken', maybe you use too many idioms.
lack of support	You need to give more evidence for your opinions.
lack sufficient development	You do not look at ideas in enough detail.
need to develop your voice	Not enough of your opinion or your analysis.
needs further revision	You need to rewrite some sections.
not managing the flow of information between paragraphs	You need to check that each paragraph leads on to the next.
not managing the flow of information within a sentence	The main point you are making in a sentence is not clear.
overdependence on sources	Not enough of your opinion or your analysis.
paragraph unity	You need to check that each paragraph follows a logical pattern – e.g. a topic sentence followed by evidence.
referencing conventions	The way you quote other writers' words and ideas and the way you list references at the end of the essay.
sentence fragments	Some sentences are incomplete – e.g. 'Because of climate change.'
signposting language	Such as 'firstly. . .', 'in addition . . .', 'therefore . . .'
sources summarised but not synthesised	You report what writers you quote say, but don't build these quotes into your argument.
too black and white – not tentative enough	If you give conclusions, these should be less general and definite.
writing lacked control	Bad grammar, spelling and punctuation.

Examinations

Taking exams is still the most common way you will be assessed at university. Taking an exam in a second language can be stressful but you can minimise stress and increase your chances of success through careful planning. This section has some general strategies that will help you succeed in university exams. Many will be similar to exams you have taken in your home country.

Before you start this section, think about an exam in which you did well in your first language. What made you successful? Write notes below:

Subject/topic . . . (e.g. human geography/water management systems)

Format . . . (e.g. essays/short answer/multiple choice)

What you did before the exam (preparation/revision etc.) that worked

What you did during the exam (strategies) that worked

There are, however, some key differences if you are taking an exam as an international student, namely:

- The format and procedure of the exam may be unfamiliar.
- The expectations of the marker may be different – for example, they want to see evidence of critical thinking skills.
- It will be harder to understand the questions.
- It will be harder to communicate your knowledge in a second language.

This section will deal with these differences.

Finding out about an exam – a checklist

It is important to find out as much as you can about an exam well in advance of the exam date. Exams in an English-speaking country may work differently from the type of exams in your education system. You can find out about exams by . . .

- reading the section about assessment you are given when you start a course;
- looking through past exam papers;
- talking to students who took your paper the year before;
- talking to other students on your course (to check that you have understood everything that may have been said about the course exams).

If you still can't complete the following checklist, then ask your lecturer. Lecturers may not want to spend class time answering lots of questions about assessment details so you could try emailing your lecturer between classes with a list of questions. He or she may choose to answer you directly or may decide to deal with everyone's questions together.

Checklist

Topics	Check these . . .	Notes
The exam day	Date	
	Start time	
	Place – building/room	
	Length of exam	
	What you are allowed to bring – e.g. dictionaries (if so – electronic or paper, monolingual or bilingual?), class notes (if so, how many pages?), set text or case study data?	
	Any special rules if English is not your first language*	
Exam format	How many questions in total? How many questions you need to answer.	
	What happens if you don't finish all the questions.	
	How important the quality of your writing is.	
	What type of questions (e.g. essay/short answer/multiple choice).	
	If you will be told the percentage mark for each question (so you can allocate more time to questions with more marks).	
Exam content	What topics will be covered. Which lectures or reading will be most important for the exam.	

* Note: universities in some countries on some courses allow extra time in an exam for students whose first language is not English. Find out early if this applies for your course, and if so, find out how you can apply for this extra time. You may need to apply for extra time a long time before your exam day.

Revising for exams

In some educational systems, you can pass exams by reproducing things that you have learnt in lectures and through reading. In many English-speaking universities, learning facts by heart is less important than using your own words and arguments. In the exam, you are asked to show that you have understood what you have learnt and can apply it in exam tasks.

Revision is still important if you want to succeed in university exams and the way you revise will depend in part on your preferred learning style.

Read the following revision tips and decide whether you think they will be useful revision strategies for you. When you have finished, check in the answer key and read what we think about these ways of revising.

TIP Useful?

	Yes	No
1 Start revising early. Don't leave it all until the last minute.	☐	☐
2 Go back over all your lecture notes and copy them out again.	☐	☐
3 Write out index cards with key points taken from your notes and reading.	☐	☐
4 Get some past exam questions and write practice answers.	☐	☐
5 Re-read all the key texts from your course before the exam.	☐	☐
6 Learn by heart essays that you think might come up in the exam.	☐	☐
7 Re-read texts from the course with reference to past exam questions.	☐	☐
8 Form a study group, make a list of possible exam questions and talk about how you would answer them.	☐	☐
9 Practise writing exam answers under time pressure.	☐	☐

TIP Smart revision

Working long hours in the library does not automatically get you more points in an exam. Make sure your revision is 'smart' – always think about the questions that you might be asked so that any reading or notes you make are purposeful. Allow frequent short breaks to stay fresh.

Exam strategies

Use this page as a checklist. Read it again before you take your next exam.

Plan your time carefully
- Allow equal time for questions with equal marks. If one question is worth 25% of the total marks, allow 25% of your time for it.
- Spend 5 minutes reading the whole paper before you start answering questions. During this time, write down any ideas or key concepts that you think of for each question.

Choose questions carefully
- If you have to choose which questions to answer, make the choice quickly. It is usually better to stick with the choice you make rather than change midway through the exam.
- If you have a choice, avoid questions if you are not sure you understand them. If you have no choice, then guess meaning from any examples given or any diagrams or notes provided.
- Take a critical stance in exams. Do not be afraid of taking an original position and supporting it with evidence, e.g. you may be able to argue that censorship actually encourages freedom of speech if you have enough evidence!

Do it right
- Read the rubric (exam instructions) carefully. The rubric may change from year to year.
- Invigilators (people who supervise exams) may announce changes or corrections at the start of the exam. If you do not understand what they say, ask for clarification.
- Do what you are supposed to do! If you

have to answer 3 questions, make sure you answer 3 questions! Check with an invigilator if you are not sure what to do.
- Don't leave any questions blank. In multiple choice questions, if you really don't know the answer, guess. For short-answer questions, by writing something on the topic you may get a mark!

Dictionaries and reference books
- If you are allowed to use a dictionary in an exam, do not overuse it. Looking up words in a dictionary takes time.
- Use it if there are words in an essay question you do not understand, e.g. 'Lord Byron's earlier work has been described as the art of the capricious. Discuss.' If you do not know the word **capricious**, look it up.
- When you are writing, it may be quicker to think of another way to write the same meaning rather than look the word up.

Write well
- You still need to write well-planned coherent answers. (See next section.)

The writing process	Time total (60 minutes)	
Understand the question	1–2 minutes	Allow for about one quarter of the total time for these three steps (approx 10–15 minutes).
Brainstorm main ideas	3–8 minutes	
Draw up an outline	8–9 minutes	
Start writing	40–45 minutes	
Edit and proofread	5 minutes	Make time for these two steps. A few minutes of careful editing and proofreading can improve your grade.

Writing under time pressure

Even in exam conditions, remember that examiners are still keen to see how well you can structure your answer and make it relevant to the question, and how well you express your ideas. To meet examiners' criteria, you need to understand what is asked. You need to think about key ideas and organisation even before you start writing, just as you would for your assignments. Here are some tips for you.

Planning your time in the exam
The chart below shows how you can manage these crucial steps in the writing process in the time allowed for each essay question, which is about 60 minutes in a three-hour paper.

Now you try. Think of the last exam you did where you had to write a lot. How long did it last? How much time did you need? How much time did you spend on each part?

The writing process	Time spent
Understand the question	
Brainstorm main ideas	
Draw up an outline	
Start writing	
Edit and proofread	

© Hayo Reinders, Nick Moore and Marilyn Lewis (2008), *The International Student Handbook*, Palgrave Macmillan Ltd

Understanding the question

Quickly analyse the essay question to establish topic focus.

Look for topic or content words, which tell you WHAT you have to deal with in your essay. (Note: if there is a quotation, look for the content words in the question that follows the quotation.) Look for the function words (e.g. 'discuss', 'compare and contrast', etc.), which tell you HOW you have to deal with the topic.

Here is an example. Can you find the 'what' and the 'how' here?

'The revolution in mobile communication technology has blurred the boundaries between what is public and private.' Discuss the impact of mobile phones on our public and private communications.

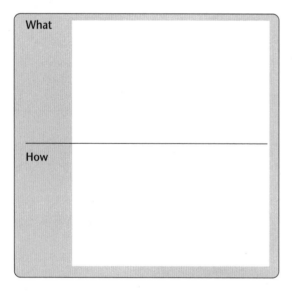

What	
How	

Check your answer in the key at the end of the book.

What exam questions mean

A simple technique for analysing exam questions is to turn the question or sentence into a real question starting with How? Why? What? Which? In Chapter 8 of this book, in the section 'Understanding essay questions', there is a task to practise this.

Here are two more complete essay questions. Try to expand them and work out what topic you are writing about and what questions you would try to answer in your essay. Check your answers in the key at the end of the book:

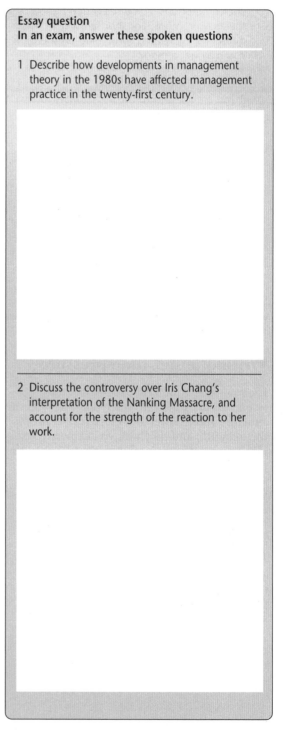

Essay question
In an exam, answer these spoken questions

1 Describe how developments in management theory in the 1980s have affected management practice in the twenty-first century.

2 Discuss the controversy over Iris Chang's interpretation of the Nanking Massacre, and account for the strength of the reaction to her work.

An A–Z of words from exam questions

You may find this glossary of terms useful when working out what exam questions are asking. Clearly the exact meaning of the words will depend on the subject you are studying; this glossary will tell you what they normally mean.

account for	Explain why something happened. This is not the same as 'Give an account of' – which asks for a detailed description.	**describe**	Give a detailed and full account of something.
analyse	Write about something in depth – identifying, describing, and criticising in detail its main features.	**develop**	Expand on something, taking it further.
argue	Put forward an idea, then give an example. Discuss what the idea means, and defend it against possible counter-arguments.	**discuss**	Examine something by careful argument. Write about the advantages or disadvantages. Debate something and consider different ways of seeing it. This is probably the most common instruction term – you should say something interesting to answer the question. You can choose your own approach.
assess	Examine something closely. Write about its strengths and weaknesses. Discuss the points for and against something. Finally, give your opinion.	**distinguish**	Explain the differences between two or more things.
calculate	Work something out using maths.	**elaborate**	Add further details to something.
clarify	Simplify something and make it clear.	**enumerate**	Make a list, giving the main features of something – and omitting details. Put the list in order.
comment	State clearly your opinions on something. Support your views with evidence or explanations.	**examine**	Enquire into something, investigate, or look closely into it.
compare	Look for similarities and differences between two or more things.	**expand**	Go into more detail.
consider	Express your thoughts and observations about something.	**explain**	Make something clear. Account for it. Clarify, interpret, and spell out a subject, giving reasons for its features.
contrast	Identify and emphasise the differences between two or more things.	**explore**	Question an issue or idea, and consider it from a number of viewpoints.
criticise	Give your judgement about something. Explore what it means, discussing all the evidence that is available.	**give an account of**	Describe something in detail, and explain it fully.
define	Write down the precise meaning of something.	**how . . . ?**	In what way, by what means or method, or to what extent does something happen, exist, or work?
demonstrate	Show how something works or operates, and prove it by giving examples.	**how far . . . ?**	Similar to questions which begin 'To what extent . . . '. You should discuss the subject, and show any of its strengths or weaknesses.

identify	Pick out the main features or the important points of something.	review	Make a survey of something. Examine the subject critically.
illustrate	Make something clear by discussing examples of it.	show	Reveal something – in some form of logical sequence or explanation.
interpret	Explain the meaning of something. Make it clear – using your own judgement, experience, or opinion.	state	Present the main points of a subject – in a brief, clear form.
justify	Show the reasons or the best arguments for something. Answer any objections likely to be made against it.	summarise	Give an account of the main points of a subject, leaving out any details and examples.
list	Make a list or catalogue of things.	to what extent	Similar to questions which begin 'How far . . .'. You are expected to discuss something, and show any of its strengths and weaknesses.
outline	Give the main features or the general principles of a subject. You can leave out minor details. Emphasise the structure or arrangement of its parts.	trace	Follow the development or history of something. Explain the changes step by step.
prove	Show that something is true or false by presenting evidence.	translate	Say something in a different way, or change it from one language to another.
relate	Show how things are connected. Show how they affect, cause, or resemble each other.	verify	Show that something is true, or confirm it.

Source: This list was adapted from one accessed from www.buzzin.net

Making sense of question words

Look at the list above and put the words into groups with similar meanings to the words in the box. Check your answers in the key at the end of the book.

analyse	argue	explain	develop	prove	compare	describe

Have a look at some exam questions from previous years and check which of these question words are common in your subject. Look especially for any questions where the words themselves are not given, and work out what you are supposed to do, for example:

The Victorians thought 'Children should be seen but not heard.' Is this still true today?

The question is asking you to compare this idea with modern ideas. The main issue here is changes in the way children are brought up and treated. The missing question word is 'Discuss'.

Brainstorming main ideas

Here are some basic tips. See also Chapter 8 for more information on brainstorming.

● Jot down several important ideas and examples that help focus the answer on the question.
● Don't keep too many ideas. Confine yourself to three or four key points.
● Focus on what you DO know, not what you DON'T know.

Drawing up an outline

Put the ideas in order to fit the question type. Keep the structure simple – you are writing under time pressure. It's OK to have an obvious structure. Many essays follow a five-paragraph format, like this:

Paragraph 1: Introduce topic and thesis.

Paragraph 2: Main point 1 and supporting details/examples.

Paragraph 3: Main point 2 and supporting details/examples.

Paragraph 4: Main point 3 and supporting details/examples.

Paragraph 5: Conclude with a restatement of your main thesis and the significance of the topic. (Keep this short and specific.)

Remember: Your principle of organisation should be drawn directly from the question. A common mistake is to write everything you know about a topic. Avoid this.

Starting to write

Write quickly, with your outline at hand. As you move ahead with the writing, you may think of new ideas or sub-points to include in the essay.

● Stop briefly to make a note of these on your original outline.
● Write them neatly in the margin, at the top of the page or on the last page, with arrows or marks to alert the reader to where they fit in your answer.
● Be clear. Signal clear relations between paragraphs with appropriate transitions.
● Avoid irrelevancies and repetition.
● Write legibly.

TIP *The clock*

Watch the clock carefully to ensure that you do not spend too much time on one question. If you run out of time, jot down remaining ideas from the outline to show that you know the material, but this is only a last option!

Because you are writing under time pressure, your lecturers will not expect you to write as accurately as if you are writing an assignment but it is still important to give yourself time to check your writing. When you check your writing, read the question again and check that you have answered it. See Chapter 9 for more information about proofreading your own writing.

Giving presentations

Giving oral presentations can be quite scary for international students and yet this might be an important part of the course assessment. This section looks at ways of preparing yourself.

Before you even start thinking about the delivery of your presentation, there are some other things to consider. Try to remember 'the four Ps':

People (audience)
Plan
Practice
Present

Many students make the mistake of not thinking about the first three of these and go straight into the actual presentation. Before you can do that you will need to think about your audience ('people') and plan your presentation, and of course practise a lot.

Who are you speaking to?

Are they students, teachers or a general audience? People you know well, or strangers? In each case you will probably *pitch* your talk differently. By 'pitch' or 'pitching' we mean ways in which you change the tone or content of your talk to suit the audience. As an extreme example, think of how you would explain how a car works to a child. This would be different from how you would talk to an adult. In a presentation you would do the same.

What is their interest in the topic?

Why would they want to listen to your presentation? Your teacher will of course be looking at the quality of your work but how about other students? Are they in the same class and do you know they are interested in the topic, or are they students from other faculties? In that case you may have to make them enthusiastic about the topic, such as by giving an interesting or funny example.

How much do they know about the topic?

If people have little or no knowledge of the topic, you will need to explain more. You will need to be careful with your language. Explain and give examples of all technical terms and give more background information.

Why are you giving this talk – what are people expecting from you?

Are you expected to give a description of something or give and explain your opinion? This is where many students go wrong, without knowing why. Make sure you completely understand what you are asked to do. If the assignment says 'compare X and Y', make sure whether this means you will simply need to give a factual description of both and point out the differences and similarities, or whether you also need to state your personal preference for one or the other. By thinking about your talk in this way, it will be easier to plan the content and order of your presentation.

If you have a presentation to give soon, use this diagram:

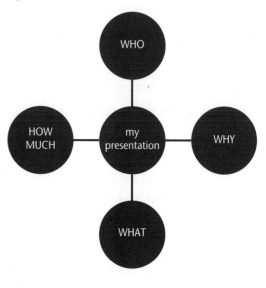

A word about timing

Use the information above to help you plan the *timing* for your presentation. Try and decide how much time you will give to each part. Have a look at the schedule below to see how much time the speaker intends to give to each part.

2 mins	introduction
4 mins	background: what is 'attrition'?*
4 mins	my study: attrition in younger learners
4 mins	results of the study
2 mins	conclusion
4 mins	questions

* One of the meanings of 'attrition' is 'forgetting'.

What does the above schedule tell you about the audience the speaker expects? What would you change if:

- Your teacher or someone else will introduce you, and everyone in the audience has a copy of your handout, which describes the background to your study?
- People in the audience all know what 'attrition' is?

Have a look at the end of the book for some answers.

Dealing with nervousness

If you are nervous about doing a presentation, you are not alone. Most people find it difficult to speak in front of an audience. One study found that people are more afraid to give a presentation than they are of death!

Luckily there are many things you can do to help you become more confident. Here are some of them.

Practice

The third 'P' in our list above is your friend. Practising a lot so that you know the content really well will make you relax more on the day. Some people try not to practise too much, so that they sound more natural when giving their presentations, but this is perhaps easier when you have more experience. Practise with a friend, in the mirror, with your dog – anything!

Practising doesn't mean you have to memorise every word. In fact, it is probably better not to. But practise giving your speech, and when you feel you know the content reasonably well, try to focus on ways of becoming more relaxed and speaking more naturally.

Breathe!

When we are nervous we usually breathe more quickly and our breaths are more shallow than normal. As a result our brains do not get enough oxygen, so that we can't concentrate as well as normal and we feel light-headed. Force yourself to take a few deep breaths and to breathe in a relaxed way. You should feel the difference almost immediately.

Trust yourself

It is incredible what we can do if we only believe in ourselves. People who get up and tell themselves 'I can't do this, I can't talk in public' usually don't do well. On the other hand, telling yourself you *can* do this, that you are even good

at it, miraculously, makes us better speakers! As you sound more confident the audience will like your talk more and you will be able to tell this from their reaction. This makes you more confident and as a result the audience will like your talk more . . . etc., etc.

Have a friend in the audience

Arrange for someone you know to sit at the front and put on a smile or friendly face. If you get really nervous during the talk you can make eye contact with him/her to make you feel better.

Imagine you are talking to a friend

Related to the previous tip, imagine that you are giving your presentation to one or more friends over a coffee, rather than in a formal situation in a room full of people. When you talk to your friends you are likely to be relaxed and your tone will be more casual. As a result, you will sound more natural and your audience will like your talk more. Some of the best speakers in the world say this is one of their greatest 'secrets'.

The language of presentations

As for the language of presentations, it is important to remember that spoken language and written language are very different. Imagine you are studying physiotherapy and you need to give a presentation explaining why runners suffer from frequent injuries.

This is what you wrote in an assignment:

> One of the causes of lower-leg injuries amongst road runners who increase their training load rapidly in the build-up to a competition is the hard surfaces on which they do much of their training load. The constant impacts that occur when training on the road result in conditions like shin splints* and . . .
>
> * a very painful lower leg injury

What would you say in a presentation? Turn to the answer key at the end of the book for a solution.

Speaking and writing – what are the differences?

Now answer these questions about speaking and writing. Check your answers in the answer key at the end of the book.

1 Which one uses more words to say the same thing?
2 Which one uses more complex sentences?
3 Which one uses shorter and more frequent sentences?
4 Which one uses the most complicated vocabulary?
5 Which one has more repetition?
6 In which one do you need to be the most accurate?

Here's why:

● When you are reading, you can re-read a section if it is difficult to understand. When listening, if you miss something, you've really missed it, so speakers use less complex grammar and vocabulary and simpler sentences when speaking. This helps listeners understand as they listen.
● In writing, the reader is often a long way away from the writer so cannot say if they don't understand. They have to be accurate. Speakers can make their language easier to understand with gesture (using their body language) and pronunciation to stress important words. And if their audience doesn't understand, they can say it again.

● When you are writing, you need to meet a word limit. You cannot write forever and ever. When speaking, there is sometimes a time limit, but no word limit. Speakers make themselves understood by saying the same thing in different ways.

So – make sure the language of your presentation is easy to understand and clear to your audience. Make sure you are speaking (using spoken language) and not reading aloud (using written language) or repeating a written text (from memory).

Avoiding too much informal language

While spoken language is often simpler than written language in everyday situations, remember that university presentations are formal situations. Your colleagues and your lecturer will be there so you should avoid using too much informal language. Your lecturer will mark you down and people will not take your ideas seriously. This may be a problem for you if you have learnt English informally at work or through spending a lot of time in an English-speaking country.

Look at the informal language that a student used in a presentation about Health and Safety rules in a restaurant. What should she have said instead? Check your answers in the key at the end of the book.

Informal language	What should she have said?
Hi guys. How's it going?	
If you've anything you wanna ask keep it to yourself until the end.	
I'm going to give you the dirt on the dos and don'ts of working in a restaurant.	
That dude Richards – he had some sweet ideas about . . .	
It's crazy not washing your hands. It is like so gross.	
Now that's it. We're outa here.	

© Hayo Reinders, Nick Moore and Marilyn Lewis (2008), *The International Student Handbook*, Palgrave Macmillan Ltd

Using visuals and other support materials

An image can say a thousand words, which helps if you are not entirely confident with your English presentation skills. Images give you something to point at and you can stop talking for a while so the audience has time to look. If your pronunciation is not your strong point, images will help your audience understand you better. Research has shown that over 40 per cent of people are 'visual learners', meaning that they depend on visual information more than on spoken words to get new information. So, including images in your presentation is a good idea. The same applies to audio- and video files and PowerPoint presentations.

PowerPoint® is a popular tool but there are a few things to keep in mind:

● Don't read out every slide. Each slide should summarise your key points or show something to illustrate what you have said, such as a picture. Don't include too much information: PowerPoint is not a replacement for a presentation!
● Related to this, don't face the screen – look at your audience and point at the screen when necessary.
● Make sure your font size (the size of the letters on the screen) is large enough for people to read from the back of the room (18pt or larger is usually good).
● Be careful with colours and animations (things moving around the screen). Usually they confuse the audience or take their attention away from the content of your presentation. You will sometimes hear people talking about the 'KISS' principle. K I S S here stands for 'Keep It Simple, Stupid'! In other words: less is more.

Presentation feedback – what should these students work on?

Read the following feedback given to students after an oral presentation. First identify the problem. In what way do the students need to improve? Check your answers in the key at the end of the book.

(a) 'There were parts of your talk that I couldn't hear, which was a shame because I think you were making good points.'

(b) 'Sometimes I found it difficult understanding you. Some of your language was very complex. Try to say things more simply and clearly.'

(c) 'I had problems following your presentation. I wasn't sure where it was going and whether you were giving an example of something you had just said or whether you were moving on to a new point.'

(d) 'It was difficult to understand your presentation because you were reading aloud.'

(e) 'It just ended. I felt you needed to say something to round it off.'

(f) 'When you described the structure of that company I found it really hard to see how the different departments work together.'

(g) 'I felt you looked at the screen more than at the audience.'

(h) 'I wasn't sure what some of the things you talked about mean.'

Troubleshooting presentations . . . some solutions

Read these solutions and match them to the feedback in the section above. Write the letter (a) to (e) next to the solution. Some solutions may work for more than one problem. Check your answers in the key at the end of the book.

Problem?	Solution
1	Imagine you are talking to an old deaf man sitting at the far end of the room, then you will speak louder and more clearly.
2	Try recording yourself when you are practising, and listening to yourself speaking to see if you are clear enough.
3	Try talking from cue cards (small cards with only 3 or 4 words written on them)
4	Pause more between sections.
5	Use more repetition, e.g. 'Let me say that another way . . . '
6	Signal, with your voice going down, that you have ended one section of your talk.
7	Signal, with your voice going up, that you are starting a new section.
8	Use discourse markers more, e.g. 'Let me give you an example'; 'My next point is about . . .'; 'I'd like to move on to . . . now.'
9	Keep your sentences short and simple.
10	Use more sentences to say the same thing.

TIP *Eye contact*

Choose your best lecturer. Watch how they use eye contact to keep students interested. Do they use it more or less than speakers in your culture would? Do they look at everyone? How long do they look at one student before moving on? When you give a presentation, do the same with your eye contact.

Summary – tips for successful presentations

Tick off the ones you already use. Try out the ones that are new.

Before the presentation

- Think about the first of the four 'Ps', people. Who are your audience?
- Make sure your presentation has a simple order, e.g. three main points.

- Plan how you will introduce yourselves, your topic and your talk.
- Plan transitions between topics or sections in your presentation.
- Make sure your visuals are clear and easy to follow.
- If using technology, test it in the room you will use.
- If you are working with a partner, practise together so you know who is doing what.
- Plan how you will conclude.
- Brainstorm a list of questions you think you will be asked.
- Practise your presentation.
- Don't try to memorise everything you will say.
- Time it before you do it.
- Record yourself and listen to it.

During the presentation

- Speak from notes. Don't read.
- Speak slower and louder than normal.
- Pause between sections.
- Don't use slang.
- Talk about the points in your visuals, don't read them.
- Use markers to introduce new ideas and new sections, e.g. 'My next point is about . . . ' or 'Next, I want to talk about . . . '.
- Use body language and intonation to make things clear.
- Watch the time.

Dealing with questions:

- Tell your audience when they should ask questions, e.g. 'There will be time for questions at the end.'
- Allow time for questions.
- If you don't understand a question, ask the person to repeat it, e.g. 'I'm sorry, I didn't catch that . . . '.
- Use questions as a prompt to talk more about an aspect of your topic.
- Use expressions like 'Yes. That's an interesting question', when you need time to think of a response!
- Don't be defensive! Say 'Yes – that's a valid point.'
- Be prepared to open questions up to the audience. This means you say 'Umm. That is an important issue. Would anyone else like to say something about that?'

Portfolio assessment

For some courses you may be asked to produce a portfolio of work, which counts towards your course assessment. On some courses, lecturers like portfolio assessment as it can show your development over the whole semester. This means you have to write a collection of different kinds of texts completed across the semester and get marked on it. For example, for a unit on a web design course, you may need to hand in:

> **PORTFOLIO**
> - a report of an interview with a client about a website they want designed
> - a plan of the proposed functionality of the website you are designing
> - a budget plan detailing the programming work involved
> - layout screenshots to show a range of design options
> - a timesheet in which you outline your time on the project
> - a detailed project plan with milestones and deliverables laid out
> - a critical evaluation of your web project showing strengths and weaknesses

Students' experiences of portfolio assessment

These students were all assessed using portfolios. Read about their experiences and decide which students were positive, which were negative and which were neutral about portfolio assessment. Check your answers in the key at the end of the book.

(a) 'The word limits for each section were less and so although I had to write lots of texts, it was much easier than doing 3000-word assignments. And much better than taking an exam.'

(b) 'On my course, it wasn't clear how each part of the portfolio would be marked. I wasn't sure how important each part was and so I didn't know how much time to spend on each part. We had to include a journal over the course and it took me so long to write but it was only 10% of the portfolio's overall mark.'

(c) 'At first, I had no idea what to do but then I had a look at some previous students' portfolios and this was so useful. I could see what was expected of me and what I needed to do to get a good mark. In the end, it worked well.'

(d) 'I had only learnt how to write a discursive essay at school but in this portfolio I had to write so many different types of texts – a proposal, a report, a budget plan, a project timeline etc., etc. You have to get good at looking for these types of writing and working out how to organise them. Do you use headings? Do you put in diagrams? Do you need a conclusion? Our lecturer didn't offer much help with this but I got advice from the Learning Centre.'

(e) 'There weren't any real deadlines – just suggested dates to complete work by. I missed a couple of deadlines at first and then I realised I was getting behind. Our lecturer wasn't very strict about this. When I realised it was my responsibility to get stuff done on time, I caught up OK.'

(f) 'Our lecturer was really clear about each part. She set up each section separately and introduced it well so we knew what to do.'

Summary – a checklist for portfolios

These are things you should check when a lecturer sets up a portfolio assessment:

Deadlines

- Do you need to hand in parts of the portfolio as you go, throughout the semester, or do you hand it in all at once?
- When do you get feedback?
- If you hand it in section by section, when are the deadlines?

Marking

- How is each section weighted? Do you get one overall mark or is each part weighted differently?
- Is the portfolio the whole assessment for the course or do you need to do an exam as well?

Word limits

- Is there an overall word limit?
- How many words should you write for each section?
- How much time is each section supposed to take?

Text types

- Are there any examples of past students' portfolios to give you an idea of what to write?
- Are there guidelines and criteria for each section?
- Where can you find similar text types?

Conclusion

Assessment is an important part of life at university. As an international student you may find it difficult as the rules may be different from what you are used to. It is like playing a game. There are rules – and you may fail if you do not follow them. In order to win, you need to work out first what question the assignment or exam is asking, and then how you are supposed to answer it. Like all games, you get better at working out what the lecturer wants you to do. It is important to try to take a critical stance in assessments at universities. Imagine how happy your lecturers will be if they have 100 assignments that all say the same thing and then read your assignment that takes an original or different view on the same subject. Because you are from another country and a different culture you may find yourself looking at a topic in a different way from other students. Use your difference to your advantage!

Chapter 11

Communicating with staff

CHAPTER OVERVIEW

By the end of this chapter you will be able to:

● decide whether your problem or question is worth talking about with a staff member
● choose the best ways of contacting staff
● communicate with the department through your class representative
● make effective use of the departmental website

Introduction

There will be times when you need to communicate directly with tutors. In Chapter 6, we talked about communicating during tutorials, but this chapter is about other kinds of communication. It's about the many times you will want to talk with staff to ask for something or answer their requests for something. As you will see, this communication may take place through email, over the telephone or face-to-face in the staff member's office. There are lots of reasons why students would want to contact staff. This section looks at those reasons and aims to help you think strategically about the best way to approach staff to get what you want.

Why contact staff?

Why do students want to go and talk to staff? Look at the following list of common reasons why students make contact with academic staff and decide. Which of these purposes would you find hardest or easiest to face?

Reason	How hard is it to ask for this? (easy) 1 2 3 4 5 (hard)	Reason	How hard is it to ask for this? (easy) 1 2 3 4 5 (hard)
You need an extension (more time) for an assignment.		You want to leave a class.	
You want some feedback on a draft that you have written.		You want to sit in on a class you have not enrolled for.	
You want to change your tutorial time.		You have a question about a lecture.	
		You're not sure what to do for an assignment.	
You want to find out about which courses to study next semester.		You don't understand the mark you've been given.	

Now you have thought about why you might want to contact a staff member. From here on you will think about how to make that contact. In the next section, we will look at the three main ways of contacting staff – by email, face-to-face, and on the telephone.

Using email

Email is commonly used by students as a way of making appointments with teachers. The good thing about email is that it is quick and convenient and teachers don't need to respond immediately. You can also check your language before you send your message (turn on the built-in spelling checker for this). One of the problems with email is that because you are not communicating face-to-face, it is easy to cause offence. Because emails are so quick to write, people sometimes forget that you should be as polite as if you are writing a letter – particularly if you are writing to people you are not close to. The same applies to text messaging (SMS), perhaps even more.

Getting the tone right

Step 1

Look at the following email requesting an appointment. There are some problems with the tone of this email. How would the lecturer who got this email feel about making an appointment with this student? Check your answer below.

> Subject: This is Miki :)

> Hi Jim – I NEED to see you ASAP to check some stuff about the assignment. I've started but got stuck with. can I come tomorrow afternoon b4 4? I have a class then. Let me know if that's OK w/u. BTW I enjoyed the class last week
> cheers
> Miki

He would probably feel very negative towards this student and would not be happy to meet them.

Step 2

Now think about what you would change to improve the tone. Rewrite the email so that it will have a more positive effect on the lecturer.

> Subject:

>

Step 3

Now compare the email you wrote with the one that follows. What has changed from the original version?

> Subject: Request for an appointment

> Dear Jim,
>
> I'm having some problems with Assignment 2 and was wondering if it would be OK to come and talk to you about it later this week.
>
> I am free tomorrow afternoon until about 4 o'clock if that is a good time for you. I am also free on Friday morning, if that works better for you.
>
> Please let me know,
>
> Many thanks
>
> Miki

Did you notice?

- the subject line is more specific. It is not common to leave the subject line blank or put your name in the subject line. Try to be as precise as possible. Many lecturers are very busy and will only read important messages quickly. If your message does not require an immediate reply, don't use the word 'urgent' or 'important' in the subject line.
- Avoid capitalisation of whole words. It sounds as if you are angry.

© Hayo Reinders, Nick Moore and Marilyn Lewis (2008), *The International Student Handbook*, Palgrave Macmillan Ltd

- It is usually better to avoid abbreviations like BTW ('By the way') or ASAP ('as soon as possible'), and texting language such as b4 ('before'), when trying to sound professional.
- The tone of the original email was too personal and informal. Remember you are writing to a teacher. In many English-speaking countries (e.g. Great Britain, New Zealand) it is fine to address your teacher by their first name, but this differs between countries and even universities. Try to find out what other students are doing if you are not sure. Even if you call them by their first name face-to-face, writing is more formal so you should be more polite.
- The first email did not give an alternative time. The second lets the teacher choose their preferred option and is more polite.

For and against emailing

Let's consider what different people think about using email to make requests of staff members. Read the viewpoints in the left-hand column. Try to think of a point for and against each one. The first one has been done for you.

TIP	*Use the Class Representative*

Ask the Class Representative to find out what policy suits a particular staff member best (see p. 168).

(see p. 168).

Text messaging

Text messages (or SMS) are a popular way for students to contact each other. Most teachers prefer to use email but some do give out their mobile phone number. Check whether they are happy to receive class-related messages, and take great care to follow the advice above about emails: it is even easier to sound impolite or unfriendly when using text messages. Always use your name in your text message as your teacher may not recognise you by your phone number!

Face-to-face requests

Of course going to the office is not the only type of face-to-face requests that staff members get.

Viewpoint	For	Against
Quick to read	Yes, each one may be quick.	But not if a person gets dozens each day.
Quick to answer		
Friendly		
Clear in meaning		
Saves time		

At the end of a lecture there is often a queue of people waiting to ask a favour. Even walking around the university grounds a staff member might meet a student who wants to stop and talk about some personal concern. Students sometimes rush up and put a request to someone who is on the way to lunch. However, let's first look at the situation where you want to go to the lecturer's office.

Issues with face-to-face requests

Ideas about privacy, personal space and interrupting people when they are working are different in different countries and even in different universities. What is normal for some lecturers in some countries may be rude for lecturers in a different country.

Here are some issues about face-to-face requests. For each question, choose the best answer and then read on.

QUESTION 1

Is it OK just to turn up at any time with no appointment?

A   Always
B   Sometimes
C   Never

For a few lecturers the answer is 'Always'. They sit in their offices with the door open and always look welcoming when students come in. These are usually people who do not teach classes of 200 or more students.

For most lecturers, there are certain times when they make themselves available to students. These times are often called 'office hours' although the person might well be there at other times, sitting behind a closed door. Check when this person's office hours are in one of these ways:

● look at the notice on the door;
● check the website;
● ask the secretary;
● email to ask for a time.

In a real emergency (and not everyone shares the same idea of what a real emergency is) then the rules can be broken and you can try

knocking on the door. For most people, a real emergency includes the following:

● A situation where someone may be hurt.
● The examination is one hour away and suddenly you feel too ill to do it.
● You have just been told that a student has broken into the assignment box and stolen an assignment.
● You have just realised that the assignment you handed in yesterday was actually one you wrote for a different course.
● Your class of 150 have been waiting for 30 minutes and the lecturer has not arrived.

QUESTION 2

What sort of requests do lecturers look at favourably?

A   Requests where the student looks distressed
B   Last-minute requests
C   Requests made early

This depends! Read on . . .

We asked some lecturers to comment on how willing they would be to say 'yes' to the following requests. Before turning to the end of the book, decide whether each was likely to have a 'yes' or a 'no' response.

1 'There's a long waiting list in the library for the book you recommended. Would you mind if I borrowed yours?'   Yes / No

2 'I know you are strict about dates for handing in assignments but as you can see, I've broken my leg.'   Yes / No

3 'I just missed a bit of your lecture this morning. I wonder if you'd mind running through that last part again with me.' Yes / No

4 'Would you mind giving me your frank opinion on whether I should advance this subject next year?'   Yes / No

TIP   *Try out your request with another student first*
You can find out if it will get a good reception and you can practise what you are going to say.

Lecturers expect to be asked about things they have not already explained in class or written on a handout. They expect that this request is special to a particular student. If the topic is more general, then ask your student representative to speak on behalf of the class. For instance, it may be that a group of students have three major assignments due for three different staff members on the same day. Then it's reasonable for the student representative to go and negotiate a different time with one of the lecturers.

The language of requests

The success of your request may also depend on the language you use and the way that you deliver the request. Your pronunciation (e.g. the way you use intonation) and body language (e.g. if you look stressed, or smile) may create an instant positive effect on your lecturer or it may create a negative effect. Read the following transcriptions of meetings between a teacher (T) and student (S).* Both of the students have requests. What are they asking for? How successful are they? What words do they use to make their requests more polite? What is the effect of the students' choice of words on their relationships with their teachers?

Wen

T: Come in. How are you?

S: Good thanks. I just wanted to change my . . . um . . . tutorial time.

T: Oh, OK. What time are you in at the moment?

S: I think I'm at . . . um . . . two o'clock on Tuesdays . . . and I've got . . . um . . . clinic on that day for accounting.

T: You've got what?

S: Clinic. Accounting clinic . . . so . . .

T: Tuesday, two o'clock (*turns papers*)

S: I'm sure that it's at two o'clock.

Jane

T: Hello. Have a seat.

S: Thanks. Actually I have . . . um . . . wrote the short story for my assignment. I was wondering could you give me some feedback and if I am on the right track.

T: OK. Yeah. You've got it?

S: (*finds and hands over story*) That's my story.

T: Oh. Let's have a read . . . um . . . [*19 sec. as T reads*] OK. Yeah that's what I mean it's a story.

S: mm-Hmmm

T: So what are you going to do with your story next?

* (The extracts of meetings between students and teachers are taken from E. Crandall (1999) 'Native Speaker and Non-Native Speaker Requests in an Academic Context', Occasional Paper, no. 12, Department of Applied Language Studies and Linguistics, University of Auckland.

Wen wants to change his tutorial time. Jane wants feedback on a draft that she's written. Both of them communicate what they want relatively successfully. Wen uses the word 'just' to understate his request. This is very common amongst native speakers and has the effect of making the request sound smaller and therefore easier to say 'yes' to. His choice of language shows that he is in control of the request, and taking the initiative, again making it easier for the teacher to agree.

Jane uses the words 'I was wondering could . . .'. This makes the request more indirect. This is a common way of making a request sound polite and is a useful technique. But don't overdo it as otherwise the teacher may think you are wasting his/her time or are hiding the true purpose of your visit.

Now, let's look at this in a little more detail.

What's a good opening line?
If your English is very good, you can probably skip this part, although it's surprising how many people rush in and ask for something without the usual phrases that make their request sound polite. Look at the following phrases and decide why they are likely to be successful. The first has been done for you. Check your answers in the key at the end of the book.

I was just wondering if . . .	*'Just'* – makes the request seem smaller and therefore easier to say 'yes' to. *Wondering* – again makes the request sound less serious and less threatening. There is less at stake than with 'Can you . . . ?'
Sorry to be a nuisance but . . .	
Excuse me. Is it possible . . .	
This is just a small request.	
Sorry I didn't make an appointment. Do you have a couple of minutes?	

TIP *Think about how your language will affect the lecturer*

- Acknowledge that you are interrupting the lecturer/don't have an appointment/can come back later.
- Get on with it! Don't waste time getting to the request.
- Practise first – work out what you will say.
- Minimise the request using words like 'just', 'small'.
- Impersonal requests using 'it' are easier to say 'yes' to than personal ones using 'you' and 'me'.

How does the conversation end?

It is important to know when to leave. If you take up too much time, you will leave a negative impression on the lecturer and he/she will be less likely to listen to you next time. Listen for clues from the lecturer. Remember, they can't leave – you are in their office!

Body language and actual words are the clues that the lecturer may expect the conversation to be over. Look out for any of these signs. The lecturer . . .

- looks down at the desk and starts shuffling papers;
- summarises an answer for the second time;
- looks at his/ her watch;
- says 'Thanks for coming', or 'I hope that answers your questions.'

What if you are still unhappy with the answer?

This is where your student representative comes in. That person has the role of negotiating things between students and staff.

Trouble-shooting lecturer–student dialogues

The following are transcripts of an actual visit by a student (S) to the office of a lecturer (T) (Crandall, 1999). For each one, think about the dialogue and answer the question. Check your answer with the key at the end of the book.

Dialogue 1 How many problems can you see in this?

T: OK. What's up? What can I do for you today?   [5 seconds of silence]

S: Yep

T: What, oh just whatever you came to see me about. Yep?

S: Yep. OK.   [Taking out paper]

T: Oh. Exam script.

S: Yeah. I failed last semester.

T: Oh OK.

S: Yep (*laugh*) you see the mark is very low.

T: Yeah.

Dialogue 2 Read the following transcript of a meeting between a student and a teacher. The meeting takes place in the teacher's office. What does the student want? Why does the teacher get impatient? Check your ideas in the answer key.

T: What can I do for you today?

S: Ah. I've come about my assignment.

T: Assignment. Oh yes. Yep. You've been to the tutorial?

S: Yes.

T: Yep [*9 seconds*] Well, what is the problem with your . . . ?

S: Ah [*9 seconds*] I don't know how to write an essay about a university.

T: And why is it difficult for you?

S: I find it hard to get started.

T: And why is that?

S: I don't have much experience in writing and I make many mistakes.

T: Ah, I see. There is an excellent writing centre at the University where you can get help with writing. . . . Etc.

Decide what you want to get out of a meeting and clearly explain to the teacher why you are there. Remember that the teacher doesn't know why you are there unless you tell him or her. Here is another way the student could have asked his question:

Teacher: What can I do for you today?

Student: I have come to talk about our next assignment. I am new to this country and found it very hard to write a good essay. How can I improve my writing skills?

Explaining what you want
Now look at the following situations. You have arranged an appointment with a teacher. How would you explain what you want? (Compare your answers with our suggestions at the end of the book).

Reason	What would you say to the teacher?
You want to sit in on a class you have not enrolled for because you think it may be more interesting than the course you are taking.	
You have a question about a lecture that you didn't want to ask in front of the other students.	
You don't understand what to do for an assignment.	
You get a bad mark for an assignment. You don't understand how it's been marked.	

Telephone contacts

Apart from the email and face-to-face contacts we have already discussed, you can, of course, use the telephone. This is great when you do not have time or you are unable to travel to the department. For example, when you are sick or overseas.

Problems of telephoning in a second language

As you will know if you have lived in another country, speaking on the phone in a second language is quite scary and one of the hardest types of talking. This is why:

● Speakers use lots of idioms on the phone and these are tricky if you are not used to them (e.g. 'ring up'/'call back'/'put you through'/'hang up'/'hold the line'/' hold on').
● Expectations of telephone conversations are different in different countries (who talks first/what they say/how long you should talk for/how to end the call, etc.).
● You can't use body language (e.g. eye contact, smiling, using your hands) to help you understand, to show that you don't under-stand, and to get your message across.
● Long pauses are not normal on the phone. You have very little time to understand what the other person is saying and say what you want to say.

Getting your message across

Here are some questions to consider before ringing. Check your answer in the key at the end of the book.

---

1 What would you say if the staff member answers the phone immediately? Which of these options seems best to you?

   (a) Ask if this is a convenient time to talk.
   (b) Give your name and state your problem.
   (c) Say whether your call is urgent or not.

2 What could you say if you hear an answerphone message? Which of these options seems best to you?

   (a) Ring off immediately.
   (b) Ask the staff member to phone you back.
   (c) Explain briefly why you have phoned.

Becoming more confident on the phone

Here are some things you can do to help you become more confident on the phone.

1 Practise what you want to say into a voice recorder and play it back. This way you can hear what you sound like on the phone and check your pronunciation. Practise leaving answerphone messages.

2 Write out beforehand what you want to say. At the very least, have a list with the main points you want to cover. You can also write down some difficult words (perhaps as you pronounce them rather than how you write them) and key phrases, like your opening or closing sentences.

3 Roleplay situations with a friend before you make the call.

4 Speak on the phone in English as much as possible – build up your confidence with more predictable requests.

5 Analyse the language of phone calls. When you are in a place where you can hear lots of phone calls, listen to the language that people use and analyse the way they introduce themselves and end conversations. Doctors' waiting rooms, cafés, and train stations are great places to hear both formal and informal phone conversations. Try out the phrases you hear, in your own phone conversations.

6 Study telephone language. Below is a reference to check out:

   B. J. Naterop and R. Revell, *Telephoning in English* (Cambridge: Cambridge University Press, 2004).

This book has a CD with dialogues you can listen to and exercises with useful language to use on the phone. It is suitable for Upper Intermediate language students. In your university's self-access centre, you will find books on Business English, which will have sections on telephone language.

Class Representatives

In many universities, one student in each class will be an elected Class Representative (Class Rep) for that class. Their job is to speak to the department or lecturer about issues that affect all the students in their class. They may have to go to training and will probably go to a formal meeting with a lecturer in the department once a semester. At the end of the semester, one of their duties in some universities is to organise a class party.

When to talk to your Class Rep

In which of these situations should you talk to the Class Rep? Check your answers in the key at the end of the book.

Read more about Class Reps

This is the link to download a handbook for Class Reps at the University of Canterbury in New Zealand:
www.ucsa.org.nz/fileadmin/downloads/classreph andbook.pdf

Here's a link to a brief introduction to the Class Rep system at Edinburgh University:
www.eusa.ed.ac.uk/src/academic/classrep_ profile.html

Situation 1	You are really confused by an assignment and have spoken to other students on your course. They are just as confused as you.
Situation 2	It is impossible to get a really important book from the library because there are not enough copies.
Situation 3	You feel that a lecturer is giving you bad marks because he/she does not like you.
Situation 4	You fail an exam and don't understand why.
Situation 5	You feel that one lecturer's classes are really boring and think he or she doesn't care about the students.
Situation 6	You want to complain about a class. You feel that there is too much testing for that class.
Situation 7	You need extra tutoring with one of your assignments.

Chapter 12

Dealing with problems

CHAPTER OVERVIEW

In this chapter you will:

- learn about managing anxiety and how to stay motivated
- find out where to find help in your new university
- discover how to manage culture shock
- learn about coping with academic issues
- learn about living on a budget and making extra money
- read about opportunities to make friends

Introduction

As an international student, expect to face problems and new challenges every day. Most international students are living away from home (sometimes for the first time), cut off from old friends and family, in an unfamiliar country, dealing with an unfamiliar culture, speaking a second language and trying to pass a university course at the same time. It's not all bad, though. Coming up with innovative solutions can be fun and experiences that are difficult at the time make great stories to tell people back at home about, later. How successful you are as a student will depend on how well you deal with these problems.

Managing anxiety

One factor that stops students from doing well at university is their own negative feelings, in other words, anxiety. As teachers, we have seen examples like these:

- Clever students who do well all through the semester but become so anxious about examinations that they don't get the results they want.

- Students who are anxious because they are not studying but can't make themselves start.
- A+ grade students who are anxious in case they get a lower grade for their next assignment.
- Failing students who feel no anxiety at all.

Do you recognise yourself in any of these descriptions?

Because motivation, personality type and anxiety are closely linked, we'll be talking about them all in this section.

What causes anxiety?

One way of thinking about anxiety is to see where you stand on the anxiety scale.

1 Being competitive   Do you find yourself comparing your results with other students' results?

   (a) very rarely

   (b) sometimes

   (c) often

Comparing yourself too much with other students is one of the factors leading to anxiety.

2 Taking tests   When you think about a future test, do you feel . . . ?

(a) not worried
(b) slightly anxious
(c) very anxious

In fact there is not much relationship between worrying and success. Some worriers do very well, some don't. The same can be said for students who hardly worry at all. For most students the answer is in actual readiness for the test, not in anxiety.

3 Your relationship with your teachers
When you think about your teachers you . . . ?

(a) don't consider what they think
(b) feel hopeful
(c) feel very anxious

Anxiety can be heightened when learners are living as immigrants in the target culture and suffering culture shock. One reason is that teacher–student relationships can be very different from country to country.

4 Your feelings about managing your studies
When you are deciding what to do for an assignment do you feel . . . ?

(a) excited
(b) a bit worried that you might not do well
(c) very anxious that you might not do well

You may find that you are expected to take much more responsibility for your studies in your new country than in the education system you are used to, especially if you are studying in a university for the first time. Finding that you have more educational freedom can be exciting for some students but can leave some students feeling lost and extremely anxious. It often takes students time to realise how much responsibility they are expected to take for their studies.

Does motivation help?

Your motivation can go wrong (or right) at several stages of your course starting with the choice of subject.

Why are you studying this subject?
For example, did you choose to study this subject? That might seem a strange question to ask, but students may be taking a particular subject for many reasons which have no connection with self-motivation. Check these out.

● Who thought this would be a good course for you?

your parents

your teachers

you

nobody

● If the answer is 'nobody' there may be other reasons why you are studying it such as:

This is a compulsory subject.

It fitted your timetable.

Your first choice (course) was scheduled too early in the morning for you to get out of bed.

As you can see, negative reasons for taking a course can make it difficult to be motivated. Still, if you want to pass, you need to try motivating yourself in other ways.

Examine your attitude to the subject
You can do something to improve your motivation. One way is to start thinking positively about the parts of your course. Try this:

● How many reasons can you find for the importance in the world of the subject you are studying?
● How many different future options could this subject give you?

Thinking about time can help too. If you are 8 weeks into a 13-week term and you are not motivated, divide up the rest of the time available, look at the lecture topics each week and ask yourself:

● What's one thing I want to get out of each week remaining on the course?

Monitor your motivation levels over time
The motivation questionnaire on p. 172 will help you measure your current motivation levels (if you answer it truthfully!). 'Intrinsic'

motivation is internal motivation – how meaningful things feel to you. 'Extrinsic' motivation is external – from other people and society. Some people will have stronger 'intrinsic' motivation than 'extrinsic' motivation. On the other hand, some people will have much stronger 'extrinsic' motivation. This is not better, nor is it worse.

'Synergy' is about connections – in your case between you and your course and with people on the course.

You should try this questionnaire at different stages of your course and keep track of your scores. For each question, place yourself on a scale of 1 to 5.

It is normal for motivation levels to go up and down over a course or even a semester but if you are aware that your motivation levels are slipping, you can try and change this around or talk to someone about it.

Write down your scores here:

date	score out of 60
1	
2	
3	
4	

Category	Key questions	Your motivation level				
Energy						
Level of activity	How much work are you putting in?	a little				a lot
		1	2	3	4	5
Achievement	To what extent do you feel like you are making progress?	going backwards		good progress		
		1	2	3	4	5
Fear of failure	How much do you feel your hard work is being recognised?	not at all				well
		1	2	3	4	5
Synergy						
Personal growth	To what extent do you feel that your course is helping you grow as a person?	not at all				a lot
		1	2	3	4	5
Course	To what extent do you feel the course is right for you?	not right			100% right	
		1	2	3	4	5
Relationships	To what extent do you feel you are working well with other people on your course – the other students and your lecturers?	not at all			working well	
		1	2	3	4	5

© Hayo Reinders, Nick Moore and Marilyn Lewis (2008), *The International Student Handbook*, Palgrave Macmillan Ltd

Category	Key questions	Your motivation level				
Intrinsic						
Interest	How interested are you in your lectures, tutorials and readings at the moment?	bored				very interested
		1	2	3	4	5
Enjoyment	How much are you enjoying your course at the moment?	hate it				love it
		1	2	3	4	5
Autonomy	How much control and choice do you feel you have over your studies?	no control			full control	
		1	2	3	4	5
Extrinsic						
Progress	How important to you are the grades you get?	don't care				care a lot
		1	2	3	4	5
Accountability	How important is your progress on the course to your family, friends or company?	doesn't matter		very important		
		1	2	3	4	5
Future hopes	How important is your performance on the course to your future career?	not important		very important		
		1	2	3	4	5

How important is personality?

Personality is one more factor affecting how anxious a student is. If you are working in ways that do not fit your personality you could get bored or turned off study. Take this 2-minute personality test and then read about the best way for someone with your personality to study. It is based around some typical decisions that international students make. For each question, decide which of the answers sounds most like you. The one that sounds most like you gets score '1'. The next closest answer gets score '2', and so on.

1 *The country you decided to study in*

When you chose a country to go to, what was the most important factor in your decision?

(a) . . . It was the most logical place for me to go and study.

(b) . . . It fitted in with my friends and family.

(c) . . . The most practical – this was the place I could get the results I wanted.

(d) . . . I liked the idea of it. It seemed the most exciting.

2 *Your career choice*

Which of these sounds most like you?

(a) . . . I want a job where I can analyse things and see what makes them work.

(b) . . . I'm interested in jobs with lots of contact with people.

(c) . . . I want to do something where I can solve problems and make a difference.

(d) . . . I want to do something where I can be creative.

3 *Your ideal teacher*

Which of these sounds closest to your ideal?

(a) . . . I like teachers who know their subject, give me the facts and get to the point.

(b) . . . It is really important for teachers to care about their students.

(c) . . . I like teachers to be practical and give me real-world learning tasks.

(d) . . . I like teachers who give me the freedom to take things my own way.

4 *Working in groups*

Which one sounds like you?

(a) . . . I prefer to think about the issues myself and then come together with the group to discuss them.

(b) . . . I think it's really important that everyone has their say.

(c) . . . The key thing is that we make a decision and get the task done.

(d) . . . I like to challenge the others and ask questions like 'What if . . . ?'

5 *Your subject choice*

How did you decide what subject to do?

(a) . . . I like working things out in a systematic way. Accuracy is important. I like to be able to understand how things work.

(b) . . . I am interested in people and feelings. I want to do a subject where I can explore and understand why people behave in the ways they do.

(c) . . . I like solving problems and seeing how things work in practice. I like applying ideas and getting results.

(d) . . . I like creating things and seeing new possibilities.

6 *Going out*

How do you choose a movie to go and see?

(a) . . . I look at all the available information – reviews, listings etc., and choose the best one.

(b) . . . I talk it through with my friends and we go and see something that suits everyone.

(c) . . . I choose one that is on at the right time and fits my schedule.

(d) . . . If it looks interesting, I'll give it a try.

7 *Handing in assignments*

When it is time to check your piece of work before you hand it in, which of these sounds like you?

(a) . . . I want it to be accurate so take a lot of care to make sure it is.

(b) . . . I end up spending so much time helping a friend that I don't really check mine properly.

(c) . . . I check it well enough to get a pass but don't waste time on it because I have other things to get on with.

(d) . . . I am not really interested in checking it. I know some sections are great. I'd rather move on to a more interesting project.

8 *Getting help and advice*

When you get stuck with something, how do you decide when to ask for help?

(a) . . . I like to figure it all out myself before asking for help.

(b) . . . I like to share my problems and talk it through with someone.

(c) . . . I will do whatever it takes to solve the problem efficiently.

(d) . . . I am open to suggestions. Sometimes people say things that help me see the problem in a totally different way.

Now add up your score for each letter:

Total score for (a) =

Total score for (b) =

Total score for (c) =

Total score for (d) =

The lowest score is your dominant personality type. Read the table below to find out how people with this personality type approach study. The right-hand column has some tips for avoiding anxiety.

Note: this questionnaire is adapted from one that can be accessed at www.engr.utexas.edu/eoe/PeerLeaders/Resources/Learning&Personality Styles.pdf. (If you are interested in finding out more about personality, you should take the full test.)

At this stage, it could be a good idea to look back at the 'learning styles' questionnaires in Chapter 3. Again, if you are trying to learn in ways that do not suit your natural learning style, you may be causing yourself anxiety.

Anxiety summary: make a plan

Finally, let's see how many of the following tips are relevant to you.

1 Consider trying to compete with yourself rather than others.

2 Remind yourself of the support that is available to you (check out the next section), for example friends and counsellors.

3 Taking action helps, even if it's only drawing up a plan of what you will start studying tomorrow.

4 Evaluate your learning. Remind yourself of signs of progress.

5 Talk with a friend about the benefits of studying in the course you are enrolled for.

6 Give yourself a reasonable amount of time before considering changing courses.

7 Plan some rewards for yourself when you have done a certain amount of study.

	How you naturally learn	How to avoid anxiety
(a) = Analyser	You learn by thinking deeply about things. You are logical and technical. You like rules and precision. You are better with concepts than people.	At times you may get stressed because you have to make decisions without understanding everything. You are too cautious and need to go with the flow a bit more. You also need to remember that other people's ideas can be useful too!
(b) = Supporter	You learn by watching people, sharing ideas and talking about feelings. You are emotional and sensitive and good with people. You are sociable and understanding.	You are sometimes too worried about what everyone thinks to get things done. This may cause you anxiety. Sometimes you need to focus more on the result and be more decisive.
(c) = Director	You learn by putting things into practice. You like getting results. You are good at problem-solving. You are good at planning and organising people and things to get the best result in the situation.	People get frustrated with you because you organise them too much. Remember, the end result is not everything – you also need to keep everyone happy.
(d) = Creator	You like action and learn by trying things out. You are a free spirit and are creative. You don't plan but do things spontaneously.	At times, remember you need to concentrate more on things that seem boring – like details. You will also need to be more consistent and work hard over time.

8 Monitor your feelings. Don't let yourself be too sad for too long.

9 Remember that other people think and learn differently from the way you do. Don't let their difference stress you out.

10 Be realistic. Even if you are doing really well, you can expect some anxious days! If you are never anxious about your progress, you should be worried!

Sources of help

Most universities have well-established support services set up for domestic and international students. These can give you help and advice when you are facing all sorts of problems. This section introduces the different agencies in a university and gives you some ideas of where you can turn for help and advice. Don't worry about going to the wrong person – if they can't help you, they will know who can. The important thing is that if you have a problem, you take action and talk to **someone**.

Who can help?

Look at the table on p. 177. On the left is the type of problem. On the right are some of the people who might be able to help. The names of the people will change between universities but there will be people who can help with these problems.

Get help early
As you can see, there is help available for every kind of problem you can possibly have while at university. The most important thing is to tell someone you have a problem early so you can get advice before your problem gets too big. No problem is too small, too simple or too terrible for a university counsellor – remember, they talk to thousands of students every year all with similar problems.

A note about counsellors
In some cultures, it is really bad to talk to a counsellor. In a university situation this is not the case. Getting help from a counsellor is considered normal and a positive thing to do. It is also confidential so the counsellor will not tell anyone about your problem without your permission.

If you go and see a counsellor for whatever problem, the counsellor will . . .

FIRST	try to understand your problem by asking you questions;
THEN	talk through choices with you;
SO THAT	you have enough information and understanding to make decisions for yourself.

Counsellors will not tell you what to do, that is your decision. Counsellors may tell you things that you don't want to hear.

In your orientation week at university, make a note of where you can go to get help with these areas.

- academic issues
- health issues
- financial advice

Culture shock

Culture shock is a series of feelings that many people go through when they move to a new country. If you have lived in another country before, you may have already experienced culture shock. If you haven't, then this section will make you aware of it so that you can prevent it from becoming a problem at university. It helps to know about it so that you can be prepared for it.

Type of problem:	Examples:	Who can help?
academic	You need study advice	an academic advisor; your lecturer; a learning centre advisor
	You want to complain about a class.	your Class Rep; your lecturer; an academic advisor
	You want to appeal against a grade/decision.	an academic advisor
	You have a problem with a lecturer.	your Class Rep; an academic advisor
	You need help in the library.	a librarian; your subject librarian
	You need help improving your English	learning centre
	You have questions about plagiarism.	learning centre advisor; academic advisor
	You are not sure which courses to take.	an academic advisor in your department
accommodation	You want to complain about a landlord. You need help finding a flat.	union accommodation office
	You can't pay the rent.	student financial counsellor
health	You feel sick. You need advice about pregnancy. You need to register with a doctor. You need advice about contraception. You want a female doctor.	university health centre
mental health	You feel depressed. You have an eating problem . (e.g. anorexia) You have worries about your sexuality. You have a question about drugs or alcohol. You want to stop smoking. You need help with stress.	student counselling service or university health centre
money	You need to find a job. You have run out of money. You need help budgeting. You have a question about tax.	student financial counsellor
international	You have a problem with your immigration status or visa. You need a translator. You feel homesick.	international student office
religion	You need somewhere to pray.	university chaplaincy service; international student office

What are the stages of culture shock?

There are generally thought to be four stages that people go through when they arrive in a new country.

A culture shock survival kit (culture-shock-proof your overseas studies)

Try these things **before** you leave for your new country.

1 Tell one of your friends at home about culture shock. Explain about the four stages and give them examples of things that people say in stage 3:

- 'The shops shut so early in this country. It's crazy. Life is much better at home where . . . '
- 'There's nothing to do here in the evenings. People are so boring in . . . '
- 'The internet connection is so slow. How do people live like this? In my country, we had better internet connection five years ago.'
- 'There's so much bureaucracy in this university. Everything takes so long. I'm sure they just make it difficult for students.'

Ask your friend to ring you every week and ask you how you are getting on. If you say things that sound like you have stage 3 culture shock, they should tell you, and help you to lighten up.

2 Make a list of all the things that you want to do in the country you are going to. For example:

- Spend a weekend in . . .
- Catch the ferry to . . .
- Spend the afternoon on . . . beach.
- Camp in the mountains near . . .
- Go to the opera in . . .
- Find yourself a conversation partner (see next section)
- Go to the art gallery in . . .

If you find yourself in stage 2, you should revisit your list and do one of the things on it. This way you stay in the discovery stage.

3 If you have a hobby like a sport, or play a musical instrument, then make sure you take any equipment you need to your new country. Having a 'hobby' outside your studies will help you feel less culture shocked.

Stage 1 **The discovery stage** You feel like you are just on holiday. Everything is new and fun and exciting. You do lots in the first few weeks and find everything interesting – there are new parts of the university and city to explore and it's all a bit unreal. Even catching a bus is fun and exciting.

Stage 2 **Things go flat** Life's OK but you realise that you are going to be in this country for a long time. You get into a routine – lectures, assignments, etc. You may find it difficult to make friends. You realise that people in the host country don't understand you that well. You have some bad days but at this stage you can live with them.

Stage 3 **The complaining stage** You start getting angry when things go wrong. You may worry about your health. You have negative feelings about people in the host country. Why is the bus always late? Why is the bread so horrible? How do these people put up with it all? You see problems everywhere and find yourself comparing things in your new country with things in your old country – all the time. Sometimes it feels that everyone in your new country is trying to make things difficult for you. You may find yourself getting depressed at this stage or very tired or just angry.

Stage 4 **And finally . . .** By now your language is better and living is easier. Gradually you are getting over the culture shock. Sure, the new country is different but it's OK. And when things go wrong you can laugh about it and about your negative reaction. The university is different from the one where you have previously studied but there are good things and bad things about it. You still miss people at home and some of the things about your country but that's OK.

And once you are studying in your new country . . .

1 Meet a friend from your country regularly, such as once every two weeks. Allow yourselves to say what you miss about your country but also reflect on how you are adapting to the change. Set yourselves goals that you can evaluate when you next meet, for example: 'By the time we next meet, I'll have joined a university society and tried out the local swimming pool.'

2 Keep a diary. Note down how you are feeling about your move, the new country, the local people, the change of university. Also write down any successes you have (friends you make, or positive experiences, etc.). If you find yourself in stage 2 or stage 3, go back through your diary and see how far you have come.

Some common areas of cultural misunderstanding

This is a task you could try in your first few weeks in a new country. Here are some topics that can cause cultural misunderstanding. They will not be a problem if you are aware of them. First read through the list and think about whether they are acceptable in your country and in your new country. Then find someone from the new country and talk about them.

	OK in your country?	OK in your new country?
1 Arriving 10 minutes late to meet a friend.		
2 Arriving 20 minutes late to meet a friend.		
3 Kissing when you meet someone for the first time.		
4 Kissing when you meet good friends.		
5 Wearing shoes inside someone's house.		
6 Touching someone on the arm when you are talking to them.		
7 Calling a lecturer by their first name.		
8 Calling someone older by their first name.		
9 Arriving at someone's house for dinner with no gift.		
10 Giving your teacher a really expensive gift – like a CD player.		
11 Asking questions about someone's age or how much they earn, on a first meeting.		
12 Asking a woman if she is married when you first meet her.		
13 Standing close to someone you don't know very well, at a party (less than a metre apart).		
14 Making direct eye contact with a teacher in class.		
15 Laughing and smiling when talking to a teacher.		
16 Making jokes about old people/women/sex/ people from a particular part of the country, with people you don't know well.		
17 Making jokes about the royal family or the president.		
18 Talking loudly with a friend on the train.		
19 Using a cell phone in the library.		
20 Getting drunk.		
21 Driving home after two or three beers.		
22 Inviting someone out and insisting on paying the full bill.		

Summary: some things that help students overcome culture shock

1 Knowing about it. (See the notes above.)

2 Making sure you keep some contact with people from your own country studying in the university and also with people at home.

3 Exercising. This stops most people worrying about things, and makes most people feel more positive about life.

4 Getting involved with people in the host country, both in the university and in the city. For example, you could take up dance classes or join a football team.

5 Focusing on your studies. Get busy – you really don't have time to worry about culture shock.

6 Setting yourself goals – e.g., 'Next week, I'm going to get out to the mountains . . . ' or 'This week, I'm going to go out for a drink with people from my class.'

7 Continuing to learn about your new country – discovering new places and people.

8 Finding someone else who has experienced culture shock and having a joke about it with them.

9 Remembering it's OK to miss your family and friends and country.

10 Talking to a counsellor if you are getting depressed.

11 Remembering you will probably not be living there forever.

Academic issues: What would you do? – A quiz

So far, we have looked at anxiety and the sources of help available to you at university. In this section we will deal with academic problems. Take this quiz and decide what you would do in each case. When you have finished, check your answers in the key and then read the advice for your personality type.

Are you a proactive problem-solver?

1 You get an email saying that you owe the library $65 in library fines and cannot use the library again until this fine is paid. Your own records suggest that you may have some fines owing but you don't think you owe that much. Do you . . . ?

(a) do nothing and keep working on your assignment – there's no time to lose

(b) phone the library and ask them about the fine

(c) pay it straight away so that you can borrow books again

2 You are set an assignment. You are not sure what the question is asking or how to approach it. What should you do first?

(a) write what you think it's asking and hand that in

(b) make an appointment to ask your lecturer what it's all about

(c) talk to other students on the course and see if they can explain it

3 You are struggling to meet a deadline. You have three essays due in the same week (3 weeks away) and you don't think you are going to be able to get them all in on time. Do you . . . ?

(a) stay up every night, work really hard and try to get them all in – you can hand one in late – it doesn't matter that much if it's a couple of days late

(b) ask one of your lecturers for an extension now

(c) do your best and then plan to ask for an extension the day before the essay has to be handed in

4 You get an assignment back and you have failed but you don't know why. You thought you did the assignment well and you don't understand the lecturer's comments. Do you . . . ?

(a) make an appointment to ask your lecturer why you failed

(b) make an official complaint about the lecturer

(c) try, first, to read the assignment of a student who did OK

5 You are trying to find a book for your course in the library. You have found it on the computer but can't find it on the shelf. Do you . . . ?

(a) go for a drink and come back later for another look

(b) decide to spend the rest of the day figuring out how the library's shelves are organised

(c) ask a librarian to help you locate the book

6 You are worried that you don't understand much of the lectures on one of your courses. Do you . . . ?

(a) make an appointment with your lecturer and tell him or her

(b) buy a top-of-the-range MP3 player and record all the lectures so you can listen to them again later

(c) seek help at the English-language self-access centre in the university

7 You are having trouble finding somewhere quiet to study. Your flatmates are too noisy and watch television all the time. Do you . . . ?

(a) buy ear plugs

(b) watch television with them

(c) ask someone in your department about available study spaces

8 You are struggling with your course – you have exams in a couple of weeks and you don't know where to start. You think you might fail. Do you . . . ?

(a) make an appointment with your lecturer and tell him or her how you feel

(b) start studying even harder, and spend all weekend in the library

(c) pack your bags and go home

9 You have a problem with your course. You don't think the assessment is fair. Do you . . . ?

(a) talk to your Class Representative (the person in the class who you voted for to

talk to your department about issues concerning the class)

(b) do nothing – it's probably no big deal

(c) complain to the head of the department about the lecturer

Finished? Now check your answers in the key at the end of the book and then read the advice for your personality type. See if you agree with the advice.

Critical thinking

Lecturers in English-speaking universities often complain that international students are not able to think critically, and may give them bad marks because of this. In the chapters on reading and writing in this book we have already talked a bit about critical thinking, but in this section we look at this topic in some more detail.

So, what do lecturers mean by critical thinking?

You may know the word 'criticise' with its everyday meaning of 'making negative comments about someone or something'. However, when talking about 'critical thinking' that is not the meaning your lecturers have in mind. There is not one sole definition of critical thinking, but here are some examples:

Critical thinkers . . .

● think logically
● put things into categories
● decide whether something is a fact or an argument
● evaluate arguments using a wide range of evidence
● weigh up evidence and come to their own conclusions
● make connections between different ideas
● apply theories to practical situations
● ask questions like 'Why?' and 'What if . . . ?'
● ask questions and see problems in the 'normal' way things happen

So, critical thinking is about *ways* of thinking, and the ability to analyse ideas and arguments.

Why is critical thinking important at English-speaking universities?

In Anglo-Saxon (British and American) culture the individual's personal development is seen as very important. Students must show that they can read, think, question, analyse and come to their own conclusions. Teachers may expect and encourage learners to discover things for themselves. They may ask questions like . . .

'What do you think?'

'How did you come to that conclusion?'

'To what extent do you think . . . ?'

For this reason, remembering a lot of facts and simply working very hard may not be enough and will probably not get you very good grades. This may be different from your own country, where hard work is often rewarded.

What sort of problems may I have with critical thinking?

The idea of critical thinking is important in lots of areas at university. For example, you will find that:

- there is an expectation that you should learn in an active/questioning/discovering way and find things out for yourself;
- the way the course is structured is different – with tutorials where you need to discuss and evaluate ideas;
- assignments often have a critical element where you need to evaluate and argue;
- the sort of feedback the lecturer gives you is different from what you are used to;
- how you speak in lectures and tutorials and the questions you ask are different;
- how you are supposed to read, and question what you read, are different;
- how you plan and write assignments is different;
- how you cite sources in assignments is considered very important;
- how you answer exam questions and how these are marked is different.

How does it feel when you are struggling with critical thinking?

It can be really hard! Read what these first-year students said about it:

'I am not a lazy student – I'm working harder and harder but my marks don't get better.'

'It is like playing a sport that you know you are good at but with new and different rules that you don't really understand.'

'I just feel lost. I don't know how to start this assignment/answer this question.'

'I'm always being asked for my opinion. I don't have one and even if I did I am just a beginner in the subject so, compared with the people who wrote the books, my opinion is not really important.'

How are plagiarism and critical thinking connected?

If students do not understand about critical thinking, they can have problems with plagiarism (see Chapter 9). Remember Umut, from our case studies at the beginning of the book? Here is the chain of events leading to her problem with plagiarism. As you read, think about how her problem is related to critical thinking and how you can avoid this situation.

1 A lecturer sets an assignment asking students to report and evaluate some research articles on a topic. She wants the students to show they have thought critically about the research and come to their own conclusions. The question reads: 'With reference to the work of *X*, *Y* and *Z* [three important researchers on the topic], to what extent do you agree with the idea that . . . ?'

2 Umut doesn't really understand the question but focuses on the bit she does understand – the first part – and starts work. She doesn't understand that she needs to give her conclusions about the research.

3 Umut reads the articles in detail and writes her assignment. She tries to report and summarise what the writers say but this is really hard. She is anxious about her English.

4 Before she hands her work in, Umut checks her essay. She is unsatisfied with her work. Her words are not nearly as good as the original articles she read and she feels very uncomfortable about changing the meaning of the original writers. So she uses some of the same sentences from the original articles.

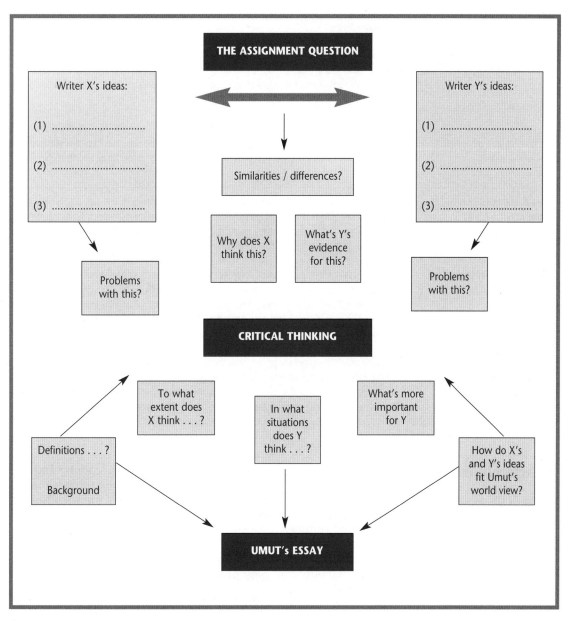

Figure 12.1 How to use critical thinking in an assignment

5 Umut hands in her work. The lecturer reads it
   and highlights all the bits that have been
   copied, and writes feedback using words like:
   'PLAGIARISM . . . SERIOUS OFFENCE . . . THIS
   UNIVERSITY . . . INTELLECTUAL PROPERTY
   . . . URGENT APPOINTMENT', etc.

Now look at the diagram in Figure 12.1 to see
how Umut should have answered the question.

So, how do you get better at critical thinking,
get better marks and avoid problems with
plagiarism?

This is a big question – if you have read this
section and our other references to critical
thinking in the chapters about reading and
writing, then you have made a good start. But
there's more you can do:

What to do . . .	How to do this . . .
Find out more about critical thinking	Many universities or departments have courses that teach more about critical thinking. Your department may make all students take one. Even if they don't, there may be seminars or workshops you can go to in your department, in the library, or in the self-access centre. Ask at the international student office or in your department.
Think about your past success	Make a list of things that you have done that have made you a successful student in the past. For each one, decide how useful it will be in a learning situation based on critical thinking.
Find out how to make the change	Talk to other students from your country who have studied in the university you are going to. Learn from their mistakes! Ask them about critical thinking. Find out what problems they had and how they got better at thinking critically. If you have a mentor, ask them about critical thinking.
Get help from your lecturers	This is especially important when they set up assignments or talk about exams. Tell them if you don't understand what they are asking you to do. Ask to see examples of other students' assignments so you can see what you have to do. Ask to see how they will mark the assessment so that they can explain how important the parts of your answer are.
Find out how to reference properly and get better at it	Go to any available workshops on referencing and using other people's ideas. Get help from your department or the self-access centre in the university. If you have problems or are not sure about referencing, make an appointment with your lecturer or an academic counsellor and take your writing with you.

Academic issues: summary

Many of the academic issues touched on here are dealt with in more depth in other chapters in the book. Be aware that the university culture may be different from what you have experienced before and it is fine to ask about your responsibilities as a student and find out what is expected of you. You will need to be proactive – if you sense a problem, do something about it and talk to someone (or a range of people), such as a fellow student, advisors in the university's self-access centre, academic advisors or your lecturers, so that you understand the issue before taking action.

Friends

Many students find it difficult making friends. It can be even more difficult to make friends when you are in a new city in a new country and you don't know anybody. The good thing is that everyone else will be keen to form friendships as well, especially in your first term.

Eight great ways to meet people in your new university

Read the following suggestions, for some ideas. Tick three that you will try.

1 *Move into shared accommodation*

You don't need to live like a hippy in a commune but university halls are great places to meet people and they are often the easiest accommodation option for international students new to a city. If you can't face living with so many other people, move into a flat with three or four others.

2 Form a study group with other students on your course

Meet for coffee and a chat about lectures or assignments and gossip about your lecturers.

3 Start a language exchange

A language exchange is when you meet someone who speaks the language you want to learn and who is learning the language that you speak. You speak for half the time in your language and half the time in their language. There may be a language exchange set up in your university somewhere – the international student office will know about it. If not, set one up for yourself. Find the Modern Languages department in your university and put a notice up with your contact details.

4 Join a university society

Universities have societies (clubs) for any interests you can imagine. Hill-walking, politics, debating, drinking, engineering, computer gaming, religion, chess, chamber music, the environment, drama, dancing, poetry, etc. To join a society, look for contact details on a poster. Often societies try to get new members during orientation week, so look out for a society that you are interested in. Even if you are not interested, you could go along anyway – you might meet some different people.

5 Join an orchestra or a sports team

If you are good (or even just OK) at something like music or sports, join a group, either at the university or in the city.

6 Get a part-time job

Earn money and meet people at the same time. Have a look in the Student's Union for advertisements from companies who need students to work for them.

7 Become a Class Rep

A Class Rep (short for 'representative') is the person in each class who goes to meetings in the department and brings up problems from the class. It is a great way into all parts of university life. You need to get elected but that is usually easy as most students are happy for someone else to be class rep. First, you introduce yourself to the class and tell everyone that if they have any problems they should tell you. You then get emails from people in your class who want answers to their questions. Then you go to a meeting with the department, and finally you pass on the answers to your class. Sometimes Class Reps have to organise the class party too. You might even find out that your department will subsidise the food!

8 Look out for events for international students

Check out the notice board in the international student office for news of any events organised for international students. It's a great way to meet people in exactly the same situation as you.

Summary

Meeting people can seem scary at first but remember – it's the same for everyone. You do need to get out of the library, though, and look for opportunities to find people with similar interests. The good thing is that with email, chat software and free internet calls, although you may be a long way from home, you can still communicate with old friends all day and all night so you do not need to feel alone.

Money

Most students face money worries from time to time. Being an international student is extremely expensive – your course fees are higher than those of local students, you may not be able to get a study grant or a student loan, you have to pay for regular flights and you may be on a visa that does not let you take a job. Money worries cause stress and anxiety. This section will help you work out a budget plan, and give you some ideas of ways to raise money while you are studying.

Three case studies

Read these three case studies and make sure you don't make the same mistakes:

Cindy, 23, Taiwan:

'I planned the academic part of my studies in Montreal really carefully – but I guess I never thought about money. My parents had made all my financial decisions for me. Well, anyway, I arrived in Canada with a large amount of cash in Taiwanese dollars that was supposed to last me for the whole semester. I changed a bit at the change office down the road from my department and just hid the rest of it in my flat. About three weeks before the end of the semester, we got broken into and we got home to find the whole flat turned upside down and my money was gone. By then, there wasn't much left – it could have been much worse. I went straight into town and put everything I had in my wallet into a bank account – it was really easy – there was even someone there who spoke Chinese.'

Kenshiro, 21, Japan:

'My parents paid for my studies in Australia so I arrived with enough in my bank account for living expenses for a whole year. I had never had that much money before so it went to my head. I bought lots of stuff when I arrived – things I was used to in Japan. A Nissan Skyline, a stereo and a new laptop. Of course it was stupid. I got into debt, had to sell the car and live off nothing but rice for months. In my second year, I learnt to budget.'

Hamed, 23, Saudi Arabia:

'In my culture, you lose face if you say you can't afford to go out with your friends because you have no money so I went out a lot with people at my university . . . and ran out of money. I couldn't believe how much I spent and I don't even drink! I learnt that it is OK to say 'No, sorry, got no money' and suggest an evening in, playing cards and telling stories instead of hitting the town.'

TIP *Keeping track of your expenses*

It is easy to spend more than you can afford, especially in another country where the currency is different and you may not know where to get the best prices for products and services. There are many free online 'expense trackers'. These allow you to type in what you spend, and at the end of the month show you how much the total is and what you spent it on. You can also use these programmes to warn you if you spend too much. Use your favourite search engine to search for 'free expense tracker'.

Ways to save money as a student

Here are some strategies for cutting your expenses. Read them through and tick the ones you already use.

- Write down everything you spend, in a notebook or online expense tracker (see above).
- Share a flat rather than renting one for yourself.
- Reduce transport costs by living close to university.
- Take advantage of 'student specials' at the cinema, pubs, hairdressers etc.
- Cook your own food rather than buying takeaways.
- Buy second-hand books and clothes.
- Buy pre-paid phone cards for international calls or use Skype (Skype is a system for calling people using a computer instead of a telephone).
- Share the cost of study books between friends.

Work out your budget

Use this plan to help you work out how much money you've got to live off each week. Fill in the amounts and work out **total a** and **total b**.

Income (write down all your income for the semester)		**Spending** (write down all your predictable spending for the semester)	
Item	**amount**	**Item**	**amount**
Study grant		Course fees	
Scholarship		Exam fees	
Savings		Union fees	
Money from other sources (e.g. family)		Health insurance (essential for international students)	
Wages		Accommodation (rent etc.)	
other:		other:	
total a =		**total b =**	

Now, work this out:

total a – total b = c _____ (This is the amount of money you have for living expenses for the semester.)

Next, work out how much you have to spend each week.

Let **x** = number of weeks in the semester (e.g. 14) + the number of weeks holiday (e.g. inter-semester break = 2).

c ÷ x = y _____ (This is the amount of money you have for living expenses per week.)

These are some of the things you will need to buy with **y**:

bills (power, phone etc.)	clothes	library fines
food	going out	other
transport	books	

© Hayo Reinders, Nick Moore and Marilyn Lewis (2008),
The International Student Handbook, Palgrave Macmillan Ltd

A treasure hunt: find the best deals in your new city

People who are new to a city or country often don't know where to find the best deals. In the orientation week when you start your course, businesses in the city will advertise to new students but it's a good idea to spend a day or so finding out ways of living cheaply in your new city.

Find these things in the city you have chosen to study in:

1 The name of a cinema that has 'student nights'

name: _____

which night: _____

2 The location of a market that sells cheap food and clothes

where: _____

which day: _____

3 The name of a suburb that is close to university but has cheap rent

name: _____

4 The place where students advertise text books they want to sell

where: _____

5 A name of a second-hand bookstore

name: _____

6 The address of a website where you can buy second-hand furniture (e.g. ebay.com)

name: _____

7 The name and location of a second hand bike shop

name: _____

where: _____

8 The name of a pre-paid international phone card, and where you can get it?

name: _____

where: _____

9 A shop that sells discount bus passes for students

where: _____

10 A hairdresser's that does cheap haircuts for students

where: _____

Ways to earn money while you are studying

Check the terms of your visa. You may be able to take a part-time job while you are studying. Some visas allow you to work for a limited number of hours, e.g. up to 10 hours per week. The first place to try is the Students' Union. They may have a notice board where companies place advertisements when they have jobs that students could do.

Here are some ways that international students earned money while at university. They may give you some ideas of how you could earn money while you are studying. Decide which ones you could do on your visa. Then rank them in terms of 'best to worst' for you.

● **Use your area of study**

'I was majoring in computer programming and was desperate for some money. I used to go to a gym and got talking to the manager one day. He needed a website — so I designed one for him. It was pretty simple and looked good on my CV.'

● **Use your talent**

'Although I studied drama, I did a lot of music at university. I formed a small band and we used to play at university parties – student balls, graduation parties etc. We used to play in a pizza restaurant and that led to some weddings. It was well paid and easy work and we could do it whenever we wanted.'

● **Use your department**

'I was studying chemistry and saw an advert for lab assistants. I worked every evening for 2 hours just clearing up and getting things ready for the next day's classes. I then became a lab assistant helping first-year students doing experiments.'

● **Use your first language**

'I got a job teaching my language to kids

studying for their high school exams. I had never taught before but that didn't seem to matter. I also got work translating documents for schools.'

● **Use your ethnicity**

'I am Japanese and got work easily in a Japanese restaurant. The pay was not good but I was feeling a bit homesick so it helped me meet some Japanese people.'

● **Use your study skills**

'In my third year, I started running workshops in the Language Learning Centre for other international students starting their studies. I also got paid to be a student mentor for new students.'

● **Use your holidays**

'Rather than go home in the holidays, I used to go and live on a farm and pick fruit. I made a bit of money and they gave you accommodation too so I didn't spend too much.'

● **Use your library skills**

'I never thought I'd become a librarian but I saw an advert and applied. I met lots of people and got to know the university library very well.'

● **Take part in an experiment**

'My lecturer was looking for participants in a psychology experiment. It was quite interesting and well paid. Easy money. I don't think I'd do medical experiments, though.'

Now, look back at the list and decide which you could fit in around your study and which would take too much time.

Balancing work and study

The problem with getting a job is that it can take up too much valuable study time. However, it might be fun; you will definitely meet people; it could be a good break from study and it may help you fit in with life in another country. If you do take a part-time job, you might decide to organise your working hours so that you work fewer hours around exam times or times when you have lots of assignments to hand in.

Grants, scholarships, loans and other sources of funding

Often students don't know about funding that they may be able to get. In some cultures, it is embarrassing to ask for extra funding. As a student, it is always better to ask than to go short.

Here are seven places to look for extra funding. Once again, tick any that you may be able to apply for.

1 An extra grant

If you already have a grant from a government or some other source, go back to them. Explain that you need more money to finish your studies, explain what has happened (e.g. your housing costs have gone up) and ask if they can give you more help.

2 Special grants

You may be doing a special subject that needs expensive equipment and you may be eligible for a grant for that equipment.

3 Photocopying or textbook allowance

Some departments offer help with photocopying costs and/or the cost of buying course materials. You may need to apply for this, so make sure you find out about it.

4 A scholarship

Some scholarships are awarded by a department or faculty and given to the students who get the best marks across the year, but you may be able to apply for others. Have a look on your university website or ask your department secretary.

5 A research grant

If you are doing research, you may be able to apply for a grant to cover the cost of hiring a research assistant or for some other expenses such as translation costs. Ask your supervisor.

6 Hardship grants

Often student unions have 'hardship grants' – this is money they keep for emergencies. For example, if you have to spend a lot of money suddenly finding new accommodation, and find you don't have enough money to buy food, you should ask your student organisation. They may be able to help.

7 A bank loan

Most banks offer overdrafts with low interest rates for students. You may be able to apply. It's worth checking the terms and conditions.

See Chapter 2 for more advice on how to apply for a scholarship.

Money – a summary

Running out of money is a serious concern for many international students but you can reduce stress by taking action:

1. Make a budget plan.

2. Minimise your expenses.

3. Earn some money.

4. Apply for all the help you can get.

Also remember – you can get help on budgeting from university counsellors at your university. Universities are very worried about people (especially international students) not finishing their studies so it is definitely a good idea to talk to financial counsellors about money problems.

Summary

As an international student you can expect to have to deal with some of the problems in this chapter (and maybe some different ones). We have tried to show some creative solutions to these problems and encourage you to be proactive. We have also tried to encourage you to find someone to listen to your problem. Whatever your problem, if you talk to someone about it, it will feel more manageable and you can reduce your anxiety. There are lots of people you can talk to at university about study, money or personal problems – your friends, the international student advisor, learning centre advisors, university counsellors, your supervisor or your lecturer, so don't suffer in silence.

Conclusion

What next?

If you have read this book from cover to cover, or if you have dipped into the parts that answer your questions, you will realise that there is so much more to find out. When we talked about ideas for building up your vocabulary we gave only some of the many examples we could have. Even with two chapters on writing we limited ourselves almost entirely to essay writing. A specialist book on university writing would tell you more about responding to case studies and writing special reports, to mention just two more examples. When we planned the content we had to keep reminding ourselves that you wanted to carry round a reasonably sized book, not something the size of a telephone directory.

We have pointed you to some sources of help that are not books. We talked about getting support by:

● accessing the many websites listed;
● joining a university study group;
● attending sessions at the student learning centre;
● talking over your problems with someone at the Student Health Centre;
● finding out about clubs that interest you.

At your own university you may find out about many more places and people, especially if you keep your eyes on notice boards and websites.

If you feel ready to read a short story, here is one. Once upon a time there was a tiny ant who worried. Each morning he got up, darted out of his hole until he found a crumb of food and then darted back. The rest of the day he sat in his hole worrying. He worried that his food might run out or that he might fall ill and nobody would know. He suspected that there might be more to life than just keeping alive but he couldn't think of any way of finding out.

Meanwhile, around the corner, in another, much bigger hole, there were dozens more ants. Each morning they too got up but they divided up the day's work between them. It was fun looking around for food in a team and bringing it back in a long line. There was always someone to watch the nest of eggs and someone else to collect the food. None of these ants felt alone.

If this was a story for children we would have to tell you the point of that story but because you are an adult you will have worked it out for yourself. Hopefully you will not be someone who rushes back from lectures to worry by yourself in your own little room.

Finally, we would like to wish you all the best for your studies, whether you are just starting as an undergraduate, moving through your first degree or looking forward to higher studies. Universities are full of amazingly varied courses and people. Make the most of both of these.

A glossary of university words

This final chapter is a list of words that have been used in this book, with their meanings. When you first arrive at a new university you will hear many new words and phrases. Some of them refer to people, some to places and some to parts of your courses. The terms in the following list are particularly common in universities which follow the British tradition. You will find differences in places where they use American terms.

WORD	MEANING
active listening	Thinking about what the lecturer is saying rather than just copying down everything.
additional or recommended reading	Extra books and articles suggested by the lecturer for your course reading.
aegrotat pass	An examination pass for someone who is too ill to take the examination. Aegrotat passes may be given to students who have done well through the rest of the course.
assessment	The way students' work is measured (assignments, tests, examinations).
assignments	Students' essays, projects etc., which count for the course grade.
attachment	A file that comes with an email.
body of the lecture	The main part of the lecture, between the introduction and the conclusion.
Boolean operators	Words you can use to make your internet search more specific.
brainstorming	Thinking of many ideas for a piece of writing.
Breaks (mid- or inter-semester breaks)	The weeks when there are no lectures.
calendar	The book that lists all official university information.
campus	All the university buildings and grounds.
catalogue, online catalogue	A list of all the books in the library.
CEO (Central Executive Officer)	The head of a university (some universities use the term 'Vice-Chancellor').
certified copy	A signed piece of paper which says the paper is a true copy of the original.
chaplaincy	The people who are interested in students' spiritual life.
conjoint degree	A degree from two different university faculties. It takes longer than one degree but not as long as two.

co-requisites	Two different courses which must be taken at the same time are called co-requisites.
counsellors	Staff who listen to students' problems.
course reader	Articles and/or chapters on the topic, photocopied and bound together for students on a course.
credit	Points towards a degree for a course you have taken at another university.
criteria (singular: criterion)	What you need before you can do something else (e.g. 'There are 3 criteria for getting into this course').
database	A collection of information, usually on a computer.
dean	The head of the Faculty.
degree	a BSc, a BA, a BCom, etc.
degree programme	All the courses you take to make up your degree.
department	One part of the university e.g. the History Department.
deputy vice-chancellor	The person who works with the vice-chancellor but at a slightly lower level.
diagnostic test	A test to tell students what they are good and not so good at.
draft	A copy you write of an assignment or an article before the final copy.
edited book	A book with chapters from more than one author.
e-journals	Electronic journals that you can find and read on a computer.
eligible	Able to do something, e.g. eligible for a course.
emoticon	Little face-pictures like these: ☺ or ;-).

exchange programme	Students from two countries both do some study in the other's country.
exemptions/ exempt	Permission not to take a compulsory subject. If you know a language very well you may be exempt from the first year course.
facilities	Places (libraries, computer rooms) and things (photocopiers) that students can use.
faculty	A large part of a university where similar types of subjects are taught. A faculty is a larger grouping than a department. In American usage it also means the staff at a university or college.
foundation studies programme	A course for students who are not yet ready to enter the university.
GPA	The marks you have already got for your previous study.
graduation ceremony	The time when you receive your degree.
handouts	Pages of information used in a course.
harassment	Harassment is unacceptable behaviour between university staff and students. Sexual harassment is a serious offence. If you suffer from harassment contact your University counsellor.
HOD	Head of Department.
IELTS	International English Language Testing System.
index	An alphabetical list of words and their pages at the end of a book.
International Baccalaureat	A school-leaving examination which is recognised all over the world.

international office	The department where staff look after overseas students.
intonation	The way a speaker's voice rises and falls to change the meaning.
Justice of the Peace	As well as signing legal documents, a Justice of the Peace will also be a witness to signatures. Depending on their training, they may also be called on to assist in some courtrooms.
keyword	A word you use on a computer to search for the topic you want.
language conversation exchange	You teach your language; the other student teaches you his/her language.
learning journals	A book where you write about your studies.
lecturing styles	Differences in the way individual lecturers speak in public.
literature	1 The novels, plays, poems etc. of a country or language 2 Books and articles on a particular academic subject.
mailing list	A list that people subscribe to in order to be able to exchange messages with anyone on the list, usually about a certain topic.
major	A main subject.
mentor	A mentor is an experienced student who is paired with a new student to help them with aspects of study and university life.
minor	A subject studied for only one or two years.
moderated discussion list	A computer address list where messages are first read by one or more people before they are sent to everyone on the list.

needs analysis	A way of finding out what your weaknesses are and what you need to improve first.
non-verbal information	Everything you find out about a message apart from the words (e.g. through the speaker's hand movements).
orientation day	The time at the beginning of the year when students are welcomed to the university.
PhD	The highest degree at a university.
portfolio	A collection of work in one subject counting as part of the course assessment, e.g. an art portfolio.
predict	Work out what is coming next when listening to a lecture or when reading.
prefix	The first part of a word which has a meaning of its own (e.g. *pre*-departure).
prerequisites	Courses you must study before you can enrol in a course or programme.
prescribed/ required reading, reading list	Books and articles that you must read for your course.
proficiency	Being good at something.
provisional entrance	Permission to start university study without the right qualifications. Students with provisional entrance who do well will be allowed to start studying at the university.
reference books	Books which students may read in the library but not take away.
references	A list of everything read and used in a book, article or essay.
research article	A piece of writing in a journal, about some original work.

research assistant	Someone employed in a department to help staff and senior students with their research.
scholarship	Money to help students with their study.
semesters	The two or three parts of the university year.
seminars	Times when students present their work orally.
short-loan collection	Books which may be borrowed for a short time only.
spellchecker	A function of a computer program that checks your document for spelling and grammar mistakes.
state-of-the-art or review articles	An article which sums up what other people have written on a topic.
study break	Time without lectures, when students prepare for examinations.
supervisor	The lecturer who guides you as you write your thesis or dissertation.
style	The way one person does something, which may be different from other people's styles. Lecturers have different styles (ways of speaking and teaching).
teaching assistants (TA)	(Mostly postgraduate) students who teach (part of) a course.
thesaurus	A book which lists words of similar meaning.
thesis	Original work by one student for a postgraduate degree.
thread	Messages about one topic on a discussion board.
tips	Suggestions or ideas for doing something better.
TOEFL	Test of English as a Foreign Language.
truncate	To shorten, e.g., very long emails may be truncated.
tutors	Person who organises tutorials (see below).
tutorials	Times when small groups of students and their tutor talk about the course content.
(under)-graduate advisor	Someone who helps students plan their first degree.
under-graduates	Students who have not yet received a diploma or a degree.
vice-chancellor	The leader (or 'head') of a university.
voicemail	A telephone answering machine. You can leave a message on someone's voicemail.

References

Materials for further study

The websites and books below are all good sources for further practice.

General English

www.bbc.co.uk/worldservice/learningenglish/news/index.shtml – learn English with the BBC through this week's news, including sport, music or work-related topics. You can do quizzes, watch video clips, listen to singer-songwriters and lots more.

www.gutenberg.org/ – the Project Gutenberg Online Book Catalogue has over 17,000 free books to download. In fact, they are books of various types, not only for learning English. You can find novels and books involving language learning there.

IELTS

www.ielts.org – thinking about taking IELTS? Or do you just need to check a few details before your test? Before you do your IELTS, you should familiarise yourself with the official homepage. All the information in the handbook is onscreen for you.

www.askynz.com/ielts/preparation.htm – get some useful preparation hints for each module of the exam, for listening, reading, writing and speaking.

http://international.holmesglen.vic.edu.au/IELTS 01.htm – information about the IELTS exam including practice tasks.

TOEFL

www.toefl.org/ – the inside information about the TOEFL exam.

Grammar

http://owl.english.purdue.edu – offers over 200 free resources and advice on a wide variety of issues affecting your writing including articles and irregular verbs.

www.edict.com.hk/diagnostic/pathways.htm – this is a useful site for testing your English skills including two diagnostic grammar tests. You will get a feedback report on how you did. In addition, you can then use this information to generate your own 'learning pathway', which will provide a learning programme based on the mistakes you have made.

www.englishpage.com/irregularverbs/irregular verbs.html – if you have problems learning past tenses and past participles then use this website to help you practise.

www.aitech.ac.jp/~iteslj/quizzes/grammar.html – lots of grammar and vocabulary exercises for elementary, intermediate and advanced learners. Why not test yourself? Some of the areas tested are prepositions, articles, idioms, and sentence structure among others.

Pronunciation

www.edict.com.hk/vlc/pronunciation/ – if you have problems with a particular sound, e.g. /s/ or /d/, then it might be helpful to look at the pictures available on this website showing you how and where in your mouth to produce the sound. You can also hear examples and see videos of someone's lip movements as they produce the sound.

Spelling

www.esldesk.com/esl-quizzes/misspelled-words/misspelled-words.htm – if you want to work on your spelling, spend a few minutes a day on this site whenever you log in. You can check the meaning and pronunciation of frequently misspelled words, then try to remember the spelling and do the quiz.

Mixed skills

http://iteslj.org/quizzes/ – contains lots of grammar and vocabulary exercises for elementary, intermediate and advanced learners.

www.englishmaze.com – the English Maze contains hundreds of dynamic speaking, listening, reading, writing and grammar activities. Choose your level and follow the maze! There are pre-maze activities to learn new language, and post-maze activities to review what you've done in the maze.

Vocabulary

www.jbauman.com/aboutgsl.html – this list contains the 2000 most useful word families of English. It has been estimated that these words make up 80% of the words used in academic texts, so it is important that you check that you know all of them. Click on 'The actual 2,284 words, with frequency numbers' to see the list.

Study skills

www.antimoon.com/ – Read how four successful language learners learnt to speak English to a very high standard using a computer program called Supermemo. It is interesting to read about their experiences.

www.skills4study.com – a leading study skills website with study tips, downloads and advice.

Vocabulary-learning sites

http://language.massey.ac.nz/staff/awl/sublists.html – the academic word list contains 570 word families, which are commonly used in many subject areas, such as the Arts, Commerce, Law and Science. Here you will find sublists which group the words in order of frequency, beginning with the most frequently used words. To be successful at university, learn these words first.

www.englishdaily626.com/ – this website has information and exercises on different aspects of English. For vocabulary, read the idiom sections.

www.lextutor.ca – The complete lexical tutor. Here you will find many vocabulary exercises and tests to find out your level.

Vocabulary-levels tests online

www.er.uqam.ca/nobel/r21270/levels/ – if you don't know which words to learn, choose a test and find the size of your vocabulary in terms of high-frequency words. Warning – the test only tells you what's wrong – not what the right answers are. Use the result to decide which words to learn. After finding your vocabulary size, click on 'learn words' to find the most suitable word list for the size of your vocabulary.

Online dictionaries

http://dictionary.cambridge.org – Cambridge International dictionaries

www.merriam-webster.com/ – Merriam-Webster dictionary

http://nhd.heinle.com/home.aspx – Newbury House dictionary

www.thesaurus.com – Thesaurus

www.dicts.info/ – the All Free Dictionaries, translation dictionary www.urbandictionary.com/ – the Urban Dictionary

www.websters-online-dictionary.org/ – Webster's Online Dictionary

www.wordsmyth.net – Wordsmyth dictionary

Specialist dictionaries

www.gecdsb.on.ca/d&g/apr00/web1.htm – Academic Press Dictionary of Science and Technology

www.chinalanguage.com/CCDICT/index.html – Chinese/Korean/Japanese to English Dictionary

www.ucc.ie/cgi-bin/acronym – Dictionary of Acronyms

www.cellbio.com/dictionaries.html – Dictionary of Cell Biology

http://foldoc.doc.ic.ac.uk/foldoc/index.html – Dictionary of Computing

www.ora.com/reference/dictionary – Dictionary of PC Hardware and Data communication

http://allpsych.com/dictionary/ – Dictionary of Psychology

http://tradition.axone.ch – Glossary of Financial Terminology

www.animatedsoftware.com/statglos/statglos.htm – Internet Glossary of Statistical Terms

www2.let.uu.nl/UiL-OTS/Lexicon/ – Lexicon of Linguistics

www.nolo.com/lawcenter/dictionary/wordindex.cfm – Nolo's Legal Dictionary Online

Further references

Beglar, D. and Murray, N. (1993) *Contemporary Topics, 3* (Longman).

Hewings, M. (2007) *English Pronunciation in Use: Advanced* (Cambridge: Cambridge University Press).

Lewis, Marilyn (1999) *How to Study Foreign Languages* (Basingstoke: Macmillan).

Lewis, Marilyn (2000) 'ESOL Students' Notetaking in Lectures', *The tESOLANZ Journal*, 8, 79–91.

Lewis, Marilyn and Reinders, Hayo (2003) *Study Skills for Speakers of English as a Second Language* (Basingstoke: Palgrave Macmillan).

Nattinger, J. R. and DeCarrico, J. S. (1992) *Lexical Phrases and Language Teaching* (Oxford: Oxford University Press).

Subject-specific writing guides

Business
- Manolo, Wang-Toi and Troffart (2002) *Business of Writing: Written Communication Skills for Business Students* (Pearson Education). Business assignments at university.
- Ashby (2003) *Oxford Handbook of Commercial Correspondence* (Oxford: Oxford University Press). Practical business writing – reports, CVs, proposals, business letters, writing references. Lots of examples.
- Comfort, Revell and Stott (1984) *Business Reports in English* (Cambridge: Cambridge University Press). Writing business reports. Lots of examples and language exercises.

Law
- Krois-Lindner/Translegal, *International Legal English* (Cambridge: Cambridge University Press). Designed for language students who need English for work (not study), but still a useful resource for law students.

Medicine
- Glendinning and Holmstrom, *English in Medicine*, 3rd edition (Cambridge: Cambridge University Press). Designed for language students who need English for medicine. This covers all four skills but has examples of medical writing – e.g., case notes, referral letters, etc.

Science and technology
- Kirkman (2005) *Good Style: Writing for Science and Technology* (Routledge). A great book on vocabulary and grammar for people who have to write technical material.

Further reading

Critical thinking

Cottrell, Stella (2005) *Critical Thinking Skills* (Basingstoke: Palgrave Macmillan).

Grammar

McCarthy, M. and Carter, R. (2006) *Cambridge Grammar of English: A Comprehensive Guide: Spoken and Written English Grammar and Usage* (Cambridge: Cambridge University Press).

Language learning

Lewis, Marilyn (1999) *How to Study Foreign Languages* (Basingstoke: Macmillan).

Learner dictionaries

Adrian-Vallance, E. (2006) *Longman Exams Dictionary* (Longman).

Rundell, M. (2002) *Macmillan English Dictionary for Advanced Learners* (Basingstoke: Palgrave Macmillan).

Listening and note-taking

Beglar and Murray (1993) *Contemporary Topics, 3* (Longman).

Lewis, Marilyn (2000) 'ESOL Students' Notetaking in lectures', *The tESOLANZ Journal*, 8: 79–91.

Pronunciation

Hewings (2007) *English Pronunciation in Use: Advanced* (Cambridge: Cambridge University Press).

Speaking

Reinhart, S. M. (2002) *Giving Academic Presentations* (Ann Arbor: University of Michigan Press).

Van Emden, Joan and Becker, Lucinda (2004) *Presentation Skills for Students* (Basingstoke: Palgrave Macmillan).

Study skills

Brick, Jean (2006) *A Student's Guide to Studying at University* (Sydney: Macquarie University).

Cottrell, Stella (2008) *The Study Skills Handbook*, 3rd edition (Basingstoke: Palgrave Macmillan).

Lewis, Marilyn and Reinders, Hayo (2003) *Study Skills for Speakers of English as a Second Language* (Basingstoke: Palgrave Macmillan).

Vocabulary

Nattinger, J. R. and DeCarrico, J. S. (1992) *Lexical Phrases and Language Teaching* (Oxford: Oxford University Press).

Schmitt, D. and Schmitt, N. (2005) *Focus on Vocabulary Mastering the Academic Word List* (Cambridge: Cambridge University Press).

Writing

Lawrence (1996 edn) *Writing as a Thinking Process* (Ann Arbor: University of Michigan).

Trzeciak, John and Mackay, S. E. (1995) *Study Skills for Academic Writing* (London: Prentice Hall).

Peck, John and Coyle, Martin (2005), *The Student's Guide to Writing*, 2nd edition (Basingstoke: Palgrave Macmillan).

Answers

Answer key for Chapter 1: Case studies

What do you think?

Notes on Chamroeun

1 There seem to be three problems here: the assignment problems, the girlfriend problems and the problems over the lecturer's interest only in the assignment.

2 The lecturer's attitude is very normal in Western universities. There is usually a division of roles, so that an academic staff member is concerned mainly with a student's studies. It doesn't mean that he or she doesn't care about the student. It means that different people at the university are employed for different purposes. In asking if the student would like to see a counsellor the lecturer is not suggesting that he is crazy, but just that there is a special person who will be able to give proper advice.

For more

Chapters 11 and 12 help you answer these questions.

Notes on Hanna

There are several problems here.

1 She doesn't know what causes high or low marks. She seems to think they should relate to the number of hours spent on the assignments.

2 She doesn't realise that many students have lower marks when they advance to a higher degree.

3 Her ideas of what makes a B grade may be at fault.

For more

Chapters 10 and 12 will give you more information on these issues.

Notes on Tanako

1 The explanation is that there is a big difference between the way we speak and the way we write, especially in academic writing. Some people, like Tanako, have had far more opportunities to speak and listen than they have had to read and write. The opposite is also true. Some students are much better at writing than at speaking.

2 One piece of advice for Tanako would be to treat her writing and speaking as different skills and to go and get some help with her written language.

For more

See chapters 8 and 9 on writing.

Notes on Laura

1 There are many, many reasons for this student's attitude and not all of them are her fault. For example:

   – Maybe the tutor is not good at including people in an encouraging way.

   – A few students may talk too fast, not leaving time for others.

   – Perhaps this student has had experience of not being understood when she spoke.

2 Our advice would be not to leave the tutorial. If she did that, she might fall behind and miss out on suggestions for the assignments. She needs reminding that many people feel shy, not just new speakers of English.

For more

See Chapter 6 on tutorials and Chapter 12 on ways of reducing anxiety for different personality types.

Notes on Phond

Unfortunately for the student she is completely in the wrong. When students think their marks are too low they are welcome to go and see the lecturer. They could ask questions like these:

What is my main problem in this answer?

What should I do to improve?

I don't understand what you wrote here.

What they cannot do, is to ask a lecturer to change a mark just because their parents will be unhappy.

Very occasionally, a genuine mistake happens in marking. In this case it's fine to say something like this:

I'm wondering if there's a mistake in my mark here because . . .

For more

See Chapter 10 on assessment and Chapter 12 on dealing with academic problems. Chapter 11 gives advice about the best way to approach lecturers with requests.

Notes on Ken

Ken is partly right that without lecture notes he could be in trouble. It does depend on the subject, of course, and on the lecturer's way of managing things. If the lecturer is in the habit of giving out summary notes for everything that's said then these could take the place of Ken's own notes. On the other hand, some lecturers do more in the hour than just explain the subject matter in another way. Some give ideas that will be useful in assignments. They might make connections with the textbook and with articles from journals that have been provided for students.

In other words, the lecture notes are probably a very important part of the course.

For more

The best advice you can offer to this student is to read Chapters 5 and 10 in this book, which deal with the topics of lectures and assessments.

Notes on Fukang

In many Western countries students are more oriented towards small groups of friends rather than large groups of students. The solution is to try and meet people individually, perhaps by asking them out for a coffee after class. Also, just because people go to sports and other events together with a friend, this does not mean they do not want to meet new people. By coming several times you will get to meet the same people and get to know them. As for studying alone, many universities have study clubs that help students to work together. You may need to do a bit of work to find them, but they do exist!

For more

See Chapter 12 for more on making friends and fitting in.

Notes on Tanya

Asking the tutor whether you can be excused is a last resort. Occasionally students are excused from particular parts of the course. For example, a student with poor sight might not have to use certain equipment or a student with a serious stammer might be excused from making speeches.

In this case, if you were her friend you might point out a few things to her.

● Through life she might need to make speeches from time to time. Why not try now with a friendly audience?
● The university counselling services may be able to offer advice.
● Friends might be willing to sit through a trial presentation to give this student the courage to speak up in class.

For more

Chapter 10 offers advice about giving spoken presentations.

Notes on Marco

Why don't lecturers hand out summaries? We can think of many answers to this question. For one thing, university is a place where people are encouraged to find out about topics partly for themselves. Think of the difference between a school class you were in when you were ten and a class you were in five years later. One difference was the independent thinking you were supposed to do.

Another reason for not handing out summaries is that when one person does this, even if that person is a staff member, you are getting just their view of what is important, not the view of the original writer.

If you were Marco's friend, you could suggest to him that he might sign on for a course in speed reading at the Student Learning Centre or get a book showing him how to read faster.

For more

You will find more ideas for helping this student in Chapter 7.

Notes on Umut

Has this student been dishonest? Not necessarily. If this is her first university essay in a new country, she may not have realised that different countries have different traditions about what may and may not be 'borrowed' for an essay. Also she may not know how to show in the essay that she is using other people's ideas. Everyone, especially in their undergraduate studies, takes ideas from books and articles. That is what they are supposed to do, but she must acknowledge that this is what she has done.

For more

For an explanation of the word 'plagiarism' see Chapter 9. The issue could also be related to critical thinking. See Chapter 12 for more on this.

Answer key for Chapter 3: Improving your English

What kind of learner are you?

To find out your total score:

1 Take your answers to questions A–H and add up the total. _____

2 Take your answers to questions I–P but reverse the points by counting 1 point if you scored 3 and 3 points if you scored 1. _____

   For 0 and 2 you can keep the same score.

3 Now add up the total and look up your score below. _____

0–12

Not sure?   Your score does not mean you are not a good language learner. Perhaps this is the first time you have thought about how you learn English. It is good to find out more about your preferences as this will help you choose the most efficient way for you. Read this chapter carefully and next time you study English, take some time to think about how you do it.

13–24

Risk-taker   You like to take risks in learning English and you have lots of confidence. Probably your speaking skills will develop quite quickly. But do also pay attention to accuracy, both in speaking and in writing.

25–36

All-round   You like to know the rules of English and be accurate but you are not afraid to speak and practise fluency. This is a good overall approach as long as you make sure you use different approaches at different times.

37–48

Careful learner   You think it is important to speak English with as few errors as possible. You don't like to make mistakes or take too many risks when using the language. You will probably become quite accurate in your English, but don't forget that language is a skill that needs to become automatic, and that you can use without thinking. Maybe you can set aside time to practise free speaking, or try writing a text under time pressure.

What kind of English course do you need?

Waleed: IELTS 6.0 is roughly upper intermediate level, so he may need to study for some time before getting to a standard when he is ready to get this score. It's important that his parents realise this. Often students may need to study full time for three months to move from low intermediate to strong intermediate, and then another three months until they are upper intermediate. Rather than going straight to an Academic English programme or an IELTS preparation course, it would be good to take a General English course first and get lots of language practice, and then maybe take an Academic English course after studying for 3 or 4 months.

Li Ping: Taking lots of IELTS tests may help her test technique a little but her English probably won't improve that much and she is already getting bored. Also, remember that to survive in English at university, she needs much more language than is tested in the IELTS test. She should think about taking an Academic English course. This will help her with her IELTS scores and will be more interesting than just doing more practice tests.

Sun Woo: He could go to a language school and take an Academic English programme but it may be worth thinking about doing a foundation course designed for international students. In these programmes, while he will still have language lessons, he will also get lots of practical content. For example, he may take a paper on statistics or choose to study subjects that are related to the course he is going to take. Often, foundation courses will cover content at the level of a final year at high school in that country. This could be reassuring – he will know that he has studied the same content that native speaker students have studied. In addition, some foundation courses offer direct entry into some university courses. This means that he may not need to take IELTS. He should check with the department at the university where he wants to study and ask them if there are specific courses that they would recommend. They may tell him that he has to do a foundation course!

Ekaterina: First, she should try taking a TOEFL test and get more of an idea of how close she is. Rather than just doing a TOEFL preparation course, it may be better for her to take an Academic English course aimed at providing her with the language skills she will need at university. This will give her input in areas of academic grammar, vocabulary and skills and strategies that will be really useful when she gets to university. Of course, it will also help her English level, which will improve her TOEFL score. Depending on the school she chooses, she may be able to take a part-time TOEFL preparation course at the same time or study for TOEFL in the school's self-access centre.

Ernesto: It's probably a good idea for him to think about enrolling in a language school and taking a high-level General English course. He may consider preparing for one of the Cambridge exams (e.g., Cambridge Advanced or Cambridge Proficiency). These courses are useful because they cover a lot of language in a relatively short period of time and, if he passes, he can get a certificate that is valid for life. They are General English exams and so don't focus specifically on academic texts but will be great for revising and extending his English. He can probably prepare for TOEFL in his own time.

Answer key for Chapter 4: Vocabulary

Types of vocabulary

According to the passage, in what ways are plants adapted for water storage?

Answer: They can have long, deep roots; shallow, horizontal roots or leaves and stems that store water for a long time.

Type	Examples
Everyday vocabulary	a / activity / advantage / after / although / among / and / as / basic / become / blow / by / common / contain / desert / develop / either / for / full / growth / has / having / heat / hours / in / infrequent / is / just / last / leaves / like / long / many / mats / much / needs / number / of / or / plants / quickly / rain / reach / return / roots / shallow / soil / sometimes / spread / stem / stems / store / stored / such / summer / supplies / supplying / surface / taken / the / they / to / total / using / water / within / years
Non-technical academic vocabulary	adaptations / capable / devoted / obtain / periods / regions / sources / sufficient / survive / unpredictable / volume
Technical subject-specific vocabulary	cacti / cactus / carssula / echeveria / euphorbias / fibrous / genera / mesembtyanthemum / metabolic / perennial / sedum / succulent / tap root
General low-frequency vocabulary	arid / cells / drought / enlarged / horizontal / lifeless / moisture / moths / parched / soaked / species / succulents / underground

Formal and informal language

A The more academic words in the list are the following:

Consider   Investigate   Describe
Summarise   Establish   Minute

B Of the three different words shown, 'killed' is the least emotive, and 'butchered' the most. The other words are, in order, from less to more emotive:

growth / big increase / explosion
successful outcome / huge success / victory
good / great / fantastic
embarrassed / insulted / trashed

C Here are some possible ways to rewrite the sentences in a more academic way:

Original: The argument is over the top.
Revision: The argument is made too strongly.

Original: That is nonsense.
Revision: These findings do not appear to be supported by the evidence.

Original: The great article.
Revision: The well-known article.

Original: I don't like this.
Revision: My preference would have been to . . .

Original: This is a bad research project.
Revision: This study does not seem have been constructed carefully because . . .

Work out the meanings of new words

Prefix	English meaning	Example
ante- & pre-	= before	pre-war period
anti-	= against	anti-war protestors
auto-	= alone, self	autonomous, autocrat
bi-	= two	bicycle
inter-	= between	interaction = action between people
intra-	= inside	intraregional = within a region
mis-	= wrong	misinterpreting = interpreting the wrong way
mono-	= one	monotone = one tone, i.e. boring
multi-	= many	multinational = for many nations
neo-	= new	neo-colonialism = new colonising
pan-	= all	pan-Pacific = all the Pacific
tele-	= far away	telephone, television

What information does a dictionary give?

1 The pronunciation in the International Phonetic Alphabet (IPA). If you don't know how to read this, have a look in the front of your dictionary.

2 The meaning or definition.

3 An example of how the word is used.

4 We learn that the verb can be used both actively (*x* accentuates *y*) and passively (*x* is accentuated by *y*).

5 We learn that 'accentuate' can be used with both people and things.

6 We can see its frequency from the number of diamonds. This word is not very frequent.

7 'V n' means that the word is a verb that is followed by a noun, i.e. it is transitive.

8 '= intensify' gives a synonym of the main word.

What information does a dictionary give? (part 2)

1 Yes. 'To call a meeting' means to organise a meeting.

2 No.

3 Not really. It is a less harsh word for 'damn', which is more offensive. (It is also a verb meaning 'to mend a hole,' e.g. in a sock.)

4 The meaning of 'break out' (amongst others) is 'to escape', in a literal sense. To 'break away' can have the same meaning but is used metaphorically.

5 On the first syllable

6 Shocking

Using a thesaurus successfully

(a) Meaning 7: 'the means or procedure for doing something <figured out the best *way* to accomplish the task>'. See the entry 'METHOD' in the thesaurus.

(b) The following words have a meaning that could work in this sentence (although you would need to change the words around so that the sentence works): approach, strategy, system, technique.

(c) Notice how the grammar of the sentences has to change:

approach: 'One of the best approaches to learning new words is using vocabulary cards.'

strategy: 'One of the best strategies for learning new words is using vocabulary cards.'

system: 'One of the best systems for learning new words is vocabulary cards.'

technique: 'One of the best techniques for learning new words is using vocabulary cards.'

(d) 'Approach', 'strategy' and 'technique' are all words that are in the Academic Word List so will make the sentence sound more academic.

Approach is closest to the general meaning of 'way'.

Strategy puts more emphasis on a process for success – something you do in order to be successful.

System emphasises the organisational aspect of making vocabulary cards.

Technique emphasises the practical aspect of making vocabulary cards.

Using a corpus: Your turn!

1 'Scared of' seems to be the most common

2 Yes, this is common. Another way of saying this is to say that 'to scare' is both a transitive and an intransitive verb.

3 This is a difficult one. It seems you can use 'afraid' in the same contexts where you would use 'scared'. But the word 'afraid' is also used more 'lightly' as in this example: 'I'm afraid I can't give you a good guide because . . .'. The meaning here is close to 'I'm sorry'. 'Scared' thus seems to have a more intense meaning.

Checking collocation

The three prepositions are:

(a) of; (b) with; (c) on.

Answer key for Chapter 5: Listening to lectures

The purpose of a lecture

1 *to make sure that students are serious about their studies*

How would going to lectures check seriousness? Some students sit in the back row and check their text messages. Just being in the room doesn't say anything about mental attitudes.

2 *to check attendance*

Some lecturers do pass around the role during lectures, and attendance counts as part of the course. Check how many lectures you can miss before having to do extra work.

3 *to give information that can't be found anywhere else*

The information may be found somewhere else but it is more likely to be scattered in several different sources (see no. 6 below).

4 *to make university learning interesting*

Yes. When the lecturer is a good communicator he or she does make the learning more enjoyable.

5 *to let students ask questions*

Sometimes there are questions in lectures and sometimes these are asked in smaller groups, such as tutorials. This is probably not the main point of the lecture.

6 *to bring together information from many sources*

Yes. See no. 3 above.

7 *to let students get to know one another*

Lectures are certainly a good time to meet other students although that is not really their main point.

8 *to present information in a new form that differs from the textbook*

Yes. The material in lectures won't contradict anything in the textbook but it might be presented in a different order or with different examples or in different words.

Why else are lectures useful?

1 Listening can make the content memorable.

2 They are a good place to meet other students.

3 Some lecturers give important handouts.

4 Sometimes lecturers show how today's topic links with a coming test.

5 It's easier to concentrate when you take notes than when you just read a book.

Predicting content from lecture titles

1 *The Case for Censorship* *(journalism)*

Why is censorship generally assumed to be negative?

What are the problems with freedom of speech?

In what situations can it be useful?

If it is used positively, how should it be applied?

Are there any working models of how it can be made to work?

What does the lecturer think of censorship in journalism?

2 *Intermittent Reinforcement* *(psychology)*

What is intermittent reinforcement?

How does it affect our behaviour?

What studies have been carried out on animals/humans on it?

What are the applications of it?

3 *The rise of social-networking websites (sociology)*

What precisely are social-networking websites?

How popular are they?

Who uses them? What age groups? Which countries?

What are the advantages and disadvantages of them?

4 *Restorative Justice: a Workable Model?* *(law)*

What is restorative justice? How is it different from Western law?

In which countries does it operate?

What are the advantages and disadvantages of it over current legal practices?

Are there reasons why it cannot operate as a working model?

Linear notes

Good points include:

- use of bullet points
- underlining section headings
- examples of each point that are easy to see – indented

- Use of punctuation – '?' to indicate interesting issues raised in lecture
- Brackets to indicate lecturers' asides – interesting ones!
- Use of abbreviations and symbols – e.g., etc., celeb. (= celebrity), $ (= money), $$$ (= lots of money), v. (= very), < (= less than)
- use of arrows to show logical connection/result

Note-taking 101

'OK. Thank you all for coming. Today our seminar is about good note-taking practice. At the beginning of last year, I did a small study of the note-taking habits of successful students, looking at the techniques they use when taking notes in lectures, and then I asked them for their advice to students who wanted to improve their note-taking. I will present some of the findings of this study and then, at the end of this presentation, there will be an opportunity for you to talk about the note-taking strategies that you found the most effective. First of all, let's look at what you should make notes on – I mean the paper – not the topics! Now, lots of students use notebooks for their lecture notes. This is fine but some students find it easier to use a loose-leaf notebook – that means one that you can take the pages out of – rather than one with fixed pages. This means that you can take the pages out and put them into a folder with your course notes. Then you can collect notes and course readings for each course in one place, in a separate notebook or section of a notebook – write name + date of lecture. Sometimes lecturers give out a handout with the main points from the lectures. You could find it useful to make notes on the handout, in the margins – this will help you organise the notes you make. Also, some lecturers put their own notes on the course website after a lecture. You can print these out and put them in your folder next to your notes. The appearance of your notes is really important too because you will need to refer to them later. If you find yourself making doodles or writing notes to your partner on your lecture notes, remember that not only is this manual activity stopping you from concentrating but it will be annoying and confusing when you look back at your notes – i.e. when you are using them to revise for an exam. It is worth losing a bit of speed in order to write legibly – this saves time in the long run. If you find you don't have time to write neatly, then you are probably writing too much. Note only key words, not every word – and think critically about what you write down. If it is not going to be useful later – don't write! The other thing you can do if you can't keep up is to leave gaps [   ] when the speaker is moving too fast. You can always check with a friend later if you see a gap in your notes. In fact, it's a really good idea to review your notes as soon as possible. You could do this with another student. Read through and improve the organisation as necessary. Looking at the layout of your notes, some students make the mistake of writing all their notes in the top quarter of the page. Leave space between points. Indent. Spread it out. Mark ideas which the lecturer emphasises, with an arrow or some special symbol. Put a box around assignments and suggested books so you can identify them quickly. In terms of developing your listening skills, pay attention to signals for the end of an idea and the beginning of another. If you hear these, they will help you follow the flow of a lecture and lay out your notes logically. Transitions such as 'therefore', 'finally', and 'furthermore' usually signal an important idea. Also, pay attention to the lecturer's voice. The voice will often go down in pitch at the end of a section and then up at the start of a new section. As a final point, often the most interesting and useful things you can gain from lectures are the examples, sketches and illustrations that the lecturer presents. Lecturers often talk about their research in relation to points they make, or tell stories from their experience. You can get the theory from a textbook, but often this experience is unpublished and cannot be got from books. They are often the most interesting parts of lectures and you can use them in your assignments and exams – so although stories may seem off the point, they may be worth noting down.

OK. Now, I'd like you to look back over your notes and . . .'

What is the lecturer saying?

These words....	mean
I'd like to talk about . . . What we're doing today is . . . This morning we'll start looking at . . .	Announcing the topic
In other words . . . So the question is . . . So . . . What I'm saying is . . .	Explaining something he or she has just said in a different way
That's not the same as . . . The catch here is . . . That's not what we really mean by . . .	This is different from something else
And that leads to . . . We now come to look at . . . Right. Well, if we move on . . .	A new subtopic is coming
For instance . . . For example . . . One of the ways this works out is . . . Let me give you an illustration . . .	Giving an illustration of something that's just been said
According to . . . I'm a great believer in . . . X would have us believe . . . The most interesting point here is . . .	These are opinions rather than facts
By the way . . . I might say here . . . As a sidelight . . . But I'm getting a little ahead of myself . . . So where was I? Well anyway . . . To get back on the track . . .	This is not part of the main lecture
That would go for X as well as for Y . . . Along the same lines . . .	This is the same as something

The lecturer's words	The purpose of the words
In today's lecture I'll be starting by discussing the need for strategies and some definitions of them. I'll be passing on some theories as well as providing you with some examples. Finally there will be some general points about how you might apply the ideas from today's lecture.	**Start from here:** To outline (signpost) the order of the lecture
Let's start with a question. Why is this topic important to you? . . .	To signal the 'real' start of the lecture To try to make the topic relevant to the students
We have various categories of learning strategies. These are social strategies, cognitive strategies, organisational strategies and metacognitive strategies. . . .	To introduce a section about the theory of learning strategies
Now let's turn to some examples of cognitive strategies for learning vocabulary. You have probably used some of these yourselves. Let's see, how many of you try to remember a word by linking it to another word you know in any language? . . .	To move on to a section giving examples
Another aspect that students say they need to learn better is listening. Think of all the contexts where you need to listen: on the telephone, in a social conversation, at a public place and of course in a lecture like this one. In some of these places you have to practise selective listening. What we mean by this term is that a person decides to block out much of what is said and listen just for some information that they need. Some of the occasions when you might practise selective listening are . . . Etc etc.	To explain a technical term

Ranking questions for usefulness

1 *Is it OK if we email you about changing the time of handing in the next assignment?*   C

2 *Excuse me. What was that point again?*   B

3 *I have a problem with reading your handwriting on the board. My eyesight isn't great.*   A

4 *Will you be telling us more about that shortly?*   D

5 *How does this point compare with what you said earlier about . . . ?*   A GOOD QUESTION

Answer key for Chapter 6: Small-group learning

What is the purpose of tutorials?

Less than 12

You have clearly had some good experiences of tutorials. Maybe they suit your learning style. You can see how they are useful.

12–18

You have mixed feelings about tutorials but on the whole can see that they are useful. Maybe you have had some difficulties having your say in tutorials you have been to. In this case, the section on 'The language of discussions' will be really important to you. Maybe small group learning is less important in your culture. Maybe you have had some negative experiences with other students or tutors.

More than 19

You have quite negative feelings about tutorials. They are an important part of university learning and you will miss out if you do not attend or participate. The section on 'Planning for tutorials' will be useful for you as this will help you see that tutorials are relevant to you.

Building discussions: reacting to what people say

(a) 8 Ask for other people's opinion
(b) 8 Ask for other people's opinions
(c) 6 Add your opinion
(d) 7 Not give an opinion
(e) 6 Add your opinion
(f) 9 Refocus the discussion

(g) 2 Fully agree with them
(h) 5 Disagree with them
(i) 4 Partly agree with them
(j) 3 Draw conclusions from what they are saying
(k) 1 Check the meaning of what they have said

Accounting for this behaviour

(a) For students like these, the teacher is the most important person in the room and the focus of their learning in the room. They may not see the point of talking to other students or the point of doing tasks in smaller groups because they want the right answer from the teacher 3; (b) These students may not feel confident and worried about speaking up in front of the whole class. They may be worried about their English language level or their subject knowledge 5; (c) These students do not seem to be participating actively in the class. They respond when they have to but are not really involved 2; (d) These students are not actively involved. They may be interested in the tutorial but are completely passive in the class. Maybe they are unfamiliar with this style of learning. Or maybe they are demotivated 4; (e) These students are fully involved in the ideas in the class but only communicate with their friends 1.

Types of questions

Students' questions	Type of question
(a) Could you please tell us what . . . means?	defining
(b) What would happen if someone . . . ?	predicting
(c) What if . . . had been written in a different century?	hypothesising
(d) Is this similar to the point you made last week about . . . ?	comparing and contrasting
(e) Reading between the lines, is it true that the poet is trying to say . . . ?	making an inference

(f)	Can we sum this up by saying . . . ?	summarising
(g)	In your opinion, what would be the most likely cause of . . . ?	evaluating

Answer key for Chapter 7: Reading

Case studies – learning from other students' experiences

Christophe learnt how to integrate his reading into the course as a whole – reading to prepare for a lecture, and then afterwards to find out more about some of the topics in the lecture. He also learnt that even if he doesn't get time to read a whole article, it's still useful. (See sections on 'Planning your university reading' and 'Increasing your reading speed'.)

Marie realised that textbooks were actually really helpful because they taught her the technical meaning of words in her course. (See section on 'Types of academic text'.)

George learnt that reading could be something that he shared with other people, and that this was a good way of saving time. (See section on 'Increasing your reading speed'.)

Rose struggled to become a critical reader and eventually understood that she was expected to question everything and not just accept it. This was different from her previous studies in her own country. (See section on 'Critical reading'.)

Andrea realised that she needed to position each text and piece of research in relation to others and herself – to work out how her field had changed over the years. (See section on 'Critical reading.')

Khaled found that reading helped his English and found that it helped him if he felt he understood the structure of a particular type of writing. (See sections on 'Types of academic text' and 'The organisation of research articles'.)

Types of academic text

Prescribed texts or recommended books (d); edited books (g); single-author books (a); journal articles (e); state-of-the-art articles (c); research reports (f); theses (h); conference proceedings (b).

The organisation of research articles

1 How was the study planned? (methods)

2 What do the results mean? (discussion, recommendations, conclusions)

3 Who is interested in the results? (discussion, recommendations, conclusions)

4 What was the study about? (abstract)

5 Why is the topic important? (introduction)

6 What did the researcher want to find out? (introduction)

7 What was the main finding of the research? (abstract)

8 Where was the research carried out? (methods)

9 What did the researchers find out? (results)

10 What research instruments were used? (methods)

11 Who else has studied this topic? (literature review)

12 What have other researchers found out about this topic? (literature review)

13 How does this piece of research fit in with what other researchers have previously found out? (discussion, recommendations and conclusions)

14 Where are the full titles of the books and articles referred to in the article? (references)

Getting help in the library

In Dialogue 1, the librarian probably feels hassled because of her workload and the queue. She is annoyed that the students do not seem to have tried to find things out for themselves. The student is a bit nervous. Maybe he is worried about his English or worried about looking stupid because he doesn't understand how the library works. The librarian helps the student reluctantly.

In Dialogue 2, while the librarian is still busy,

she does not get annoyed with the student because:

- He uses her name (she is wearing a name badge).
- He asks her how she is.
- He introduces his request ('I'm having trouble finding this book').
- He has come prepared.

How not to read

There are two main problems with the way this student is reading. First, they are not taking a critical approach to their reading. This means they are not actually thinking when they are reading either, and are trying to soak in the information. They need to take a more active approach to their reading. They also ought to think more carefully about the reading techniques they need to use to get the most out of the text more quickly. Both these issues are dealt with in the next few sections of the chapter. You can waste a lot of time reading like this. But it is easy to fall into this way of reading when you are using a second language because . . .

1 The vocabulary is difficult.

2 The subject is complicated.

3 The structure or organisation of the text may be unfamiliar.

So . . .

4 You don't want to miss important stuff!

Coming up with your own reading question

Situation 1: Which presentations look the most interesting at each session time? What time are they? Which room are they in? I need to do some shopping at some stage during the conference. When's the best time to do this so that I don't miss something good? How do I get to the conference location from the station?

Situation 2: What font should I use? What line-spacing is required? Have I complied with the referencing conventions? Who do I hand the assignment in to? Do I need a cover sheet? If so, where do I get it from? Will I need to sign anything when I hand it in? What time is the office open until?

Situation 3: How similar were these experiments to what I have to do? What were the strengths and weaknesses of their methods? What results did they get? What results should I expect?

Situation 4: What happened in each story? What were the probable causes of the accidents? What were the consequences of each accident?

Situation 5: What aspect of health policy was each looking at? What were the major findings of each study? What questions do I want answered in the lecture?

How do students read?

1 scan reading; 2 reading for gist; 3 skim reading; 4 reading intensively; 5 reading between the lines.

A reading strategy checklist

Work out how many points you scored and see what this says about the reading strategies that you currently use.

You scored . . .
less than 20 You are currently using a limited range of reading strategies and could benefit from trying out some more of the ideas from this chapter. You could try recording the strategies you use when you are carrying out a reading task, and comparing them with those of another student who you know is a more successful reader. One way of doing this is to talk through your reading approach into a voice recorder and then listen back to it and decide what changes you need to make. You could say things like 'I am looking at the heading and need to check the meaning of two words in my dictionary. Next I'm going to write down some questions I want answered.' You could also probably benefit from talking to a language advisor in a university learning centre about how you read, and together, draw up a plan of how you should seek to improve.

20–30	You are using a reasonable range of reading strategies although you are probably still wasting time when you are reading. You may still benefit from comparing the strategies you use with those that other students use and trying out some of the strategies outlined in this section. If you want more ideas, make an appointment with a language advisor and talk through your current approach.
more than 30	You are currently using a good range of reading strategies. If you feel your reading is successful, keep the following points in mind. The important thing with strategy use is that you use the appropriate strategies at the appropriate time. Make sure you keep applying strategies consciously. You also need to keep evaluating your strategy use and decide whether the strategies you are using are achieving results.

Reading online vs. reading paper-based texts: same or different?

1 *You still need to read critically.* Definitely! The internet allows everyone a chance to express their views. Writers no longer need to go through a publishing company! This is very democratic, however, as a reader, you need to be just as critical about texts you find online as you would be about texts in books. Ask yourself these questions:

– Who wrote the text? What do you know about them? Are they cited in journal articles you have read?
– What organisation are they from?
– Are they trying to sell something? Or defend a particular opinion?
– Where is the evidence for their conclusions? How did they find this evidence?
– What evidence is not discussed?
– If they are citing an opinion, how widely accepted is this view, or is it actually just the opinion of a few people?

2 *You can use the same reading strategies (skimming, scanning, reading intensively etc.) when reading online.* Yes. You still need to read efficiently and need to avoid too much slow 'bottom-up' processing. Scanning is much easier with a computer. Look at the next section for advice.

3 *It's easier to get distracted and waste time when reading online.* Possibly. If you are clear about what you need to read and have clear questions you want answered when you are reading, it is easy to evaluate pages that you open. If you are not clear about why you are reading something and what you need to find out, you can easily get distracted and waste time. Sometimes online links can take you somewhere useful. Often they take you somewhere you don't need to go and you can lose track of why you wanted to read that particular page. For example, you may be reading about early car designs on www.wikipedia.com and the article mentions 'steam engines'. You click on the link and find yourself on a page about steam engines, which is very interesting but not what you went online for.

4 *It's worse for your eyes.* Yes. For advice on this, look at the section 'Reading online: looking after your eyes'.

5 *You find the same text types online.* A lot of the same text types, e.g. book reviews, research reports, journal articles, are accessed online plus a few new ones: online discussions, e-lists and of course websites etc.

6 *It's better for the planet.* Maybe. You may use less paper. However, lots of pages are printed that are never read. And e-waste (rubbish from old computer parts) is an increasing environmental problem.

Reading online: looking after your eyes

What should Jason do differently?

1 Take frequent breaks from his computer.

2 Think about printing pages off occasionally.

3 Think about plugging his laptop into a monitor.

4 Make the text bigger.

5 Set up a proper workstation so he can sit up straight, set the monitor up properly and make sure he has good lighting.

Answer key for Chapter 8: Essays at university

Understanding essay questions

1 Analytical; 2 Expository; 3 Argument;
4 Argument; 5 Analytical; 6 Argument;
7 Analytical

Simplifying the essay topic

Below are the simplified questions and the number of the essay questions they relate to.

What is . . . like?   7
What is similar about . . . ?   9
Why is . . . important?   4
What happened . . . ?   2
What was the result of . . . ?   10
What is the purpose of . . . ?   1
Why should . . . ?   6
What is the difference between . . . ?   5
What causes . . . ?   3
Why did . . . happen?   3
Why . . . ?   6

Rephrase the question

These are just one or two examples for each question. You may have used different words.

Essay question	Simple spoken questions
Give an account of the war of . . . against . . . including. . . . In what ways is this war unlike the . . . War? (Classical Studies)	What happened in the war? What's the difference between this war and . . . ?
Discuss the ways in which . . . derived influence from . . . ? (Physics)	How did . . . affect . . . ?
What, according to . . . is the relationship between . . . and . . . ? (Physics)	How are . . . and . . . similar?
Examine the significance of. . . . (Physics)	Why is . . . important?

Types of writing

(a)   Process
(b)   Problem/solution
(c)   Cause/effect
(d)   Comparison/contrast
(e)   Classification
(f)   Definition and exemplification
g)   Analysis

Design a questionnaire

Here are some questions that would get you started.

(a)   What questions could you ask to find others of your language level and needs?

   1   *What is your English level? (IELTS/TOEFL score)*

   2   *What problems do you have with* **grammar**/**vocabulary**/**pronunciation**/**writing**/**speaking**/**listening**/**reading** *at university?*

   3   *What sort of help do you need from the university with these skills?*

(b)   Once you have identified these people, what questions could you ask, to survey their opinions?

   1   *Which of the following university services do you know about? (List the ones you know.)*

   2   *Which of them have you used?*

   3   *How useful were they? (not at all useful   quite useful   very useful)*

   4   *What problems did you have with the services?*

   5   *How could the services be improved?*

Answer key for Chapter 9: The essay writing process

Practise writing thesis sentences

Topic 1: While it may seem illogical that companies selling products that are recognised to be harmful to health are allowed to market their products through sport, it would be impossible to limit sports sponsorship to "healthy and ethical" companies for a number of reasons.

Topic 2: Some immunisation programmes have been highly successful, however, there are many reasons why immunisation is not always the best way to fight disease.

Topic 3: Although tourism is frequently reported in the media to benefit local people, in practice this is often overstated and any benefits tend to be at the expense of the environment.

Topic 4: For restaurants to be successful they need a combination of good staff, good food and a good location, amongst other factors.

Investigate

The thesis sentence is:

While I understand how the victim feels, it would be crazy to introduce the type of dog control legislation that he advocates.

There are many possible titles. Here are some ideas:

> 'NO' TO ANTI-DOG LAWS
>
> DON'T BLAME DOGS
>
> PROSECUTE OWNERS, NOT DOGS

Your own idea for a title was probably a good one too!

The parts of the introduction

Yes – the writer agrees that there should be compulsory schooling for all and intends to outline her argument in the essay.

Example of an essay introduction	Purpose of the different sentences
(1) Ideas about when and whether children should have compulsory education have varied through the ages and from country to country. (2) In some countries the choice has been left to individuals and in others the government has made one rule for everyone. (3) Most countries of the world now have compulsory schooling between certain ages but the form of the schooling may vary between institutions. (4) Variety may sound like a democratic idea but in practice, how does it work out? (5). In this essay the case will be made for national education to include certain fixed areas of learning. (6) The reasons will be explained in terms of equity for individuals and the good of the nation.	1 Gives a general historic and geographic background to the topics. 2 This sentence becomes more specific than the general statement. 3 States a fact. 4 The writer raises doubts in the reader's mind about something that is happening. 5 Thesis statement. 6 The shape of the essay is announced.

The order of the introduction

'THE EXPERIENCE OF STUDYING AT UNIVERSITY'

The writer states that many students have a positive experience studying overseas. However some don't.

With the movement towards globalisation in recent decades, both business and education have become more international.

It is becoming increasingly important for individuals to experience life in another country to make them more employable in a world job market.

While many people clearly benefit from the experience of studying at university in another country, for some students the experience is far less positive.

By looking at a series of individual case studies, this essay will outline the ways in which young people can benefit from study overseas.

The case studies also suggest that for some individuals, the sacrifice made for an overseas education may not ultimately be worth it.

Is it or isn't it?

1 *I had good long quotes, sometimes half a page long, but I always acknowledged where they came from at the end of the essay.*

This is not clear. It depends on whether the student used quotation marks and put the author's name in the text or in footnotes.

2 *Every time I used someone else's ideas I used quotation marks and their name and date.*

Not plagiarism but the student needn't always use quotation marks. It's fine to paraphrase as long as you add words such as 'As X has pointed out . . .'.

3 **I think it's safest not to quote. You could plagiarise without knowing.**

Certainly not plagiarism but not a good university essay either. You are supposed to refer to sources other than your own thinking.

4 *I take ideas from the textbook but I always change the words.*

If the student doesn't give the name of the source then this is plagiarism.

5 *If I take ideas from a book, I always say whose ideas they are. The internet is so huge, I can easily cut and paste and get away with it.*

It's good that this student is acknowledging ideas from books. Remember, your lecturer will probably have read far more on the topic of your assignment than you have! However, copying and pasting from the internet is a plagiarism too. Students will get caught. Many universities use software that scans assignments and checks them against material on the internet and against past assignments that have been handed in.

The whole essay

Is the world a better place today?

a. Quotation.

b. A sentence supporting the main argument of the essay.

c. An example of entertainment.

d. One point that goes against the main argument (we call this a counter argument).

e. An example of what people did to send greetings 100 years ago.

f. A summary of the main point of the paragraph.

g   Examples of causes of death.

h. A round-up of counter-arguments then a restatement of the thesis.

i. A definition (of the word 'better').

Joining ideas in a paragraph

Furthermore = to say more on the same point

On the other hand, Conversely = to give an opposite view

Similarly = to say more on the same point

As an example = to illustrate a point

In other words = to say the same thing another way

Even though = to concede a point but then rebut it

Despite the fact that = to agree slightly (to concede a point)

This is not the same as saying= to make things clearer

This point is also made by . . . = to refer to someone's published view

Spot the errors

Type of error	Example	How serious is it?
typo	superfical (should be superficial)	type 1
grammatical	quick (should be quickly)	type 1
lexical	wonders (should be wanders)	type 1 or 2
cohesion	however (should be 'even more so')	type 2 or 3

Answer key for Chapter 10: Assessment

Ways in which you may be assessed

1 (e); 2 (a); 3 (j); 4 (c); 5 (k); 6 (g); 7 (l); 8 (h); 9 (b); 10 (f); 11 (d); 12 (j).

An example of assessment criteria:

Preparation

- use of literature;
- quality of arguments;
- integration of theory and case study;
- careful reading;
- use of primary literature in relation to secondary sources;
- imagination in interpretation;
- conclusions drawn.

The content of your talk

- set out clearly the problem or position to be discussed;
- select what you consider to be the most important aspects of it, and explain why;
- consider different ways of approaching it;
- answer questions from the other students or your lecturer about your chosen topic;
- explain and clarify points in the subsequent discussion.

How you talked

- Delivery
- organisation of time;
- audibility;
- structure and signposting;
- use of overheads or handouts.
- Discussion
- encouragement and involvement in discussion
- awareness of wider issues raised (including the ability to recognise and stick to the main issue);
- coherence of response to questions;
- use of the imagination in interpreting and understanding questions posed to the group.

1 You need to give a presentation, answer questions on your topic and then lead a discussion.

2 The lecturer is most interested in 'academic content and quality of argument/analysis'. Notice how many of the criteria refer to critical thinking skills: quality of arguments; imagination in interpretation; conclusions drawn, select what you consider to be the most important aspects of it and explain why; consider different ways of approaching it; use of the imagination in interpreting and understanding questions posed to the group.

Text patterns in essay feedback

1 Types of comments

Positive comments

You have presented a competent discussion of the article with an analytical approach that conveys aspects of the researcher's work in a systematic way.

Detailed comments with criticisms

The section that needed more consideration was the final part, in which I would have liked to have seen a fuller account of the practical implications of the study. Mostly the essay is well written; however, at times, I found it difficult to follow your argument and had to re-read sections to understand your logic. I felt that more signposting would have helped me with this.

Final positive comment

Overall though, the assignment was a balanced critique of the issues that arose from the research and it was good to see that you mentioned many of the limitations of this kind of research that we have discussed in class. Well done.

Grade B–

2 This student should:

● Read the question really carefully and make sure he / she has responded to all parts in sufficient depth.
● Be really careful to make sure that their argument is clear by using signposting language (see Chapter 8) or sub-headings. He / she should also spend more time editing for organisation.

Spot the criticism

(a) In some parts the argument was *not clear*. The lecturer wants to see a sentence in the essay's introduction like this: 'In this assignment, I will first examine the issue of . . . before . . . and finally . . . '. If the lecturer needs help 'navigating' the essay, she is finding it hard to read.

(b) The problem here is the way the student is referring to other writers in the text. This means that when the student writes about someone else's ideas, he or she must say whose ideas they are by including the name of the original writer and a publication date, e.g. (Carter, 1990), or if the student is using the words of another writer in a direct quote, then they need quotation marks ('. . .') around the words as well as the writer's name and year. This is a very serious issue. See Chapter 9 on plagiarism.

(c) This essay was inaccurate. There may have been typos, missing words, sentence fragments (these are sentences that are not complete, e.g. 'Because of the war.'), spelling problems or punctuation errors. See Chapter 9 on proofreading your work.

(d) The student didn't answer all parts of the question. When writing and after writing, it is important to check the question again and re-read the criteria so that you can make sure you've answered it. Many assignment questions have more than one part, e.g. *Describe the chief causes of the rise in global terrorism in the early years of the 21st century and assess the impact of tighter security procedures on everyday life in the West.*

(e) This means that the student needs to give his or her opinion and get this across in their writing rather than just writing what other people have said before. See Chapter 7: on critical reading.

(f) The lecturer expected the student to read more articles on the topic and synthesize these (bring their main points together)..

(g) 'A coherent whole' means somethingthat is a complete piece of writing that reads well together. This is a problem with 'coherence' (how the essay is organised). It may be useful for the writer to go back to some familiar essay shapes – e.g. general to specific, or from problem to solution, or claim to counter-claim, and fit what they want to say into these shapes.

(h) There is no problem with this one.

Revising for exams

When you are revising, choose active, critical and interactive methods. This means you should always make sure you are doing something with the information you are trying to learn and not just repeating it. When possible, try to revise with other people so that you can test each other. The following are useful revision methods: 1; 3; 4; 7; 8; 9.

NB: Method 6 is a bad idea because you are unlikely to get exactly the same question in your exam, and your learnt example may stop you from thinking through your answer.

Understanding the question

What

Cell phones – texting; communications – at home/in public.

How

1 Describe the growth in popularity of cell phones

2 Say how this has changed the way we communicate – i.e. we have discussions in the street/train/car that previously we would have had in private. We can be contacted 24 hours a day and people expect an instant answer.

3 Talk about the effect of this e.g. our private conversations can be heard; telecom companies (and the police) can track our communications and contacts more easily – privacy law.

What exam questions mean

1 *What happened in the field of management theory about twenty years ago? What was the management practice like then? What is it like now? Why is it different? How is it different? Are the changes significant? Why?*

2. *Why is Chang's interpretation controversial? Who agrees with Chang? Who disagrees with Chang? What alternative interpretations are possible?*

Making sense of question words

analyse: criticise, assess, review, examine explore; **argue**: justify, discuss, comment; **explain**: interpret, give an account of, relate; **develop**: extend, elaborate, expand; **prove**: verify, show, illustrate, demonstrate; **compare**: distinguish, contrast, compare; **describe**: give an account of, show.

Giving presentations: a word about timing

From the schedule we can see that the speaker expects that the audience will not know him/her and possibly may not know exactly what (s)he will be talking about. The audience probably also does not know much about the topic 'attrition', as the presenter is spending several minutes explaining it.

If you know that someone else will introduce you and that the audience knows the topic of your talk, you can leave this part out. Just say hello and start your talk. This will give you two minutes which you could use for questions or elsewhere. Also, if your audience knows quite a lot about your topic, you don't have to spend four minutes explaining what it means. It could, however, still be a good idea to briefly remind people.

The language of presentations

You might say: 'Often runners start running much longer distances when they are training for a race. Some of these runners increase their running distances too quickly and much of this running on roads and hard surfaces. When runners run on roads, there is a lot of impact with each stride. This repeated impact causes lots of injuries to the lower leg. One of these injuries is called shin splints . . .'

Speaking and writing – what are the differences?

1 Which one uses more words to say the same thing? *speaking*

2 Which one uses more complex sentences? *writing*

3 Which one uses shorter and more frequent sentences? *speaking*

4 Which one uses the most complicated vocabulary? *writing*

5 Which one has more repetition? *speaking*

6 In which one do you need to be the most accurate? *writing*

Avoiding too much informal language

Informal language	What should she have said?
Hi guys. How's it going?	*Thank you all for coming.*
If you've anything you wanna ask, keep it to yourself until the end.	*There will be time to ask questions at the end.*
I'm going to give you the dirt on the dos and don'ts of working in a restaurant.	*I'm going to talk about some health and safety rules for people working in restaurants.*
That dude Richards – he had some sweet ideas about . . .	*Richards (1992) made some good points about . . .*
It's crazy not washing your hands. It is like so gross.	*Not washing your hands is both disgusting and dangerous.*
Now that's it. We're outa here.	*Thank you for listening. If there are no further questions, then we'll finish.*

Presentation feedback – what should these students work on?

(a) This student needs to work on pronunciation – speaking louder and more clearly than when they are speaking normally.

(b) This student needs to remember that spoken language is simpler than written language.

(c) This student needs to work on how they introduce their presentation and use signposting language

(d) Reading aloud is boring and difficult to understand.

(e) There was no conclusion.

(f) The speaker could have used an image to show the structure of the company.

(g) Be careful not to read from the screen when using PowerPoint. Keep eye contact.

(h) Think about the 'who' of your presentation. Who are you speaking to? How much do they know about the topic?

Troubleshooting presentations ... some solutions

Problem?		solution
(a)	1	Imagine you are talking to an old deaf man sitting at the far end of the room, then you will speak louder and more clearly.
(b)	2	Try recording yourself when you are practising, and listening to yourself speaking to see if you are clear enough.
(d)	3	Try talking from cue cards (small cards with only 3 or 4 words written on them).
(c)	4	Pause more between sections.
(b) (d)	5	Use more repetition, e.g. 'Let me say that another way . . .'
(c)	6	Signal, with your voice going down, that you have ended one section of your talk.
(c)	7	Signal with your voice going up, that you are starting a new section.
(c)	8	Use discourse markers more. e.g. 'Let me give you an example'; 'My next point is about.'; 'I'd like to move on to . . . now.'
(b) (d)	9	Keep your sentences short and simple.
(b) (d)	10	Use more sentences to say the same thing.

Students' experiences of portfolio assessment

(a) Positive; (b) Negative; (c) Positive eventually; (d) Neutral; (e) Positive; (f) Positive.

Answer key for Chapter 11: Communicating with staff

For and against emailing

Viewpoint	For	Against
Quick to read	Yes, each one may be quick.	But not if a person gets dozens each day.
Quick to answer	Yes if done immediately.	But not if they are not given priority.
Friendly	Yes if the student chooses polite words.	But not if the student writes as if to a fellow student.
Clear in meaning	Yes if the student reads it through before sending it.	But not if the email is written and sent hastily.
Saves time	May save the student time.	But the student who takes the trouble to visit may show more commitment.

What sort of requests do lecturers look at favourably

1 All except one said they would not lend books to students because the return rate was too low. However, they did say that a request like that would make them look at discussing ways around the problem with the library, such as putting the book as a desk copy only.

2 All lecturers said that medical reasons were acceptable as excuses for late assignments, especially if they were accompanied by a certificate.

3 No lecturer took this request seriously.

4 Everyone said they would take this request seriously although one said it would be good to have advance warning to give time to look up the student's marks.

What's a good opening line?

Sorry to be a nuisance but . . .

Sorry – this is more common in English than in many other languages. Apologising shows that you respect the person you are talking to and also admits that you are interrupting them.

Excuse me. Is it possible . . .

Excuse me – again makes it clear you understand that the person is busy and you are interrupting them. *Is it possible?* – it is more abstract and less personal than you/I.

This is just a small request.

This makes the request seem small and therefore easier to agree to. A good strategy.

Sorry I didn't make an appointment. Do you have a couple of minutes?

As above, there is an apology for interrupting the lecturer . . . *a couple of minutes* = 2 or 3 minutes. This is easy to agree to – even if the request actually takes longer.

Trouble-shooting lecturer–student dialogues

As you could see, there are similarities in these two dialogues.

Dialogue 1

1 The student leaves silence once the lecturer has greeted him.

2 The student waits too long before letting the lecturer know the topic of the interview.

Dialogue 2

The student comes to see the lecturer because she has a problem with the assignment. The lecturer appears frustrated because she does not know why the student is there and what the student wants. It took three attempts for the student to state that she had a problem with the assignment and she took nine seconds to say this. This is a long time for someone who is busy and probably has a queue of people waiting outside their office. It took several more attempts for the teacher to find out that the problem was really about the student's writing skills.

Explaining what you want

Reason	What would you say to the teacher?
You want to sit in on a class you have not enrolled for because you think it may be more interesting than the course you are taking.	'I'm really interested in your course on . . . Would it be OK to sit in on the class this week?'
You have a question about a lecturer that you didn't want to ask in front of the other students.	'I really enjoyed your lecture . . . the other day. Can I ask you a question about something you said?'
You don't understand what to do for an assignment.	'I am not exactly sure how to do the next assignment. I'm going to . . . [say what you think you should do]. Does that sound right?'
You get a bad mark for an assignment. You don't understand how it's been marked.	'Can I ask you about my last assignment? I didn't get a good mark but don't understand why.'

Getting your message across

1 (a) This would be a polite start but until you state your name the person answering may not have a good answer. After all, if there are many students in the class he or she might not recognise your voice and might think you are the person he's just left a message for in administration or computer services.

(b) Yes, it's a good idea to start with your name but remember to leave some pauses as you state your problem. The lecturer may want to make a suggestion before hearing the whole problem.

(c) It's probably better to let the lecturer decide if the problem is urgent, unless of course you mean REALLY serious.

2 (a) Some people are annoyed by a clicking phone. Others are relieved they don't need to do anything. It's hard to give a definite suggestion here. Just don't keep ringing back and clicking off every five minutes.

(b) Not a good idea unless you are a senior student. Imagine having dozens of students asking you to phone them back. Will you always be there by your landline? You can't expect the university to pay for cell phone calls.

(c) This sounds like a good idea. You could add that you will either phone back or email.

When to talk to your Class Rep

The following situations are personal issues and should be dealt with in other ways:

Situation 3 'You feel that a lecturer is giving you bad marks because he/she does not like you.' If you don't want to talk to the lecturer directly, contact a counsellor in the Student Union (see Chapter 12). Note: The Class Rep should not deal with harrassment cases.

Situation 4 'You fail an exam and don't understand why.' Talk to your lecturer directly.

Situation 7 'You need extra tutoring with one of your assignments.' Talk to your lecturer or get help from a language advisor.

Answer key for Chapter 12: Dealing with problems

Are you a proactive problem solver?

Add up how many points you have got.

1 (a) 1 point   (b) 2 points   (c) 3 points (see Chapter 6)

2 (a) 1 point   (b) 3 points   (c) 2 points (see Chapters 7 and 9)

3 (a) 1 point   (b) 2 points   (c) 1 point
(see Chapter 11)

4 (a) 2 points   (b) 1 point   (c) 2 points
(see Chapters 9 and 11)

5 (a) 1 point   (b) 3 points   (c) 2 points
(see Chapter 6)

6 (a) 2 points   (b) 3 points   (c) 2 points
(see Chapter 4)

7 (a) 3 points   (b) 1 point   (c) 2 points
(see Chapter 11)

8 (a) 2 points   (b) 1 point   (c) 3 points
(see Chapter 12)

9 (a) 2 points   (b) 1 point   (c) 3 points
(see Chapter 12)

Now read the advice for someone with your scores:

9–13   Your approach to academic problems is an individual one and you tend to stick your head in the sand and ignore problems. If you get a bad mark, you either ignore the problem or work harder than before but without really addressing the issue. This approach may have worked well for you before, but sometimes it would be a good idea to seek help and take a more proactive approach to academic problems otherwise things may not get better quickly enough.

14–21   You have a sensible approach to academic problems. You naturally think about things and talk them through with someone before taking further action. This is a good strategy – you are reflecting on the issues, giving yourself time to work things out and using the people around you but you ARE still dealing with the academic issues that you face.

22+   You tend to overreact to academic problems and take immediate and drastic action. While it is good to do something about your problems, the danger of this approach is that you don't actually address the source of the problem. You should try to reflect about your problems, talk to other students and staff and get some ideas before diving towards a solution which may cause more problems.

Index